Beyond Books

Beyond Books

Adult Library Programs for a New Era

Jenn Carson

ROWMAN & LITTLEFIELD

Lanham • Boulder • New York • London

Published by Rowman & Littlefield
An imprint of The Rowman & Littlefield Publishing Group, Inc.
4501 Forbes Boulevard, Suite 200, Lanham, Maryland 20706
www.rowman.com

6 Tinworth Street, London SE11 5AL, United Kingdom

Distributed by NATIONAL BOOK NETWORK

British Library Cataloguing in Publication Information Available

Library of Congress Cataloging-in-Publication Data

Names: Carson, Jenn, author.
Title: Beyond books : adult library programs for a new era / Jenn Carson.
Description: Lanham : Rowman & Littlefield, [2023] | Includes bibliographical references and index. | Summary: "Having Adult Library Programs That Work will enable librarians to prepare effective programs that already have proven results, decreasing stress, prep time, and the feeling of being overwhelmed that can result from trying to come up with new ideas on a deadline"—Provided by publisher.
Identifiers: LCCN 2022025361 (print) | LCCN 2022025362 (ebook) | ISBN 9781538139745 (cloth) | ISBN 9781538139752 (paperback) | ISBN 9781538139769 (ebook)
Subjects: LCSH: Libraries—Activity programs.
Classification: LCC Z716.33.C368 2022 (print) | LCC Z716.33 (ebook) | DDC 025.5—dc23/eng/20220621
LC record available at https://lccn.loc.gov/2022025361
LC ebook record available at https://lccn.loc.gov/2022025362

To my mum, for always taking me to the library and letting me drag home the maximum number of checkouts each week. And when I blew through all the books in the Children's Department before middle school, letting me borrow from the adult section. Except Stephen King books, because every mother has her limits.

Contents

Foreword

Within the first five hundred words of *Beyond Books: Adult Library Programs for a New Era*, Jenn Carson writes, "The biggest lesson I've learned from my two decades of public service is that you can't, and shouldn't, do it alone."

Why is this hard? Well, in the context of adult library programs, it is hard first and foremost because this is an emerging topic. Here in the United States, we don't even track the prevalence of adult library programs. Our Public Library Survey administered annually by the Institute of Museum and Library Services (IMLS) collects data on the number of "young adult" and "children's" programs offered by America's public libraries but does no tracking of adult library programs. Instead, in our national accounting, adult programs are only hinted at, not directly assessed. In this silence, there is a lot of confusion. In particular, the roles of library workers in adult library programs remain poorly understood and poorly supported.

This confusion can be found in one of the earliest texts on the subject, Michigan rural librarian Raymond Ranier's *Programming for Adults: A Guide for Small- and Medium-Sized Libraries*. Ranier writes,

> Librarians have had to move their long-standing paradigm from knowledge steward to information broker to entertainment director . . . None of us who decided to join the library world were trained—or even warned—that we would soon be functioning somewhere along the lines of Julie, the activity director on the *Love Boat* (2005, viii).

In 2022, there are a lot more resources for library workers interested in providing programming for adults, most notably the American Library Association's Programming Librarian website, to which Carson is a regular contributor. Nonetheless, there remain a lot of gaps in our understanding of this topic. What are the most effective ways for library workers to connect adults to programs, classes, and lifelong learning opportunities without stretching ourselves and our libraries too thin?

Written before and during the global COVID-19 pandemic, this book is battle-scarred and full of hard-won lessons about what makes this work worth doing, as well as how to do it. Like a lot of us, Carson had an "existential crisis" during the pandemic. Before March 2020, she had offered a ton of hugely successful adult programs, but during the pandemic, things that worked no longer did so.

In this topsy-turvy world, Carson came to realize the critical importance of articulating, as she does in the book's conclusion, that "sometimes it is ok to take a step back, reassess, change gears, and, most importantly, take care of yourself and ask for the help or space and time to do that."

As a community-engaged scholar, I've learned again and again from my students, my colleagues, and the countless public library workers who have taken time out of their busy schedules to work with me that the African proverb is true: "If you want to go fast, go alone. If you want to go far, go together."

In the new era brought about by the COVID-19 pandemic, this must become our mantra. Gone are the days of librarians providing adult programs by themselves. Those days have been superseded by the new age of us figuring things out together, often on the fly.

As Carson reflects on her own COVID-19 journey, "If technology breaks down and a Zoom program goes sideways, we figure it out as we go along." The "we" here encompasses the library staff, the program participants, and even the wider community.

We can go far, and we can grapple with life's exigencies, if we work together. To quote another aphorism of unknown provenance, "We may not have it all together, but together we have it all."

We also need to expand the "we" to include those historically left out: One of Carson's aims in this book is to broaden what is considered a viable adult demographic in the library. She also provides us with the skills to expand the "we" to include new community partners who can help us fill gaps in our skill sets, supplement our budgets, and reinvigorate us when we're feeling sapped. Plus, partners can help us reach new audiences and better serve our communities!

What differentiates *Beyond Books: Adult Library Programs for a New Era* from what has come before are three things:

1. Carson's background in youth services
2. Carson's background as a yoga/fitness instructor
3. Carson's experience as a library director, particularly during the COVID-19 pandemic

Regarding the first point, the pioneers of what have become known as library programs for emerging adults have been almost entirely teen and youth services librarians. There is a reason for that: Those who have cut their teeth working with teenagers and youth tend to see things more broadly than those who come to adult programs from a background as, say, a more traditional reference librarian. As Carson writes, "The library can be that place [adults] let loose and find their autonomy again." In other words, the library can be a place for playful learning for adults. We have been doing this, or trying to do this work, for years with teens and children. Carson shows us how we can do the same work with adults.

Regarding the second point, as someone who bridges two worlds that historically have not had a lot of overlap (libraries and yoga/fitness), Carson naturally seeks out and sees the great potential of community partnerships. Her career has been based around bringing things together that may, on the surface of things, not naturally seem to go together. I first connected with Carson in 2016 after discovering her phenomenal Yoga in the Library website, which states, "Let me tell you my vision for the future . . . I walk into any public or school library, in the country or the city, big or small, and see posters advertising yoga programs."[1] Does Carson imagine every librarian will become a yoga instructor? No, absolutely not! Instead as someone who bridges these two worlds, she has a unique view of the critical importance of the process of bridging itself. This process of bridging is what enables libraries like hers to offer what are quickly becoming traditional, rather than nontraditional, adult programs, such as yoga programs.

Finally, as a manager of a library, Carson does this work in ways attuned to the logistical realities of running a library. Her strong business acumen shows us how to make the case for these programming partnerships and then how to fund and evaluate them. The first three chapters of this book build a foundation for the work that is then put to work in the second half of the book: The fun stuff!

Just like we buckle our seat belts before we hit the road, we also need to hone our administrative acumen to prepare ourselves to start our adult programming journey on the right footing.

Whatever your cup of tea, you'll find something of interest in this book. As Carson writes, "Let's go exploring!" Just as libraries have books for all readers, so too can they have programs for all sectors of your adult population. Where will your explorations lead? This book has information on how and why to offer everything from "So, You Got a New Digital Device for Christmas?" to "Attracting Pollinators to Your Garden."

There are other books and other online resources with *ideas* of programs your library *could* offer and that have been offered at libraries, but *Beyond Books: Adult Library Programs for a New Era* is the only book I know of that gives readers the tools they need to be successful as a provider of adult library programs, regardless of topical area.

Those tools center around cultivating and tapping into cultures of collaboration in your library, in your community, in your region, and beyond. Are you ready for *Adult Library Programs for a New Era*? Keep reading!

Noah Lenstra

Note

1. https://www.yogainthelibrary.com/sample-programs.html.

Preface

A New Era

Are you tired? Overwhelmed? In need of some adventure, or do you need a nap? Maybe you've picked up *Beyond Books: Adult Library Programs for a New Era* because it is required reading for your library school curriculum. Or maybe you are a burnt-out programming librarian who needs fast, cheap, already-planned programs you can deliver next week. Maybe you are an academic librarian struggling to get students to use the library outside of research and exam cramming. Or you are in a rural branch held together with part-time staff and struggling to get anyone to attend your adult programs beyond your Thursday night book club that's existed for thirty years. Maybe you are a CEO staring down your strategic plan and knowing you need concrete directives and measurable outcomes you can incorporate in your public services section and also know it needs to be written in a relatable language that can appeal to both your frontline staff and various shareholders. Are your program numbers dropping? Has your funding been cut? Do you need to move most or all your programming online due to a pandemic, staffing issues, or a natural disaster?

Either way, I bet you are tired. I bet you need fast answers. I bet you want programs that work and don't cost a fortune. I bet you don't want to have to do everything by yourself anymore. I know, because after years of frontline library work, and especially after these last few years in a pandemic where it felt like everything that I loved about my job has been taken away, and I am tired and, frankly, heartsick. In the name of library service, I've delivered programs in churches, schools, water parks (yes, you read that right), town halls, walking paths, bookmobiles, parking lots, playgrounds, farmers markets, town squares, stuffy office buildings, gyms, and, yes, even online. I've done it on bikes, yoga mats, waterslides, and bouncy castles, with my hands full of Nerf guns, cake, kale, water balloons, and, yes, even my keyboard. I've survived a hundred Zoom sessions and lived to tell the tale. I feel like, in many ways, I've grown up in a library. My mother got me my first library card as soon as I was old enough to print my name, and I haven't looked back. The biggest lesson I've learned from my two decades of public service is that you can't, and shouldn't, do it alone.

No matter what your reasons are for picking up this book, if you are interested in offering affordable and memorable adult programs that have patrons begging to be on your waitlist, you've come to the right place. My desk might be messy and methods occasionally unorthodox, but if there is one thing I'm known for in libraryland, it's throwing a party everyone wants to attend, whether that's online or in person. And I know how to do it while maintaining boundaries and insisting on nonnegotiable self-care tactics. If we work together and take care of ourselves in the process, we can get a lot done without burning out. I know it, because I'm still here. Follow me over the next ten chapters while we explore some killer program ideas that will get grown-ups aged eighteen to 118 into your building (or online platform or outreach location) and coming back for more.

Our first chapter is going to explore the fascinating history of radical adult programming in libraries. For example, did you know the Cornell Law Library installed *a squash court* in the 1930s?![1] The second chapter is going to look at what we mean when we say "adult"—which means different things to different people—and the more recent term "adulting." We'll talk about how intergenerational programs are so important but also why it is imperative that adults have their own space to explore ideas without kids intruding (and other humans they are responsible for, like aging parents). The library can be that place they let loose and find their autonomy again, and I'll show you how to help create that atmosphere. Sometimes it feels like we don't have the emotional or physical bandwidth to even get through our days, so we want to show other adults the ways libraries can expand their connectivity, either in person or online.

Chapter 3 is going to get right into the nitty-gritty of how to pull this off: who is going to pay for it and how, what sort of legal issues we need to worry about, what staff have to say and do to get these programs off the ground, and how to convince shareholders it's a good idea to have martial arts or beer (or motorcycle engines) in the library. I've made a career of pushing the proverbial envelope, but I've always done it with the support of my staff, trustees, and town officials (or at least most of them), and I've always done it safely and within budget. And yes, I even go on vacation (usually to train in Brazilian jujitsu). They don't call me the "Lethal Librarian" for nothing (see figure P.1).[2]

Chapter 4 and beyond is where we start having fun. This is where we explore some innovative program models that are going to make you excited about going to work again. Think juice bars, beer brewing, mushroom growing, bike maintenance, rock painting, choke holds, kiteflying, and bookbinding. And don't worry, you don't have to teach them all yourselves. I'm going

Figure P.1   The author in her Jiu Jitsu uniform. *Source*: Brendan Helmuth.

to show you how creating community partnerships with people who are already obsessed about interesting (and perhaps obscure) topics are the ticket to your adventure-filled calendar of events. So, what are we waiting for? Let's go exploring!

Notes

1. Julian Aiken, Femi Cadmus, and Fred Shapiro, "Not Your Parents' Law Library: A Tale of Two Academic Law Libraries," *Cornell Law Faculty Publications* (2012): 655, accessed January 15, 2022, https://scholarship.law.cornell.edu/facpub/655.

2. Sarah Butland, "The Lethal Librarian," *Maritime Edit*, no. 11 (Winter 2019–2022): 41–43.

Acknowledgments

Three years. A pandemic. A million tiny distractions and several minor crises, and the book is finally in your hands. There's no way that could have happened without the cheerleading of many individuals, especially my chosen family, and you know who you are.

This book was originally the idea of Charles Harmon, my editor at Rowman & Littlefield, who felt libraryland desperately needed a book about "adult programs that work." He trusted me to deliver the goods, knowing I would have tested all my concepts firsthand with the public and then write honestly about what was worth trying and what was better left as one of "Jenn's crazy ideas." He was patient and understanding as I was stuck in lockdown, working from home, while solo parenting (and teaching!) two children. As my deadlines became moving targets, and my stress and guilt over it piled up, he never once made me feel like a failure or disappointment, and for that, I am beyond thankful.

When I first asked Noah Lenstra to write the foreword to this book, as he has extensive research experience in healthy living programs and the importance of library partnerships (not to mention my ongoing admiration and long-distance friendship), he didn't even hesitate. Despite just securing tenure and being absolutely swamped with his own projects and teaching schedule.

I am blessed to be friends with many fine photographers who happily show up at the library and take pictures for me, since I don't own a cell phone and am usually too busy running the show to think about snapping pics. This book also couldn't have been written without the many partners and volunteers that make these programs happen.

Readers, these are the kinds of people you want on your team. The myth of the solitary writer, toiling alone, confident in their mission and bound to no one, is an illusion. Writers are both robust and fragile creatures who need as much moral support as they do physical. We must be resilient and stubborn in order to withstand the blows of criticism and rejection and the long periods of isolation and self-doubt required to be a published author. We must be very okay with eating a lot of leftovers and peanut butter sandwiches and letting the dishes pile up. We absolutely couldn't accomplish that without an entire support network cheering us on, showing up with chocolate and caffeine, reminding us to shower and drink some water, and quietly avoiding all talk of our negative reviews on Goodreads. Like Shelagh silently picking up all the garbage bags of children's clothes I had piled on my porch for months and taking them to the donation bin so I could meticulously organize all the photos in the book. Or Brendan feeding my cat and chickens and Shelley watching my children when I needed to go to conferences to give talks about this stuff. It's the little things that are actually big things. And for all that, this neurotic writer is forever grateful.

1

✦

A Brief History of Adult Programming in Libraries and Why It Is Important

If you stop the average person on the street and ask them what sort of programs they'd expect to find at a library, they might suggest "stories for kids?" If you press further and ask what we might offer for adults, you'll likely hear "book clubs," or "teaching people how to read," or perhaps even "computer classes." Unless that person has been to a public library recently—or knows and loves a librarian—they will assume libraries are quiet, dusty places staffed with shushing old ladies in cardigans. Of course, as every modern library employee knows, they couldn't be more wrong.

If you spend too much time on Twitter, you'll undoubtedly grow tired of hearing about the decline of libraries in the age of Google and Amazon, but the great irony is that while the circulation of material goods decreases, program numbers are actually going up. According to the "2017 Public Library Data Service Report" conducted annually on behalf of the Public Library Association (PLA), over the last five years, library programs in the United States and Canada have (per capita) "grown at a rate (6.3 percent) twice the decrease in circulation per capita (-3.0 percent)."[1]

I've witnessed this firsthand as a regular library patron since the mid-1980s and as a library employee since 2008. Twenty years ago, a typical medium-sized branch library might have had a few programs a week (most of those aimed at children); now they have a few programs a day (geared to various demographics). Libraries might be moving fewer books, magazines, and DVDs, but there are certainly more people coming through the doors. The branch I currently manage, in a town of less than 5,300, had 35,390 people through the doors in 2019 (our last non-pandemic year), and we held 676 programs, and 418 of those were for a total of 3,550 adults.[2] This isn't to say that adult library programs are a new idea. Copperas Cove Public Library has a square dance club that's been operating since 1970.[3] In the 1930s, Cornell Law Library installed a squash court so patrons could unwind with a little physical recreation and also sharpen their mental alertness and acuity needed in the legal court.[4] The circulation desk was reported to hand out books *and* towels. Lewis Morse, Cornell librarian and avid squash player who oversaw the installation, believed a squash court to be as important to legal education as a classroom or courtroom.

When philanthropist Andrew Carnegie funded 2,509 public libraries worldwide at the beginning of the twentieth century, he did so with the mission that everyone—man, woman, and child of any ethnic background—should have access to knowledge in order to improve their lot in life.[5] This was a radical idea at a time when most libraries required paid subscriptions and were segregated. Carnegie, a once-penniless young man in Scotland who became the richest man in the world, strongly believed that anyone was capable of pulling themselves up by their bootstraps, and it was the duty of the well-off to provide opportunities for enrichment of the poor. During the Great Depression, the Carnegie Library in Washington, DC, was referred to as the "intellectual breadline," since no one could afford food but they could read all they wanted for free.[6]

As such, we cannot discount the importance of libraries as safe and welcoming safe spaces in our community. As Jennifer Pagliaro reports in the *Toronto Star*, that city's extensive library system continues to hear in public consultations about "the need for people to gather but also to be alone together—a need to fight off social isolation in a growing city."[7] This need for community space is no different in rural settings like my own small-town library where many citizens commute long distances to the city or work in isolation on farms and at home-based businesses. In a place where there isn't a lot to do, the library becomes a centralized hub where people of all ages, economic classes, and ethnic backgrounds can socialize or sit quietly and read the newspaper and sip coffee in each other's proximity. On college campuses, libraries offer programs that give students a break from academics, like yoga and meditation, and give them a chance to connect outside the classroom (or frat parties).[8] In urban centers, where citizens are flooded with options for activities—most of which cost money and have hidden social rules like requiring a certain level of dress or hygiene that can be a form of systemic classism or racism or bigotry—libraries offer a refreshingly welcome playing field. In sociologist Eric Klinenberg's recent book about the importance libraries play in social infrastructure, he interviews a public library worker in New York named Andrew, who runs a teatime program for adults. Andrew perfectly sums up why librarians everywhere do the work that we do:

> There's a term you don't hear these days, one you used to hear all the time when the Carnegie branches opened: *Palaces for the People*. The library really is a palace. It bestows nobility on people who can't otherwise afford a shred of it. People need to have nobility and dignity in their lives. And, you know, they need other people to recognize it in them too. Serving tea doesn't seem like that big a deal, but the truth is it's one of the most important things I do.[9]

Carnegie also believed that it was more important to have many smaller branches than one large central library in urban centers, in order to be where the people are. He was concerned young men, in particular, would find "other objectionable places if libraries are not convenient."[10] In contrast to enticing people away from bars and dance halls, librarians have given up such moralizing practices and instead started offering events that feature wine-tasting or beer-brewing, video game competitions, cannabis cultivation workshops, or dancing lessons and speed dating events. We've even garnered controversy recently over the inclusion of drag queen story hours (for children and adults) in library programming.[11] We've taken our philanthropy to the max by hiring social workers to help patrons access the services they desperately need, such as mental health counseling or locating affordable housing.[12] Many of our libraries have patrons who are suffering from financial instability and housing insecurity, and there has been an entire movement built around this, encapsulated in Ryan Dowd's book *The Librarian's Guide to Homelessness*[13] and the feature film *The Public*. We tackle food insecurity by offering cooking classes, community fridges, and seed libraries. Libraries in densely populated areas have begun training staff on how to deliver Narcan in order to prevent opioid overdoses, and companies have been donating the product to branches in the United States.[14] Multiple times per year, I offer self-defense training in our library (I'm also a Brazilian jujitsu coach) and have even provided this training to staff during professional development days.

In addition to providing these sorts of services in-house, public services librarians are also increasingly traveling offsite to prisons, bars, parks, churches, and even beaches to reach underserved and previously unreachable populations. In 2019, for example, my library delivered programs at the farmer's market, in a water park, in schools, at church halls, at a large community theater, on a lawn down by the river, in our parking lot, on the sidewalk, at daycares, at gymnastic camps, and more. Whatever your personal feelings may be about libraries catering to people with challenging and diverse (and sometimes life-threatening) needs, few librarians can successfully argue that the library today needs to remain a place for books and books only (or that it even could be). As Barbara H. Clubb writes in the *Encyclopedia of Library and Information Sciences,* third edition, "Increasingly, in many parts of the world the public library is becoming a third community place—apart from home and school or home and church—a community gathering place where there is no pressure to buy, consume, or perform as well as a place that provides encouragement for exploration, discovery, connection, and civility."[15] She goes on to discuss how the library as place doesn't just include the physical stone or brick edifice we traditionally recognize but also bookmobiles, bike libraries, donkey and camel libraries, or floating libraries and book boats. James Rettig predicted this same trend in academic libraries back in his 2003 article "Technology, Cluelessness, Anthropology, and the Memex: The Future of Academic Reference Service." Reference and reader's advisory, he affirms, will continue to be place-based but "will no longer be place-bound."[16]

Beyond face-to-face program delivery, we must also consider the benefits of offering passive programs to adults, such as coloring pages or meditation corners, or lending objects such as snowshoes, yoga mats, kites, bikes, or board games. There are also myriad opportunities (depending on your location) to partner with local cultural or recreational institutions to give away free passes to waterparks, bowling alleys, museums, art galleries, and living history sites. This might be just the ticket for a busy parent looking for a low-cost activity to do with their family or a young couple looking for a fun date night idea. When planning adult programs, thinking on a deeper and broader scale than you may have previously considered—while briefly terrifying—can be exhilarating. By diversifying your program offerings, it can buffer your library's attendance statistics from the capricious tastes of the public. You don't want to put all your time and resources into offering book clubs only to find the same three people showing up, meanwhile the majority of your patrons are binge-borrowing TV shows from your DVD collection, reading *People* in the lounge, playing *Dungeons and Dragons* at the study tables, or asking for directions to the food bank. This is where knowing your audience is so important and why it is imperative for library directors and other administrators to actually spend time with the public in their branches (I know— a novel concept—leave your office!). If your library administration or board has issues with this (which we will discuss further in chapter 3), you can let them know that these aren't new ideas. The IFLA/UNESCO Public Library Manifesto (see textbox 1.1) is now over a quarter-century old. We need to accept and meet people where they are and participate in the interests they have (or would like to have!), in order to keep them coming through our doors (real or virtual).

TEXTBOX 1.1

The Public Library Manifesto (an excerpt)

The public library is the local center of information, making all kinds of knowledge and information readily available to its users.

The services of the public library are provided on the basis of equality of access for all, regardless of age, race, sex, religion, nationality, language, or social status. Specific services and materials must be provided for those users who cannot, for whatever reason, use the regular services and materials, such as, for example, linguistic minorities, people with disabilities, or people in a hospital or prison.

All age groups must find material relevant to their needs. Collections and services have to include all types of appropriate media and modern technologies as well as traditional materials. High quality and relevance to local needs and conditions are fundamental. Material must reflect current trends and the evolution of society, as well as the memory of human endeavor and imagination.

Collections and services should not be subject to any form of ideological, political, or religious censorship, nor commercial pressures.

Missions of the Public Library

The following key missions that relate to information, literacy, education, and culture should be at the core of public library services:

1. Creating and strengthening reading habits in children from an early age;
2. Supporting both individual and self-conducted education as well as formal education at all levels;
3. Providing opportunities for personal creative development;
4. Stimulating the imagination and creativity of children and young people;

5. Promoting awareness of cultural heritage, appreciation of the arts, and scientific achievements and innovations;
6. Providing access to cultural expressions of all performing arts;
7. Fostering inter-cultural dialogue and favouring cultural diversity;
8. Supporting the oral tradition;
9. Ensuring access for citizens to all sorts of community information;
10. Providing adequate information services to local enterprises, associations, and interest groups;
11. Facilitating the development of information and computer literacy skills; and
12. Supporting and participating in literacy activities and programmes for all age groups and initiating such activities if necessary.[17]

Public libraries have long been recognized for their commitment to adult literacy, as well as for supporting distance education programs by providing study space, computers and printing needs, reference help, and by proctoring exams. Academic libraries, of course, also offer their expected expertise in academic support and enrichment for both students and staff. Interestingly, a study of the Free Library in Philadelphia (the location of my alma mater, Drexel University) showed that those with college degrees were more likely to use the public library (60 percent) than those with a high school education or less (45 percent).[18] So while it is very important to offer continuing education opportunities to those looking to improve their academic or economic standing, many of our patrons may also be looking for opportunities for social connection or—dare I say—the edification obtained through culture and play. We need to change the perception of "lifelong learning" from something drab and perhaps even morally obligatory—which overburdened adults working full-time and often raising kids or caring for adult family members may feel overwhelmed by—into an opportunity to play and have fun, perhaps while acquiring new skills or cultivating friendships. According to Audrey Barbakoff, adult services manager at Kitsap Regional Library, and fellow *Library Journal* (LJ) Mover and Shaker (2013), the most successful adult programs are all play-based and fall into three categories: getting together, getting outside, and getting dirty.[19] I think she's on to something, and many psychologists would agree. About ten years ago, I had a therapist tell me that I made everything work, even things that were supposed to be "play." I vowed then and there to try to incorporate more fun into my life. Carl Jung's play therapy has long been prescribed to help children process difficult emotions.[20] According to William Glasser's famous choice theory, one of the four fundamental psychological needs of adults is fun/learning.[21] Dr. Stuart Brown from the National Institute of Play told NPR that play is enjoyable because it is temporary and voluntary, a suspended space where the outcome isn't as important as the enjoyment of the process.[22] Think of the difference between a patron coming to the library to play a fun game of target shooting with Nerf guns versus a police officer who is required to complete a target test in order to renew their firearm license for their job. One is simply low-pressure enjoyment with peers, and the other is a competitive test where the outcome has real-world impact. Ask any police or military officer which is less stressful, and I'd bet my money on the Nerf guns. Dr. Brown compares it to someone playing poker with their buddies versus someone gambling to win a jackpot. The latter is a high-stakes job, not play. It is a radical idea in our accomplishment-driven culture: to do something just for the fun of it. To do an activity that doesn't "have a point."

The next few chapters will explore this somewhat radical notion that libraries can inject more fun and adventure into their adult programming, with or without books as the backdrop. You'll be given program models for events that *could* be considered frivolous and a waste of taxpayers' money (like buying and flying kites!) and a few that are more traditionally "educational" (like learning how to identify trees). My goal is that you walk away armed with the confidence to present these programs and ideas to your staff, colleagues, trustees, and administration knowing that bringing play and pleasure into the lives of adults in your libraries isn't just good for statistics but good for your soul.

Notes

1. Ian Reid, "The 2017 Public Library Data Service Report: Characteristics and Trends," *Public Libraries Online*, December 4, 2017, http://publiclibrariesonline.org/2017/12/the-2017-public-library-data-service-report-characteristics-and-trends/.

2. Haut-Saint-Jean Library Region, *Annual Report 2018–2019* (Edmundston, NB: New Brunswick Public Library Service, 2019), 23.

3. "Double C's Celebrate 47 Years of Square Dancing in Cove," *Leader Press* (Copperas Cove, TX), May 1, 2017, https://www.coveleaderpress.com/news/double-c%E2%80%99s-celebrate-47-years-square-dancing-cove.

4. Julian Aiken, Femi Cadmus, and Fred Shapiro, "Not Your Parents' Law Library: A Tale of Two Academic Law Libraries," *Cornell Law Faculty Publications* (2012): 655, accessed January 15, 2022, https://scholarship.law.cornell.edu/facpub/655.

5. "Carnegie Library," *Wikipedia*, accessed January 20, 2022, https://en.wikipedia.org/wiki/Carnegie_library.

6. Susan Stamburg, "How Andrew Carnegie Turned His Fortune into a Library Legacy," *NPR*, last modified August 1, 2013, https://www.npr.org/2013/08/01/207272849/how-andrew-carnegie-turned-his-fortune-into-a-library-legacy.

7. Jennifer Pagliaro, "They're the 'Beating Hearts' of the City's Neighbourhoods. So Why Are Toronto's Public Libraries Still Chronically Underfunded?," *The Toronto Star*, last modified January 20, 2020, https://www.thestar.com/news/gta/2020/01/18/the-best-thing-a-library-can-be-is-open.html?fbclid=IwAR3wckuaop0aDjv6NYb0gPEeMAu2J9hIawlRDT-PslLM9Nz0UEDQPOQEOAg.

8. Jenn Carson, *Yoga and Meditation at the Library: A Practical Guide for Librarians* (Lanham, MD: Roman & Littlefield, 2019).

9. Eric Klinenberg, *Palaces for the People: How Social Infrastructure Can Help Fight Inequality, Polarization, and the Decline of Civic Life* (New York: Crown, 2018), 53.

10. Pagliaro, "They're the 'beating hearts.'"

11. "Drag Queen Storytime Is 'Controversial' and 'Potentially Divisive,' Says Okanagan Library CEO," *CBC News* online, September 21, 2019, https://www.cbc.ca/news/canada/british-columbia/kelowna-drag-queen-story-time-1.5292257.

12. Sarah K. Zettervall and Mary C. Nienow, *Whole Person Librarianship: A Social Work Approach to Patron Services* (Santa Barbara, CA: Libraries Unlimited, 2019).

13. Ryan Dowd, *The Librarian's Guide to Homelessness: An Empathy-Driven Approach to Solving Problems, Preventing Conflict, and Serving Everyone* (Chicago: ALA Editions, 2018).

14. Timothy Inklebarger, "Company to Supply Free Narcan to Libraries," *American Libraries* online, October 24, 2018, https://americanlibrariesmagazine.org/blogs/the-scoop/narcan-company-supply-free-narcan-to-libraries/.

15. Barbara H. Clubb, "Public Libraries," *Encyclopedia of Library and Information Sciences,* third edition (Boca Raton, FL: Taylor & Francis, 2010), 4356.

16. James Rettig, "Technology, Cluelessness, Anthropology, and the Memex: The Future of Academic Reference Service," *References Services Review* 31, no. 1 (2003): 17–21.

17. UNESCO and International Federation of Library Associations and Institutions (IFLA), *IFLA/UNESCO Public Library Manifesto 1994*, accessed January 20, 2022, https://repository.ifla.org/handle/123456789/168.

18. Pew Charitable Trusts, "The Library in the City: Changing Demands and a Challenging Future," *Philadelphia Research Initiative* (Philadelphia: PEW, 2012), 13.

19. Audrey Barbakoff, "Learning through Play in Adult Programs," *RA News*, August 2014, https://www.ebscohost.com/novelist/novelistspecial/learning-through-play-in-adult-programs.

20. John Allan and Keith Brown, "Jungian Play Therapy in Elementary Schools," *Elementary School Guidance & Counseling* 28, no. 1 (1993): 30–41. http://www.jstor.org/stable/42869127.

21. William Glasser, *Choice Theory: A New Psychology of Personal Freedom* (New York: Harper Perennial, 1999).

22. Sami Yenigun, "Play Doesn't End with Childhood: Why Adults Need Recess Too," *NPR*, August 6, 2014, https://www.npr.org/sections/ed/2014/08/06/336360521/play-doesnt-end-with-childhood-why-adults-need-recess-too.

2

✛

Who is an Adult?

Before we get into the *where* and *how* of running adult programs, we better examine who exactly is considered an "adult" and why it is important to cater to this age demographic. For much of human history, an "adult" was someone who was of age to marry, reproduce, go to war, and work for pay (though there is, of course, a long history of child labor and child marriage as well). The most widely recognized designation for maturity is the "age of majority," when a person assumes the legal ramifications of adulthood. The most common age for this worldwide is eighteen.[1] This should not be confused with the age of voting, license, marriage, consent, drinking, and so on, as these vary greatly by country and region. The average voting age worldwide falls between eighteen and twenty-one, depending on the country, with the highest percentage being eighteen.[2] Some countries, like Argentina, have set it as low as sixteen. Many countries, such as the United States, have a draft registration requirement for young men ages eighteen to twenty-six.[3] Canada's (voluntary) minimum draft age is eighteen; it is seventeen with parental consent.[4] UNICEF considers the marriage of anyone under the age of eighteen to be a fundamental violation of human rights.[5] In Canada, the legal minimum age for marriage is eighteen, or sixteen with parental or judicial consent. That said, in some provinces—like my own, New Brunswick—the age of majority is nineteen, not eighteen, and therefore, the minimum age for marriage is also nineteen.[6] The minimum age in the United States varies widely per state, with some having no minimum as long as there is judicial or parental consent.[7]

Biologists, psychologists, and other researchers also look beyond these legal markers to study age from a less chronological and more relational and anatomical perspective. They want to understand how old someone is biologically, socially, or psychologically.[8] Even within the broad range of adulthood, there are various generalized judgments based on categories of age demographics from the era you were born. These dates vary widely between researchers, so I'll use typical ranges here: Lost Generation (b. mid-1800s to 1900 and now deceased though still in recent memory), G.I. Generation (b. early 1900s to early 1920s, a few remaining members are still alive), Silent Generation (b. mid-1920s to early 1940s), Boomers (b. mid-1940s to early 1960s), Generation X (b. mid-1960s to early 1980s), Millennials (b. mid-1980s to mid-1990s), Generation Z (b. late 1990s to 2010), and Generation Alpha (b. 2011 to current day).[9,10,11] Each generation comes with its own purported quirks, such as Millennials preferring texting over phone calls and Gen-Xers being cynical and independent. Some libraries have tried to cater to these alleged groups by offering programs targeted directly to them by name or by a subject matter they hope will pique their interest, such as "20 Somethings' Trivia: *Game of Thrones*."[12] There's even a book called *The Generation X Librarian: Essays on Leadership, Technology, Pop Culture, Social Responsibility and Professional Identity* speaking directly to my age-cohort of library staff.[13] There are multiple other books on generation-specific programming and collection development, such as *Boomers and Beyond: Reconsidering the Role of Libraries* or *A Year of Programs for Millennials and More*, as well as many articles online and in print journals.[14,15]

Can we really use chronological age to define maturity or presume someone's tastes? I'm a late-era Gen Xer who has never owned a cell phone and I still prefer sending Facebook messages and emails over making phone calls, but that's just because I find it more efficient and less invasive. Anyone who works with the public has met a toddler who seems much more astute than their peers, a ninety-year-old that seems zestier than most, or a young adult that shuffles around seemingly exhausted by life. I know teens that love tea cozies and grandfathers who like surfing. Even if we have age limits on programs for safety reasons, we often encounter patrons who try to bend these rules, claiming things like, "my pre-schooler is mature for her age; she can handle scissors and a glue gun." Likewise, we find some kids sneaking graphic novels out of the adult collection that would horrify some grown adults or into a screening of an R-rated movie, and others the same age that are terrified of monsters and still like playing with dolls. Given the uniqueness of each person, I'm cautious about presuming we know what people like, or how they will behave, based on their chronological age (or gender—nothing grinds my gears more than presuming you'll like an activity based on your assumed gender, but that's a whole other book!), but we do need to explore some boundaries.

What about taking this thought experiment a step farther down the rabbit hole? Does a patron with dementia or an intellectual disability still count as an "adult" if they aren't able to tie their shoes, communicate (verbally or non-verbally), or go to the bathroom without help? Should they be "allowed" to attend library programs that require manual dexterity or basic math skills? And what about acute physical disabilities that impede these basic culturally accepted hallmarks of "maturity"? It is beyond the scope of this book to debate the controversial topic of whether someone with a cognitive disability that impairs their functioning should have the same rights and/or responsibilities as a neurotypical adult. Once we start sorting and labeling other humans based on (sometimes startlingly biased criteria), it all becomes a frighteningly complex mess. Frankly, I want nothing to do with starting an argument, but here I am writing a book about library programs for adults, so let's lay out some ground rules in case it comes up at your workplace.

As we can see from the examples above, there are multiple ways to categorize who is a "minor" and who is an "adult" and then further classifications within that division. How do we typically address this in libraryland? Most library administration agree upon three or four main classifications (both for materials and programs): juvenile (newborn to twelve years of age), teen or young adult (ages thirteen to nineteen), adult (generally ages eighteen or nineteen and older, but varies widely depending on your local rules/laws), and senior (age fifty-five-plus, and this mostly applies to programming as we don't generally have "senior" material collections). My own library system (which consists of sixty-three branches province-wide) has the following "suggested" divisions for programming: child (ages zero to twelve), youth (ages thirteen to nineteen), adult (ages twenty to fifty-nine), and older adult (ages sixty and above), but these can vary in branches based on staff discretion and the event's topic. So, for example, at my branch, we have two separate *Dungeons and Dragons* programs: one after school for youth (ages twelve to eighteen) and one in the evening for adults (ages nineteen and older), on separate days and times. The rules also vary widely for what age people can be alone in the library without a parent or guardian. In my system, it is age thirteen, but that still doesn't make them an "adult," even if they are unaccompanied. The rules for R-rated movies at the cinema are anyone under seventeen must be accompanied by a parent or guardian, and we can apply that same rule in libraries for screenings. I'm going to assume you already have local rules for borrowing adult-content books, which would also apply to book club attendance. Programs serving alcohol, or outreach done in bars, should follow the same rules that businesses use in your community. But what about a smoking-cessation program? A sex education program? My feelings on the matter are that if it is educational and doesn't glorify unprotected or nonconsensual sex, illicit drug use, or unnecessary violence, it should be for anyone. You or your administration may reasonably disagree. If you feel overwhelmed just reading this, take a deep breath. For the general purposes of this book and its programming content, I'm just going to define anyone age eighteen or over in the library as an "adult" and leave it at that. If you want to fight about it, find me on social media.

Personally, I have a soft spot for intergenerational programs, for a number of valid reasons. For one, they promote socialization and communication between different age demographics, and that is always a good thing. At one time, extended families were more likely to live under one roof, with older relatives helping to raise younger ones, which allowed for a lot of cross-generational interaction. In today's global economy, and with a high instance of divorce and single-parenthood, families are often spread all over the country, sometimes even the world. In *Palaces for the People*, Eric Klinenberg explores how this impacts our aging population and how libraries mitigate this isolation in many ways:

> For older people, especially widows, widowers, and those who live alone, libraries are places for culture and companionship, through book clubs, movie nights, sewing circles, and classes in art, music, current events, and computing . . . The elderly can also participate in some of these activities in senior centers, but there they can do them only with other old people, and often that makes them feel stigmatized, as if old is all they are. For many seniors, the library is the main place they interact with people from other generations. It's a place where they can volunteer and feel useful. It's where they can be part

of a diverse and robust community, not a homogenous one where everyone fears decline.[16]

He goes on to explain how libraries—as free community commons—also lessen isolation among new parents, young adults, and children. Intergenerational programming impacts children and teens as well as seniors. I couldn't agree more, as I've witnessed it happening in my own library and experienced it as a patron. I've written about this extensively on my Programming Librarian blog for the American Library Association; the benefits of multiple age demographics comingling go both up and down the age ladder.[17] In school, most kids are stuck in classrooms all day, interacting with others their own age. With smaller at-home family sizes and the birth rate decline in North America, most children don't have the benefit of siblings or cousins that are many years older or many years younger to play with. As Peter Gray discusses in *Free to Learn*, when younger children interact with children a few (or more) years older than them, they get to:

- learn through observation, which encourages them to take risks and stretch outside their comfort zone;
- play in the zone of proximal development, where they must collaborate with others of a higher skill set to participate; and
- receive emotional support and encouragement, which helps them feel loved and supported by older peers they look up to.

The benefits are also high for older children interacting with younger ones. They get to:

- nurture and lead, which builds empathy and teaching skills, making them better parents and mentors later in life;
- learn through teaching and demonstrating, which reinforces and enhances their own skills; and
- benefit from the creativity-enhancing effect of being around younger children.[18]

This is known as scaffolding, a term developed by Jerome Bruner at Harvard, and it affects adults too.[19] We benefit from sharing our skills with those younger—or less skilled—than us (those aren't mutually exclusive), and we also benefit from learning from those older—or more skilled—than us (again, not to be confused as necessarily the same thing, but there may be overlap). One of the best parts of this sort of sharing is that it breaks down ageist myths and stereotypes, challenging our preconceived notions about other age groups. For more information about intergenerational programming, I highly recommend the City of Edmonton's *Toolkit* on the subject, which can be found as a free downloadable PDF online.[20]

If we decide everyone that is eighteen or older is an "adult" and we're going to design some programs just for them—then what? As discussed previously, it is hard to classify people's interests based on when they were born, even if your strategic plan dictates you need to reach more "seniors" or your boss asks you to come up with some programming to attract "young people." The public doesn't care about your statistics; they just want to have fun. You may have heard about the national trend to offer "Adulting 101" classes targeted at Gen Z and Millennials (Kelly Ripa even got all hot and bothered about it).[21] These programs focus on everything from how to make a grilled cheese sandwich with an iron in your dorm room to how to change a lightbulb. The premise is these skills aren't generally taught in school (or at home), and they need to be learned somewhere. But often, librarians report, seniors or older adults show up too.[22] Perhaps a spouse has died and they never learned how to sew a button, change a tire, or balance a budget because their partner always did it. Or perhaps they want to know proper email etiquette to help them get a better job or writing skills for a college application, even if they aren't fresh out of high school. My point is that we shouldn't assume just because someone is a certain age that they know everything about being a "grown-up." Some people don't apply for their first mortgage until they're well into their forties (student loans plus a recession make it tough). Some people are busy raising a family or holding down two (or more) jobs and never learned how to properly clean an oven, and they just let it get grimy or they moved so often they never needed to (or they didn't own one). Some people weren't raised by parents who had any financial literacy skills, and so they've muddled through adulthood and now find retirement looming with no savings and massive debt. Maybe they never learned to tie a tie because they never needed to wear one until they had to attend someone's funeral. In other words, we shouldn't judge someone's skill set based on their age.

Does that mean that every program in this book is designed for all ages to attend? If so, what would be the point of having "adult programs" at all? While I think intergenerational programs are an outstanding way to build community and enhance skills (and I will make note in many program models of how the program could be expanded to be more all-age encompassing), I also think some-times adults really need a break and deserve to just hang out with other adults. While some of the programs in this book will take an educational tone, all of them are designed to acknowledge that adults not only want to but also deserve to have fun (without kids around!). Whenever I get interviewed about my unconventional approach to librarianship, I always admit that I create programs I'd want to attend. My library is the kind of place I'd want to chill out in even if I didn't work there all day. This is a benevolent sort of selfishness, I think. As a forty-year-old single mother of two with a mortgage, truck payment, and aging parents, I'm deep in the throes of being a grown-up. I'm writing this as a rallying cry to my people. We need more opportunities (and cultural permission!) to play. I mean, honestly, last night, I dreamt I was grocery shopping and got annoyed that juice boxes weren't on sale and woke up grumpy. If that's not peak adulthood, I don't know what is. So, without further ado, let's get started on having some fun!

Notes

1. "Age of Majority," *Wikipedia*, accessed January 20, 2022, https://en.wikipedia.org/wiki/Age_of_majority.

2. "Voting age," *Wikipedia*, accessed January 20, 2022, https://en.wikipedia.org/wiki/Voting_age.

3. "Selective Service System," *Wikipedia*, accessed January 20, 2022, https://en.wikipedia.org/wiki/Selective_Service_System.

4. "List of Enlistment Age by Country," *Wikipedia*, accessed January 20, 2022, https://en.wikipedia.org/wiki/List_of_enlistment_age_by_country.

5. "Child Marriage," *UNICEF* online, October 2021, https://data.unicef.org/topic/child-protection/child-marriage/.

6. "Marriageable Age," *Wikipedia*, accessed January 20, 2022, https://en.wikipedia.org/wiki/Marriageable_age.

7. "Marriage Age in the United States," *Wikipedia*, accessed January 20, 2022, https://en.wikipedia.org/wiki/Marriage_age_in_the_United_States.

8. Susan Krauss Whitbourne, "What's Your True Age?," *Psychology Today* online, June 23, 2012, https://www.psychologytoday.com/ca/blog/fulfillment-any-age/201206/what-s-your-true-age.

9. "List of the Oldest Living People," *Wikipedia*, accessed January 20, 2022, https://en.wikipedia.org/wiki/List_of_the_oldest_living_people.

10. Igor Karasev, "Which Generation Are You From?," *Igor Karasev* blog, June 22, 2018, https://medium.com/@igorkarasev/which-generation-are-you-from-4ce5410755f7.

11. "Generation Alpha," *Wikipedia*, accessed January 20, 2022, https://en.wikipedia.org/wiki/Generation_Alpha.

12. "20 Somethings' Trivia: *Game of Thrones*," *Baton Rouge Parish Library Infoblog*, July 17, 2013, https://ebrpl.wordpress.com/2013/07/17/20-somethings-trivia-game-of-thrones/.

13. Martin K. Wallace, Rebecca Tolley-Stokes, and Erik Sean Estep, *The Generation X Librarian: Essays on Leadership, Technology, Pop Culture, Social Responsibility and Professional Identity* (Jefferson, NC: McFarland & Co, 2011).

14. Amy J. Alessio, Katie LaMantia, and Emily Vinci, *A Year of Programs for Millennials and More* (Chicago: ALA Editions, 2015).

15. Pauline Rothstein and Diantha Dow Schull, *Boomers and Beyond: Reconsidering the Role of Libraries* (Chicago: ALA Editions, 2010).

16. Eric Klinenberg, *Palaces for the People: How Social Infrastructure Can Help Fight Inequality, Polarization, and the Decline of Civic Life* (New York: Crown, 2018), 37–38.

17. Jenn Carson, "Blog: A Range of Ages: Mixed-Age Play at the Library," *Programming Librarian*, September 17, 2018, http://programminglibrarian.org/blog/range-ages-mixed-age-play-library.

18. Peter Gray, *Free to Learn* (New York: Basic Books, 2015).

19. "Jerome Bruner," *Wikipedia*, accessed January 20, 2022, https://en.wikipedia.org/wiki/Jerome_Bruner.

20. City of Edmonton, "Intergenerational Programming Toolkit," *Edmonton* online, accessed February 11, 2022, https://www.edmonton.ca/city_government/documents/PDF/afe-intergenerational-toolkit.pdf.

21. Anne Ford, "Adulting 101: When Libraries Teach Basic Life Skills," *American Libraries* online, May 1, 2018, https://americanlibrariesmagazine.org/2018/05/01/adulting-101-library-programming/.

22. Ibid.

3

✢

Implementing Adult
Programs in Your Library

According to the 2017 *Public Library Data Service Report* conducted by Counting Opinions (SQUIRE) Ltd. (CO) on behalf of the Public Library Association (PLA), circulation numbers are slowly going down, but program numbers are rising much faster.[1] Over the last five years, public library programs in the United States and Canada have grown (per capita) at a rate twice the decrease in circulation per capita (+6.3 percent versus -3.0 percent). A different survey that same year shows that over half of American Millennials (ages eighteen to thirty-five at the time of the survey) used a public library in the past year.[2] A Gallup poll from 2019 showed that adults visited libraries more than cinemas, sporting events, museums, and parks.[3] Ian Reid, commenting on the *2017 Public Library Data Service Report*, concludes that if "the growth in programming continues, it may be constrained by potential capacity issues, such as hours open, staff resources and space, although these may not be of immediate concern depending on where/when and how programs are delivered (in-library, online, asynchronously, in community). Nevertheless, expanding the number of hours open to accommodate more programming (perhaps at more convenient times) implies a potential increase in commitment for additional resources, including staff. Correspondingly, there will be a need for libraries to justify those commitments."[4]

So what's a programming librarian to do? This chapter will explore some of the logistics and challenges of implementing successful adult programs in your library, with the hopes that you can feel confident you've got all the proper policies and procedures in place before you begin. But I do urge you not to become calcified in your planning and to keep in mind that having a flexible and adaptable mindset is always the sanest approach when dealing with the public, as incidents will often arise that you couldn't possibly have prepared for in advance, and we'll talk about that too. My approach not only favors micro-adjustments and early course corrections to ward off disaster but to also know that sometimes failure is inevitable! Oh well. Onwards!

Funding

Big gulp. Let's get this one out of the way because it is the roadblock that gets thrown up most often when I talk about programming. As soon as I start spouting off all my—fabulous, of course—ideas, someone always interjects with: "Yeah, that's all well and good, but how are we going to pay for it?" If your library is like most public or academic libraries, your programming budget is much, much smaller than your allocations for salaries and collections. As we've discussed previously, even though programming is becoming more and more of a draw to bring people into our buildings, and an essential part of our service offerings, often our budget and staffing don't reflect this increase in traffic, and we are forced to play perpetual catch-up. Until we can successfully advocate for larger program budgets (which I fully recommend and have done myself), there are three main sources for generating extra funds and one other solution. The other solution is offering interesting programs that don't cost anything. For example, starting a weekly running or walking club, which I discuss extensively in *Get Your Community Moving*, won't cost you a dime.[5] The three main sources for external funding are grants, partnerships (which we'll explore in detail below), and donations.

I spend a great deal of time researching and applying for grant funding. If you can access a grant database, such as Grant Connect, this can help you find sources of funding you might not otherwise be aware of.[6] Another way to narrow down your search is to look outside of traditional library or education grants, such as those available through national library foundations or the American Library Association's (ALA) initiatives, and instead look for funding directly related to the topic of your program. Many of these are tailored for nonprofit organizations, such as libraries. For example, if you are interested in offering yoga, meditation, or healthy living programs, search for grants that apply to "wellness" or "mindfulness" or physical literacy initiatives. If you are interested in offering programs to do with technology, look for STEM grants or grants for teaching older adults digital literacy skills. For arts and culture programming, look to arts foundations and associations, such as Canada Council for the Arts.[7]

Another way to drum up funding to pay for library programming is through creative fundraisers. There are also book sales, the sale of library bags and other swag, special dinners or events, or soliciting donations through your local library foundation that go directly to programming initiatives. What about instead of Adopt-a-Book you create Adopt-a-Program, and people could sponsor their favorite services? Many of my runners sponsor running-related programs, and many of my yoga students donate funds to continue the yoga programs they love so much. For more fundraising ideas, I highly recommend checking out the ALA's Programming Librarian blog.[8] Search under "fundraising" for all kinds of great suggestions.

Partnerships

Library partnerships are my bread and butter. They are, in my opinion, where most of the magic happens. No librarian—no matter how enthusiastic—or even collective staff can possibly deliver a plethora of engaging and unique programs without support from volunteers, patrons, and other community members, such as local businesses and nonprofits. Not only is it impossible from a time management perspective, but we also don't have the limitless skills or stamina to churn out endless programs. By figuring out what sort of skill sets your volunteers and staff already have, and would be willing to share, and then closing any gaps by reaching out to community members, you can cover a lot of ground. So, for example, let's say you wanted to offer a dance program in the library but didn't have anyone on staff willing or able to teach it. You could see if there were any volunteers who had dance skills, or if anyone could refer you to someone in the community. Or you could call the local dance academies and see who was willing to come to the library to teach a beginner dance class and what types of dancing were available. Most people will offer a lower fee to nonprofits like libraries or (even better!) offer their services for free. Partnering with businesses to provide free or discounted food, supplies, or other services (like bike repair!) is another great option. For example, every year, our local grocery stores, coffee shops, and farmers support our programs by donating food and seeds (for our seed library). Others offer us discounts on bulk orders. Some businesses will also sponsor programs in exchange for their name on the poster or a sandwich board, or to have their banner on display at the event. For example, our local Manulife Financial branch (owned by a member of our running club) sponsors our Kids' Kilometre Fun Run every year by buying book prizes or donating swag for giveaways. In exchange, we include their name in our marketing materials and put up their sandwich board on the day of the event (see figure 3.1). We also make sure to publicly thank them in the media and to the audience on the day of the run.

Figure 3.1   A partner-sponsored running program. *Source*: Brendan Helmuth.

I encourage you to make a list of all the potential partners you can think of that could provide expertise, cash, donations in kind, or other services. Expand your vision beyond the usual suspects and think beyond the books. What about bringing in someone from the martial arts dojo to give a demo or having the 4-H Club give a presentation on raising backyard chickens. The sky's the limit!

Administrative and Staff Buy-In

Before we get any further down the adventurous adult program rabbit hole, we need to talk about a dirty little secret many libraries share: there are usually people in most library staff (from the top to the bottom of the hierarchy) that abhor library programs. Or, at the very least, they don't think they should extend beyond book clubs and storytime (in public libraries) and author talks and writing workshops (in academic libraries). The jam-packed monthly calendar at my public library would make them roll their eyes. I know this intimately because I have employees and colleagues who feel this way and aren't even shy about saying it. They subscribe to the notion that libraries should be quiet (at all times), never provide outreach services, and stick to what they are stereotypically good at (providing information, preferably text-based). You will have to work hard to win these people over to the "programs and outreach services provide valuable skills, information, and fun opportunities!" camp. Some of them will never join.

Some programming librarians and administrators would advise you to start at the top and convince your institution's leaders that adult programs are very important. Show them the research cited in this book or examples of what other libraries around the world are doing and explain how a program-heavy library can have increases in circulation, traffic, and, likely most important from their viewpoint, donations. While I think it is essential to get buy-in from your bosses (asking forgiveness later works in some cases but isn't the best practice, in my experience), I would wait to do that until *after* you get your frontline staff on board. More on this in a moment.

If you don't already provide a lot of adult programming—and you're not a one-person library—you'll need to sit down with your adult and public/student services librarians, any programming paraprofessional staff, and even your circulation and reference staff (who will see an increase in traffic, phone calls, and general questions). I would bring whoever oversees your marketing (including social media presence and website) in on this, too. Get a general feel for how they all think current adult programming (if there is any) is going and what recent challenges and triumphs they have faced. Actually listen and make notes. Start small by asking what they think about some ideas you've had rolling around in your brain (maybe from this book!), and most importantly, work together to discuss them as a team. The more they feel like they are making a contribution and they aren't just being mandated to do something without their valuable input (and it *is* highly valuable), the more likely it will be successful. Have them create a list of the top three (or five, or ten, depending on your size and available resources) adult programs they might like to try out in the next year. Then create another list, as discussed above, of possible partners to support these programs (you can bring out your own list if they are struggling for ideas, but make sure that most of this comes from them). Then decide, as a group, who would like to be involved with each project, depending on the strengths, available time, and work plan of the members. If you manage employee performance agreements and reviews, consider adding adult programming initiatives to their objectives and yearly goals. If you are involved in strategic planning for the organization, think about how increasing adult traffic in your library fits your three-, five-, and ten-year plans. The sections that follow will give you a good idea of what needs to be discussed with your employees and volunteers, including the already-mentioned partnerships and budgeting components.

Once you've done this preliminary brainstorming, and you have a reasonable amount of buy-in from your frontline staff, then book a meeting with your boss, senior management, board of directors, or other shareholders who you will need permission from to carry out your plan. Lead with metrics that suggest adult programs can really boost library services, a short history of their success (including any local successes you've had in the past), and then reveal your detailed proposal for how to roll this out. Bonus points for showing how these programs fit in with your current strategic plan and overall mission. Make sure to include funding projections and staffing allocations. You may not get everyone's approval on the first attempt (or ever), but showing up with a well-researched presentation and detailed action plan will go a long way to proving this isn't just a passing trend and is something your library should be capitalizing on.

Legal Issues

Depending on the type of programs you wish to offer, it would be wise to consider whether you need liability waivers, also known as "hold harmless" forms. These declarations are designed to make the patron aware of any risks that could come to them during the activity and that the library, its staff, and volunteers are absolved of any responsibility for injury. These forms are essential, in my opinion—and probably the opinion of your institution's legal counsel—for any programs that involve physical activity, such as dance, yoga, running, snowshoeing, and so on. You can find a link to samples of these waivers on my website.[9]

As backup protection, you may also wish to require that any outside instructor have their own liability insurance. Depending on your building's policy, a contracted party may not be covered. I carry personal liability insurance as a yoga teacher. I'm covered by my library's policy when I teach in our building but not offsite or when I teach in other studios on my own time. It's better to be safe than sorry. My policy doesn't cover teaching jiujitsu or self-defense outside my library, so I rarely teach this offsite, unless the institution I'm teaching at has its own coverage. In my experience, personal liability insurance isn't that expensive if you or your instructor can afford it, and it is worth the peace of mind.[10]

If you plan to take photos or videos of patrons during events to use in promotional materials or share on social media, you'll need patrons to sign a photo or video release waiver. This waiver indicates their willingness (or refusal) to be photographed or recorded. It is especially important to be mindful of including minors or adults with cognitive disabilities. Have parents/guardians/

caregivers sign off and give you the okay before sharing their photos. As a best practice, unless we know people really well, we try to only share photos that don't expose faces, and we don't list the names or tag people.

Lastly, it is important for any volunteer or outside instructor to get a criminal record check done if they will be working with someone in the "vulnerable" sector (i.e., the elderly, disabled, children, teens, etc.). Depending on your jurisdiction, you may be able to also look up online whether they have any recorded sex offenses, if your state or county keeps a registry. A clean record check doesn't guarantee the person won't cause harm and shouldn't create a false sense of security, but it is an act of due diligence for employers in an institution such as a public library. Colleges and universities may have their own individual policies and procedures for this matter, which I urge you to look up and follow.

Marketing

When considering how to advertise your adult programs, it is best to try to put yourself in the mind of those you are trying to target. Where would they go to get their information? Our library currently uses Facebook, our website, our town's website and social media platforms, print posters, print calendars (which we also share digitally), and a digital newsletter to advertise our programs. And, of course, word-of-mouth marketing from our staff, volunteers, and patrons.

Facebook is, by far, our most consistently used marketing tool. The site is currently consumed mostly by Millennials and Gen-Xers, but those over sixty-five are the fastest-growing segment of the population engaging with the platform.[11] Teenagers and children are the least likely to use Facebook. The best time of day when Facebook gets the most users is between 11 a.m. and 2 p.m. on Wednesdays and Thursdays. According to a survey done in October 2021, 43.5 percent of Facebook users aged thirteen and up worldwide were female, and 56.5 percent were male.[12] There are multiple ways you can promote adult programs on Facebook. Creating event listings is popular; that way, people can indicate they are "interested" or "going" to an event and share with friends. Though sometimes the numbers of people who are "interested" can be very misleading, so I would suggest requiring people to call (or email, if you prefer) for registration (if you require registration, we'll discuss this more in the "Logistics" section). I've had 180 people indicate they are "interested" in an event to only have two that show up. You can also make posts (including a photo to grab attention) about the event. Or you can record a video talking about the program and post it or do a Facebook Live event during the program to get people watching and interested. You can do the same on Instagram and share across these platforms interchangeably, as you can link the two accounts.

It's been suggested that it is better to perfect using one social platform than trying to manage all of them all the time, especially if you don't have a specific staff member dedicated to the task.[13] That said, it doesn't hurt to cross-post content. So, while you may use Facebook to create event listings, you can still share digital posters or images of the event on Instagram or live-tweet during the program, or share links to your online calendar on Twitter.

It's essential to have an engaging and interactive web presence so patrons (or potential patrons) can find out your location, types of services and collections, hours of operations, and check out your calendar of events. If you aren't sure what a successful library website should look like, I highly recommend visiting *Piola*'s list of "The 25 Best Library Websites for 2019" to see what other libraries are doing right.[14] It includes snapshots of each website's mobile view, which must be tantamount to the desktop platform, since so many people now access information on their smartphones. Most people will first go to your website to look for a calendar of events, so make sure this is easily accessible from the home page. You'll also want to have icons linking to your Facebook, Instagram, Twitter, Snapchat, blog, or other platform profiles so people can follow you for updates.

In the non-digital world, many libraries are still operating print marketing campaigns, using a combination of flyers, posters, calendars, bookmarks, and other promotional materials. At the L. P. Fisher Public Library, we have had a really good response to our monthly, double-sided print calendars. People like to take them home and put them on fridges or pore over them to see which events they'd like to attend. On one side, we have the calendar with all the dates and times listed (starred if they require registration). And on the other side, we have short descriptions of the programs. We encourage people to call, email, or check out our Facebook page for more information. We also send this calendar out to people on our email newsletter.

Never underestimate the good old viability of a well-written press release or calling your local radio station to do a free public service announcement. We get a lot of free advertisement from the press showing up to cover our events or from staff calling or emailing the local radio station to let them know what's happening. There's hardly a week that goes by that we aren't featured in our local newspaper for something. If you have a free public access television station, you may even consider having a weekly or monthly spot for your public library where you could talk about upcoming programs, interview local authors, and plug new books, DVDs, and other resources. On campus, make sure you have a good contact at the college radio station so you can promote events on air. Some libraries even have their own podcasts!

Logistics

What sort of logistics do you need to think about when executing a well-run adult program? First, what is the location? This will determine the time and date. You can't plan to use a room for an event if that room is already booked for something else. So, the first task is sussing out what available locations best fit the program and then picking an eligible date and time. The date and time should correspond with the target demographic. If you want to reach Millennials or Gen-Xers, probably don't plan a program in the middle of a weekday, unless you are targeting stay-at-home parents. Likewise, most elderly patrons prefer daytime programs to late evenings, especially in the winter when it gets dark early and the roads might be bad. Keep in mind that many adults work shiftwork, so offering a program multiple times on various days (provided you have a large enough available audience) might reach more people. Be mindful of school holidays when many people will be away or with their families. But, then again, if you are planning a multi-generational program, hosting during a school holiday week may give families a chance to attend the program together. Likewise, in academic libraries, don't schedule programs near exams or over breaks, unless they are exam-related or designed to reach students and staff who may be sticking around campus.

What is the capacity of your room and the number of your available supplies? Also, what is the capacity of your attention, or the attention of your staff members, volunteers, or hired instructors? This will greatly depend on the subject of the program; a public lecture could be easily given to hundreds of passive listeners, but a workshop that requires a lot of instructor-participant interaction is going to need to be kept small, perhaps between five to fifteen people, depending on available supplies, space, and the teacher's comfort level.

As mentioned previously, it is also important to determine whether you want patrons to sign up for the event ahead of time. This is very useful if you have a restricted budget or space capacity. It also gives people slightly more accountability to show up, though, in my experience, you will still have people who are no-shows. In small communities, you usually get to know who those people are pretty quickly and adjust your expectations accordingly. Some libraries charge a small fee to register for a program, which they believe makes the patron more likely to attend; some require participants to pay for supplies. In a 2017 survey conducted by *Library Journal*, one in five public libraries in the United States claimed they charged admission fees for programs and events.[15] In some states or countries, that practice would be in violation of laws or library policies.[16] Make sure to understand your local laws and library rules and follow those. My library's practice has always been to remove as many barriers to participation as possible, including program fees.

What is your timeline? From the moment you decide you want to make this project happen to the day you roll it out, how long do you have to prepare? Make a list of all the things you need to get done and assign those tasks to members of your team (which may just be you!) and their order of importance.

Lastly, when thinking about program logistics, beyond gathering supplies, you also need to think about how best to set up the room ahead of time. Do you need a bare floor for dancing? Tables for crafts? Comfortable chairs for seniors? A projector and specific cables? Do these need to be tested first? A quiet space for meditation? An accessible change room for yoga or a theatrical performance? A tent? A stage? A liquor license? Some of these scenarios can be arranged ten minutes ahead of the start time, and others are going to require more careful planning. And if you aren't the one who will be setting up the room, make sure you talk to whoever is *and* also leave detailed instructions in case that person is out that day. You don't want to walk into a space a few minutes before go-time only to find the room's not ready. That's the stuff of a programming librarian's nightmares!

Outreach

What happens if you want to (or have to) take a program offsite? Maybe you're thinking about offering a beer-tasting program but can't serve liquor at your library, so you're moving it to a local pub or brewery? Maybe you'd like to offer yoga or a dance class, but your library doesn't have a suitable space? Maybe you'd like to take your patrons out in nature for a hike? Maybe you are trying to reach an underserved audience that you'd have trouble attracting through the doors otherwise? Whatever your reasons for considering offering outreach services to your adult patrons, the most important aspect of any successful program is having a solid plan and part-nership in place. Your partnership will be with the outside location you are taking the patrons to (or going to recruit new ones!), such as a museum, recreation center, women's shelter, bowling alley, senior's center, community hall, beach, restaurant, or even the municipal sidewalk. Even if you plan on offering a program in a public space, like a city park, sidewalk, or campus green space, you'll still need to notify the municipality or campus administration of your intentions. You may even need to apply for a permit, especially if you're setting up a tent or blocking streets or a parking lot for something like a 5K fundraiser. Make sure to include this in your planning timeline. How you handle your relationship with your partner(s) when it comes to booking, implementation (including clean up!), and following up after the event will make all the difference between whether you get to go back or not.

When planning outreach, don't forget to consider transportation. We'll touch on this some more in the accessibility section that follows, but for now, start con-sidering what options you might be able to offer your patrons. Is there anywhere within walking/wheeling distance from your library that would be a good loca-tion for outreach? Are there chartered buses available for a reasonable fee? Public transportation to your site? Does it cost to pay for parking there? Are the building and planned activity accessible to everyone?

Accessibility

For those of us that have the privilege of being able-bodied, we often forget that not everyone has the ease of access that we enjoy. Take a walk around your library, parking lot, and entrances with a stroller in hand and see how easy the building and grounds are to navigate with a set of wheels. The same awareness (or lack thereof) goes for economic or other societal privileges. One of the reasons I've long been an advocate for offering movement-based programs, such as yoga or Zumba classes in libraries, is that libraries are places where everyone is welcome, the buildings are usually (or should be!) accessible, and the programs are (usually) free. Offering programs at the library also lowers the intimidation factor for many people. Thinking about taking an art class at an art school when you are unsure of your skills is much scarier than showing up to a free, drop-in program at the public library. Likewise, showing up for a free yoga class or meditation session during exam week at the college library is much less intimidating for many students than going to the gym with all the fit, spandex-wearing athletes or a Buddhist hall with its unspoken rules and precepts to follow, or some other meditation center off campus. When planning your adult programs, keep these key areas of accessibility in mind:

- Is your building or offsite location physically accessible for those with a dis-ability? Think beyond just the width of doors and wheelchair ramps but look to see if the doorknobs are easy to open, if there are sidewalks or only grass or gravel, if the lighting is acceptable for someone with low vision, or if the counters are at different heights for different needs.

- Are there accessible washrooms at the location you'll be visiting? Are they working? Do they provide access to free menstrual products? Do they have safe sharps disposal containers?
- Can everyone hear you or see your mouth while you are speaking to the group? Is there a mic available you could use? Remember to speak clearly and not too fast. This is not just for those hard of hearing but also important for patrons whose first language isn't English (or whatever language you are delivering the program in) and may be struggling to understand.
- Are there enough chairs available? Are the heights of the desks or tables adjustable?
- Is your program being provided in a manner that respects the dignity and independence of a person with a disability? Would they be able to integrate with the rest of the group with relative ease and not feel singled out?
- Are there assistive devices available for patrons experiencing disabilities so that they may be able to partake in the program? Examples would be speech-to-text software on a computer during a computer class or a chair and modified poses available for those who need them during a yoga class.
- Is a guide/service animal able to accompany a patron during the program?
- Is a patron able to bring along a support person to the program? Has a space been reserved for them?
- If there are any disruptions in service (such as an accessible washroom being out of order) or barriers to access at the location, has the patron been notified ahead of time so they can make a sound decision about whether they'd like to participate? Imagine the frustration and possible embarrassment you would experience if you made an arduous trip to attend a function only to find out you couldn't use the facilities.
- Have the staff, volunteers, or partners involved in the program been trained on how to provide the service to people with varied disabilities? Does anyone on staff have mental health first aid training? Non-violent intervention training? Implicit bias training? Trauma-sensitive program delivery training? If no, why not?
- Have you considered multiple modalities for delivering this program? Such as in-person delivery but also simultaneous digital delivery through an online videoconferencing software program or through posting a recording on social media later, such as maintaining a YouTube channel for recorded performances and programs.
- Is the print on your handouts large enough and clear enough? Are electronic documents formatted so they can be read by a screen reader?
- Are your videos captioned?
- Do any of your staff speak multiple languages, including American Sign Language, and could someone provide translation services if needed during a program?
- Are your program participation or registration costs low or nonexistent to allow as many people as possible from all socioeconomic backgrounds to participate?

- Are people of all genders or sexual orientations welcome in this program? If it is targeted toward a certain audience, such as a "Women's Self-Defense Class," "Mom and Baby Yoga Class," or "Men's Book Club," is that for a valid reason? Have you discussed ahead of time what to do if someone shows up presenting as a different gender and wants to join?
- Are there clear sight lines and clearly marked entrances and exits in your program space? Are there intermittent or abrupt noises that are unnecessary and could disturb a patron with a strong startle response or sensory processing issues? Can the patrons be made aware of this ahead of the program if the noises need to be included? For example, I always warn my yoga students before I ring the singing bowl, so I don't startle anyone with an unexpected noise. What is soothing to some induces a panic attack in others.

If you can't answer yes to most or all of these questions, I urge you to think about ways to modify your program delivery to help make as many people feel as welcome as possible. I know this isn't always easy. For example, if you are offering a snowshoe hike at a nature preserve, the reality is that some people just won't be able to go. Is there an alternative outdoor physical activity that could be offered in addition so as to give people more options? If you'd like to learn more about ways libraries can be more accessible to groups such as users with mental health issues, those with learning and/or attention issues, patrons with developmental disabilities, users with sensory disabilities, patrons with service animals, people who need assistive technology, and patrons with physical disabilities (realizing there is often overlap among these groups), please check out the valuable, free toolkits provided by the American Library Association on their website.[17]

Training

It stands to reason that most library staff members delivering programs are trained to do so (generally), but if you are offering more radical and adventurous programming, and it is something you think might become a more regular occurrence, or if you are in a large system, something that might be offered in other branches, consider offering training about the things you've learned while delivering the program. If your staff members or volunteers have special skills, consider having them present a workshop during a professional development day or deliver a webinar to share those skills with other people in libraryland.

Make sure if you are bringing in outside instructors for programs, they have all the required training to deliver the service properly, such as making sure a yoga teacher has a minimum of 200 hours of training, or if a doctor or therapist is licensed, or if an accountant is up-to-date with this year's tax forms before hosting a tax clinic. When an invited guest speaks at your library, they are representing the quality of service your clients are used to you providing, so do your best to make sure to meet their expectations. Not everyone is going to love everything you do, and that is why it is so important to solicit feedback—and know how to evaluate it objectively—which is the last topic that will be touched on in this chapter. I once had a licensed doctor of Chinese medicine provide a program about acupuncture and even performed it on volunteers from the audience (see figure 3.2). Not

Figure 3.2   A patron learns about acupuncture from a licensed practitioner. *Source*: Jenn Carson.

everyone loved watching people get stuck with needles, but . . . that's the program they signed up for!

Program Evaluation

I have a love/hate relationship with feedback. It's not because I can't handle criticism (though I'm not sure I *love* it) but because I find it difficult to solicit in a way that ensures I receive an authentic delivery. There are few things that irk me more than having someone tell me how much they enjoyed something to my face only to hear later they complained about it all over social media or to a bunch of people in the parking lot. Some participants won't say anything, good or bad, even if you ask directly, or anonymously, or bribe them with treats. Then there are the patrons with especially strong opinions who will tell you *everything* they are thinking, whether it is valid, or useful, or not. So, as a programming librarian, you can find yourself in a bit of a sticky wicket because once you hold your first exciting adult programming adventure, you are going to need some sort of markers to tell if it was a success and if you should do it again. As much as you might want to work from the assumption that everything went well if no one complained, it is important to elicit feedback from your patrons, and it is equally important to actually *listen* to them, and then do something about the data you gather. Don't hand out evaluation forms if no one is going to read them or alter program delivery based on the information. Don't ask patrons if they enjoyed a program if you are just going to get defensive if they complain about something. Don't solicit staff feedback if you aren't planning on doing anything about it. This will only breed mistrust—or worse, apathy—among your staff and clients. Gathering opinions must be done in a way that everyone's voice gets equal weight, which is why it is so important to solicit feedback from a broad selection of the population because no particular patron is more important than any other (despite what they—or your fundraising committee—may tell you). The same goes for your staff and partners. The employee who cleans up the room after the program is just as valuable as the person delivering it or the partner footing the bill. Your patrons may have loved your glitterfest, but I bet your janitor didn't. And trust me, you don't want to get on the wrong side of the cleaning crew. Our job is to make sure we are meeting as many possible needs as we can with the skills, resources, space, and time we have—based on our particular organization's mission and strategic plan—so it is essential to solicit feedback from the people we are paid to serve. My favorite evaluation forms are short and sweet:

1. What did you like about this program?
2. What do you recommend we could do better next time?
3. Would you recommend this program to a friend?

My preferred method for gathering feedback is anonymous evaluation forms, and I've included a link to a sample from my library service in the endnotes that is more in-depth than the one above.[18] You can hand these out at the end of a program for specific commentary on that event. Or alternatively, you can create a general survey to distribute in the community, perhaps at your annual general meeting. Ask what patrons would like to have offered in the year ahead and what they enjoyed in the previous year. You can also send links to digital surveys via social media or email newsletters (provided you have permission to send newsletters, this varies by each country's privacy laws). There are lots of free online survey software available, like Survey Monkey, for you to take advantage of. Remember to solicit the opinions of the marginalized and the illiterate, who may or may not attend your current programs, feel comfortable with paper or electronic forms, or be particularly social due to social anxiety or other mental health issues. Take a moment for engagement when you are doing outreach, especially to underserved groups, and ask people what they'd like to see more of at the library, or what services they would benefit from. Also, on the subject of partnerships, don't forget to include questions about how your patrons (or potential patrons) may wish to contribute to your library's programming by volunteering to share their skills. And lastly, don't forget to gather feedback from your staff about program planning and execution—their opinions matter too!

Notes

1. Ian Reid, "The 2017 Public Library Data Service Report: Characteristics and Trends," *Public Libraries Online*, December 4, 2017, http://publiclibrariesonline.org/2017/12/the-2017-public-library-data-service-report-characteristics-and-trends/.

2. A. W. Geiger, "Millennials Are the Most Likely Generation of Americans to Use Public Libraries," *Pew Research Centre*, June 21, 2017, http://pewrsr.ch/2tOt8gQ.

3. Justin McCarthy, "In U.S., Library Visits Outpaced Trips to Movies in 2019," *Gallup* online, January 22, 2020, https://news.gallup.com/poll/284009/library-visits-outpaced-trips-movies-2019.aspx.

4. Ian Reid, ibid.

5. Jenn Carson, *Get Your Community Moving: Physical Literacy Programs for All Ages* (Chicago: ALA Editions, 2018).

6. "Grant Connect," *Imagine Canada*, accessed February 11, 2022, https://www.imaginecanada.ca/en/grant-connect.

7. "Bringing the Arts to Life," *Canada Council for the Arts* online, accessed February 12, 2022, https://canadacouncil.ca/.

8. American Library Association, *Programming Librarian* (blog), accessed February 11, 2022, https://programminglibrarian.org/.

9. "Liability Waivers," *Jenn Carson* online, accessed February 12, 2022, http://www.jenncarson.com/resources.html.

10. My personal liability insurance costs about $200 CAN per year.

11. Jenn Chen, "20 Facebook stats to guide your 2021 Facebook strategy," *Sprout Social* online, February 17, 2021, https://sproutsocial.com/insights/facebook-stats-for-marketers/.

12. Statista Research Department, "Distribution of Facebook Users Worldwide as of October 2021, by Gender," *Statista* online, January 28, 2022, https://www.statista.com/statistics/699241/distribution-of-users-on-facebook-worldwide-gender/.

13. "10 Tips to Master Social Media at Your Library," *EBSCO* online, accessed February 12, 2022, https://www.ebsco.com/sites/g/files/nabnos191/files/acquiadam-assets/10-Social-Media-Tips-for-Public-Libraries-Infographic.pdf.

14. "The 25 Best Library Websites for 2019," *Piola* online, May 2, 2019, https://meetpiola.com/the-25-best-library-websites-for-2019/.

15. Jennifer A. Dixon and Steven A. Gillis, "Doing Fine(s)? | Fines & Fees," *Library Journal* online, April 4, 2017, https://www.libraryjournal.com/?detailStory=doing-fines-fines-fees.

16. Jamie Matczak, "Charging Fees for Library Programs," *Wisconsin Valley Library Service (WVLS)* online, September 20, 2018, https://wvls.org/charging-fees-for-library-programs/.

17. Melissa Tracy, "Understanding Accessibility Challenges for Patrons," *American Library Association (ALA)* online, February 5, 2018, http://www.ala.org/news/member-news/2018/02/understanding-accessibility-challenges-patrons.

18. Government of New Brunswick, "Appendix B: Sample Program Evaluation Form," *The New Brunswick Public Library Service Policy 1085* (July 2017), accessed February 12, 2022, http://www2.gnb.ca/content/dam/gnb/Departments/nbpl-sbpnb/pdf/politiques-policies/1085_library-programs_appendix-b.pdf.

4

✛

Food and Drink Programs

While libraries may be the last place anyone would think there would be food-related programming—The spills! The smells! The potential bugs and rodents!—there has been a shocking increase in food and cooking education in institutional America. It largely began with the creation of former first lady Michelle Obama's Let's Move! initiative, which ran from 2010 to 2017 and contained a large "healthy eating" component.[1] The program was designed to combat the obesity epidemic and alarming food insecurity facing US citizens. If you are unfamiliar with the term "food insecurity," it refers to a social and economic condition where access to food is limited or uncertain, causing far-reaching mental and physical stressors for those afflicted (see textbox 4.1). It can be caused, for example, by not having access to a full-service grocery store in a neighborhood where the majority of residents don't own vehicles or have mobility issues. Carrying large amounts of goods on public transportation is difficult, and multiple trips are costly and time-consuming. Residents have to rely on convenience stores to purchase goods, which may be overpriced and rarely farm-fresh, or end up eating at fast-food restaurants that offer affordable (but unhealthy) options just to keep their families fed. This can also happen in rural locations where the nearest farm market (which may also be seasonal) or full-service grocery store is many miles away. This creates what is known as "food deserts."[2]

TEXTBOX 4.1

The Effects of Food Insecurity

Among women, food insecurity has been linked with:

- Obesity
- Anxiety and depressive symptoms
- Risky sexual behavior
- Negative pregnancy outcomes such as low birthweight and gestational diabetes[3]

Among children, food insecurity has been linked with:

- Anemia
- Asthma
- Depression and anxiety
- Cognitive and behavioral problems
- Higher risk of being hospitalized[4]

We may think of malnutrition as something that only happens in developing countries or to those on society's margins, but as Tracie MacMillan explores in "The New Face of Hunger" for *National Geographic*, one-sixth of Americans don't have enough food to eat, even though most of those families have at least one adult working full-time.[5] That translates to about 11 percent of households in the United States and 9 percent in Canada being considered food insecure.[6] In contrast with most European countries where the number is closer to one-twentieth, the reality of suburban starvation in North America is shocking, causing some to refer to this demographic as the "SUV poor."

On top of the painful irony of being hungry yet clothed, housed, and employed, the SUV poor are often overweight. Their children are too. This results from having to rely on high-calorie/low-nutrition products from food banks, fast-food joints, and convenience stores. When you only receive $150 per month in food stamps and you can buy eight boxes of pasta for the same price as a bag of organic grapes, most families will go with the option that fills bellies longer. When you are pressed for time because you are working three minimum-wage jobs to pay bills, you go with what is fast and easy. The result is children and adults suffering from deficits in essential nutrients while bearing the physical and emotional effects of being overweight—a stigma with long-lasting repercussions.

Food insecurity and lack of what I call "food literacy" (having a working idea of the nutritional value—or lack thereof—of foodstuffs and how to grow, prepare, and eat them) doesn't just affect working families, the elderly, or infirm. What we think of as typically young, healthy, vibrant college students are also stressed about getting enough to eat. When I was the student life coordinator at the New

Brunswick College of Craft and Design (situated in the gentrified downtown core of the province's capital city of Fredericton in New Brunswick, Canada), one of the top issues facing our students was a lack of access to fresh produce and afford-able meals. The nearest full-service grocery store was a bus or taxi ride away, though there was a small meat market that also sold produce and some canned and boxed goods downtown. There was also a weekly farmer's market within walking distance from the college, but in our cold climate, produce availability is seasonal and can be cost-prohibitive. If you don't get there bright and early (and most college students are averse to rising at 6 a.m.), most of the good stuff is gone. And honestly, most of my students had no idea what to do with potatoes, let alone something more exotic-sounding like kohlrabi. Students, as most aca-demic librarians reading this can attest, live on a diet of ramen noodles, energy drinks, coffee, cheap takeout, and peanut butter sandwiches. I quickly learned I could produce impressive numbers at school functions if I provided free food. Giving away pizza and sandwiches wasn't enough; students were still hungry and often sickly. I worked with the student association to create a (free!) weekly food delivery where local farmers and markets would donate excess produce and dried goods that were near or at their sell-by date. Or they provided produce that wasn't market-pretty but still perfectly edible (like crooked carrots or too-small apples). With the help of student volunteers and one paid helper, I would arrange pick up and delivery of the items and distribute them from the student lounge. It was often gone in a matter of hours or less. We offered cooking and storage tips to go along with the items, because often, students had no idea what to do with a bag of spinach or Swiss chard. It continually shocked me how students in their late teens and early twenties lacked real-world skills, like knowing how to deposit a check in their bank account or peel a cucumber, despite being able to build a website or create impressive 3D models. Luckily, cooking and food prep skills are easily transferable.

While this may sound radically innovative, we weren't reinventing the wheel—similar programs have taken place in colleges, libraries, churches, and community centers all over the world. Noah Lenstra (who wrote the foreword to this book) has been diligently keeping his finger on the pulse of health and wellness programs in libraries with his Let's Move in Libraries project, of which I am an advisory board member.[7] During 2020, as the COVID-19 pandemic was raging in Canada and the United States, I asked him what he thought about libraries' contribution to ending food insecurity, and here was his take:

In addition to distributing food to those who need it, public libraries increas-ingly work with partners to educate community members on how to grow and prepare food, as well as on the basics of nutrition and meal planning. These include such initiatives as teaching and community gardens on library grounds, introductions to knife skills and other food preparation skills, how-to cooking classes focused on specific dishes, introductions to new flavors and tastes, and the basics of meal prep using tools like the USDA's Choose My Plate online tool (https://www.choosemyplate.gov/). All of these programs were offered in a virtual format during the COVID-19 pandemic by librarians that posted videos to platforms like Facebook Live and YouTube, or that sent seeds in the mail to gardeners rather than having them check them out in person . . . By serving as summer meal sites in the US Department of Agriculture's Summer Feeding Program, over 2,000 US public libraries (as of 2019) enrich young peoples' minds and bodies . . . Even during the COVID-19 pandemic, these efforts continue, with libraries offering grab-and-go lunches to vulnerable families at libraries across the nation (see https://youtu.be/Q6Ig_zo1tj4).[8]

For more information on how public libraries are addressing food insecurity, you can check out Lenstra's open-access article, "Food Justice in the Public Library: Information, Resources, and Meals," and also visit the California State Library's program website: https://lunchatthelibrary.org/.[9]

While libraries cannot solve the deeper systemic dysfunction that causes food insecurity or save the world amid a global pandemic or other disasters, we can work to mitigate some of the ill effects of our culture's inequalities. This chapter will look at ways that public and academic libraries can offer food-related programming to help mitigate some of the difficulties around food preparation, access to high-quality meals, and education about healthy eating. Chapter 8, "Health and Wellness Programs," as well as my previously published book, *Get Your Community Moving: Physical Literacy Programs for All Ages*, offer program ideas to help patrons combat obesity and the emotional toll of food insecurity.[10] Chapter 9, "Business and Finance Programs," also offers key programming ideas for helping your patrons create realistic budgets for stretching their food dollars farther. And lastly, Chapter 10, "Nature and Gardening Programs," offers program suggestions for helping patrons grow their own food at home or in a community garden. But this chapter isn't only about combating food insecurity in your neighborhoods; it also offers some fun tips to bring in potential patrons that may be intrigued that a library is offering something tasty besides books. Who knows, maybe they'll initially come for the free food but return over and over again once they see how many amazing services we offer!

Program Model: Water Bottle Decorating

Want an eco-friendly program that also promotes healthy hydration? This easy workshop could be targeted to very specific groups or left as an intergenerational program for anyone. You could do this with the general public or pick a demographic: sports teams, work teams as part of professional development, school groups, as an outreach program at a homeless shelter or nursing home—the sky's the limit! At the L. P. Fisher Public Library, our program was open to the general public, and we welcomed anyone ages five and up (they had to be able to hold a paint pen steadily and not lick it). The following program model is designed for a general adult audience, but feel free to modify it to suit your own crowd. Gather some BPA-free water bottles (we like the stainless-steel ones best!), some paint pens, and have fun personalizing those ubiquitous adult sippy cups we all lug around.

Advance Planning

Step 1. Figure out your target demographic and the day and time you want to hold the workshop. It should take one or two hours, depending on the size of the crowd and how many pens you must share and how many helpers you have on hand.

Step 2. Book the room you'll be using. This program could also be done outdoors, weather dependent.

Step 3. Find the funding to pay for your materials (or find sponsors to provide the materials). See the section "Budget Details" that follows for tips and tricks.

Step 4. Gather the supplies (listed in the "Materials Required" section). Posca pens are the brand we use. These are acrylic-based products that come in a variety of colors and have various nib sizes. It's best to provide both: thick for fill-in work, and thin for outlines, lettering, and details. The pen format makes them easier to manage than traditional paint for those with small hands or those with arthritis or other issues affecting their grip. I also recommend having baby wipes on hand, which easily clean up messes and mistakes. Coloring books or design books can provide inspiration, and it is good to have scrap paper for doodles and testing out colors and ideas. You may like to provide stencils if you feel your group would prefer something more structured and less open-ended (see figure 4.1). For water bottles, we watched the sales, and when some seventeen-ounce off-brand stainless-steel, vacuum-sealed models were half-price, we bought twenty of them. Try to find ones with minimal logos, which get in the way of the paint. We were also gifted ten bottles from a local fine arts college, which had a small version of their logo on the side. I recommend using something to cover the tables so that paint doesn't get everywhere. The environmentally friendly option is old newspapers or cut-up cardboard from the recycle bin, but plastic tablecloths work too.

Step 5. Decide if you are making this a drop-in program or if you require registration. Registration is recommended since you will have a finite number of bottles unless you hit the bottle jackpot or people are bringing their own from home. Plus, you will want to know how many pens and other supplies you'll need. Make a sign-up sheet or whatever your library does to record registrations for events.

Step 6. Notify staff so they can let patrons know about the program. Advertise on Facebook, Twitter, and any other social media your library uses. In an academic library, notify faculty in case they would like to attend. Or, if you are planning it with a specific audience in mind, make sure to schedule it with them in advance. Make a poster and add it to your print and online calendars.

Step 7. Prepare photo and video releases if you plan on taking photos/video to share online.

Step 8. Depending on your artistic abilities, level of comfort, and the size of your group, you may wish to recruit a helper or teacher. I asked local artist Jody McCleary to join us to help with instruction and troubleshooting. Jody and I also made our own decorated water bottles ahead of time to try out the materials and be able to show patrons examples of what could be done.

Figure 4.1 **Three adult patrons try using stencils to decorate their water bottles.** *Source*: Jenn Carson.

Materials Required

- Paint pens
- Baby wipes
- BPA-free water bottles (if providing, or patrons can bring their own)
- Scrap paper and pencils
- Coloring books, lettering, and/or graphic design idea books
- Stencils (optional)
- Plastic tablecloths or old newspapers
- Photo/video waivers (if using)
- Evaluation forms (if using)
- Written instructions on a whiteboard or paper handouts (so you don't have to repeat yourself)

Budget Details

$50–$200+. This is not a cheap program, but the good news is it is very easy to find sponsors and funding for it. Many local businesses, nonprofits, sports teams, or other entities are likely very willing to supply water bottles in exchange for free advertising. The only drawback is these may have logos on them. Want a sneaky tip? Those paint pens will cover right over most logos unless they are raised. Watch for water bottles on sale. Speaking of the pens, these aren't inexpensive either. A basic six-pack of black-and-white ones will cost $10 to $20, depending on if you can find them on sale. For a large crowd or a variety of colors and nib sizes, expect to spend at least $100 on the pens. The good news is that you might be able to get the local art supply store to donate some or give you a discount in exchange for their logo on the poster or a special mention on social media. The baby wipes run $3 to $10, depending on how eco-conscious you can afford to be (the unscented, bamboo ones are lovely but expensive). The ones with alcohol, though harsher on the skin, are better for taking off paint. You can also ask people to bring their own water bottles from home, most people have lots hanging around, but this may alienate those that don't have one to bring and may create a perceived class disparity between those with fancy, brand-name, double-walled stainless steel and those with giveaway plastic freebies. Do what you can afford.

As mentioned earlier, some of our bottles were donated, and the rest of the program supplies came to about $360 CAN for twenty people. I applied for a grant through our Western Valley Wellness Network and ran the program during Wellness Week in October in order to qualify for full funding. Because of this, the program cost the library $0, though I did have to buy the items out of pocket and then get reimbursed. If you look around for grants and sponsors, that could easily be your reality as well if you have enough cash flow to buy items ahead of time. Think outside the box, and you may even be able to get funding or a product donation through your local water commission, nature conservation council (which wants to rid the environment of disposable plastic water bottles), or sporting goods/outdoor adventure store or home goods store.

Day-of-Event

Step 1. Set up the tables, gather all supplies, and lay everything out. Assemble your staff and volunteers (and visiting artist, if you have one) and go over the game plan. If it is a beautiful day and you have a park on campus or are near the library with picnic tables, you could consider doing it outdoors. That would cut down on the paint smell and maybe make messes less risky. It also makes passersby curious about your library and its cool programs.

Step 2. Once everyone is assembled, explain the directions very clearly (see textbox 4.2). It's helpful to have the instructions printed out or written on a whiteboard for people who arrive late (or weren't paying attention) or just to refer to. It will save your voice if you have a big crowd or are outdoors. Feel free to shorten my directions; these are mostly for you to get a good visual ahead of time. I highly recommend decorating a bottle yourself to get the hang of the pens.

TEXTBOX 4.2

Directions for Water Bottle Decorating

1. Plan your design ahead of time. Use the books on the tables for inspiration and try out using a pencil (not the paint pens!) on the scrap paper first. The more time you put into planning the design, the easier it will be to execute on the bottle.
2. How to use the pens: to get the paint flowing, you need to depress the tip a few times until it starts to come out. Don't hold the tip down for too long or it will all bleed out (see figure 4.2).
3. Thin nibs are best for outlines, lettering, and adding small details at the end. Thick nibs are good for coloring in.
4. Make sure to let each color and coat dry before adding the next or else it will smear and the colors will mix on the pen nibs, ruining both colors. You must be especially careful about this with light colors such as white or yellow, or you'll end up with disgusting light-grey-brownish paint pens.
5. Since there are not enough pens for everyone to get their own set of colors, we must share. Keep all the pens you aren't using in the middle of the table, and only take the color you need right now.
6. If you make a mistake, use a baby wipe to clean it up. Let the bottle dry before painting again.
7. If you need help or have a question, raise your hand, and one of our instructors will come over to help you.

Step 3. Walk around and help people with their painting, stencils (if using), getting the pens working, finding the colors they need, and answering any questions they may have (there will be lots). Don't forget to take pictures and video, if you are doing so. You'll want to share the amazing creations on social media. A group shot at the end with everyone's bottles is always nice to have.

Step 4. Keep an eye on the time and remind people when you are fifteen, ten, and five minutes to ending, so they have time to finish up their projects. Inevitably, you will have some people who could sit there all day adding more and more details or reworking a specific spot (and they may try to). Unless you have unlimited time, you'll need to firmly nudge these people along. Start reminding them early, or they will resist.

Step 5. Distribute evaluation forms (if using) and ask people to use the provided pencils (not the paint pens!) to complete them. I recommend keeping the evaluation to three short questions:
   1. What did you like about this program?
   2. What do you recommend we could do better next time?
   3. Would you recommend this program to a friend?

Step 6. Clean up and pack away the leftover supplies. Store paint pens in a ziplock bag or plastic container in case they leak and to help keep them from drying out.

Figure 4.2   Instructor Jody McCleary shows an adult patron how to use the paint pens. *Source:* Jenn Carson.

Literacy Tie-In

If you'd like, prepare an eye-catching display to correspond with the event (this can also be done on digital platforms for e-books!). Choose books, films, and periodicals that have to do with environmentalism, especially water conservation or access, and the importance of hydration. Adding some books about the science of water is fun too! Try to find something that would appeal to different types of patrons. Below is a short list of some diverse materials you could use for a water-friendly display. Bonus: you can re-use this display for Earth Day. I'm sure you can find many more titles, as it's a fascinating topic, but this will get you started.

Periodicals:

- *Mother Earth News*
- *Orion Magazine*
- *Resurgence & Ecologist*
- *Water Canada*
- *Yes! Magazine*

Print or audiobooks:

- *Beauty Water: Everyday Hydration Recipes for Wellness and Self-Care* by Tori Holmes
- *Downriver: Into the Future of Water in the West* by Heather Hansman
- *The Drought-Resilient Farm: Improve Your Soil's Ability to Hold and Supply Moisture for Plants; Maintain Feed and Drinking Water for Livestock when Rainfall Is Limited; Redesign Agricultural Systems to Fit Semi-arid Climates* by Dale Strickler
- *The Fourth Phase of Water: Beyond Solid, Liquid, and Vapor* by Gerald H. Pollack
- *The Hidden Messages in Water* by Masaru Emoto
- *Infused Waters: 50 Simple, Gorgeous Drinks for Ultimate Hydration and Health* by Georgia Davies
- *One Well: The Story of Water on Earth* by Rochelle Strauss and Rosemary Woods
- *Quench: Beat Fatigue, Drop Weight, and Heal Your Body through the New Science of Optimum Hydration* by Dana Cohen and Gina Bria
- *Water: The Epic Struggle for Wealth, Power, and Civilization* by Steven Solomon
- *Water: The Fate of Our Most Precious Resource* by Marq de Villiers
- *Water: A Very Short Introduction* by John Finney
- *The Water Will Come: Rising Seas, Sinking Cities, and the Remaking of the Civilized World* by Jeff Goodell
- *The Whole Story of Climate: What Science Reveals About the Nature of Endless Change* by E. Kirsten Peters
- *Young Water Protectors: A Story About Standing Rock* by Aslan Tudor, Kelly Tudor, et al.

DVDs:

- *Before the Flood* (2017)
- *Chasing Ice* (2014)
- *Poisoned Water* (2017)
- *Poisoned Waters* (2009)
- *Revolution* (2013)

Helpful Advice

- Stencils are sometimes messy because the paint seeps underneath them, making for a blurry edge. If the stencils aren't the self-adhesive kind, you have to tape them on or else try to hold and color at the same time, which is tricky. Not recommended with children or those lacking in patience or dexterity.
- Some pens require shaking first (read the label), as these usually have a ball bearing inside that rattles. Shake prior to the program. Be mindful if you are using them with a group that has sensory processing issues, as they may find the sound irritating (not to mention the smell).
- The best way to make sure everyone has equal access to the paint pens is to get one full color set per table and everyone at that table must share. We couldn't afford this, so we had one pack of black and white (various nib sizes), one pack of metallic (thin nib), and one pack of bright colors (thick

nibs). We distributed them as best we could among four tables, and then if people needed a specific color/nib size, they raised their hand, and Jody and I would dash about trying to find them what they were looking for. If we saw spare pens lying about, we'd grab them and hold them in the air, calling out like an auctioneer: "Light blue, big nib light blue here, get your big nib light blue. Anybody need a big nib light blue? You sir? You want a big nib light blue? Wanna trade? Trade for a thin metallic gold? Sold! One big nib light blue sold for a thin metallic gold! Anybody want a thin metallic gold?" And so on . . . It wasn't particularly efficient (or quiet), but it was fun and entertaining. The kids especially looked forward to their turn to auction off their paint pen, but you might find adults are just as enthused.

- Make sure the water bottles you acquire are BPA-free.[11] If they are bringing their own from home, that's up to them, but you can encourage "Bring BPA-free bottles!" in your marketing.

- If you want to make the finished design last longer, you can spray the bottles with a fixative, but this is expensive (about $10 to $20 per bottle) and must be done outdoors. It reeks. Also, it should preferably have three coats, which will take awhile, as you'll have to wait for each coat to dry. I didn't think this was feasible for our program's length, budget, and format, but I did bring in a bottle of spray fixative from home to show patrons an example of what could be purchased and used at home if they wanted. I emphasized it would help their art last longer (months versus weeks, depending on how rough they were with them). Don't put the decorated bottles in the dishwasher.

- Make sure to let patrons and staff know ahead of time that the acrylic paint does have a slight smell. Most people won't even notice, but anyone with environmental allergies might be offended by it and choose not to participate. They are safe to use indoors and with children. If any gets on the skin, have patrons wipe it off right away with a baby wipe or soap and water. Don't allow any children under the age of five to participate; you don't want them to put the paint in their mouths.

- Like most library programs, prepare for the fact that not everyone who signed up will show and people will show up who didn't sign up. This worked out happily for us because the exact number of people who didn't show left us the right number of bottles for people who randomly appeared wanting to paint. I'll leave it up to you and your policies whether you accept surprise arrivals or if you want to save leftover bottles for another time (or for staff!).

- I really recommend taking one of the bottles to use as a "demo" bottle. You can draw a design on it ahead of time or part of a design to show people the process and how to get the pens flowing and how to use them properly. The demo bottle can also be used for practice by patrons.

- Perfectionist pro-tip: you can gently scrape mistakes off with your fingernail or a plastic butter knife.

- If recruiting an artist-volunteer to help or even run the program, ask them about their experience with these materials, they may have lots of good tips to share. Our volunteer even got a discount at the local art supply store, which we took advantage of by having her purchase our pens and then reimbursing her.

- Make sure you leave enough time for this program—anything less than an hour will make patrons frustrated and feel rushed.
- Want more? Now that you got these awesome markers, have some more "decorate this"-style programs. You can also use them to label all sorts of things in the library. May as well get your money's worth—use them up before they dry out!
- If the pens are out of your budget (or mess-tolerance), this program can also be done with high-quality waterproof stickers. You can get fun packs of thirty to fifty stickers on Amazon for about ten dollars.

Program Model: Recipe Swap

This program is incredibly versatile and can be used both online and in person. The model that follows offers options for either. The basic premise is that you encourage patrons to share their favorite recipes while you promote the library's cookbook collection. Depending on your organization's policies and health and safety procedures, you may even be able to have patrons bring sample cooking from home to share (taste tests are the best!). If not, it can still be fun to share just the recipes themselves. Patrons can get very creative sharing their food photos or videos online—presentation matters! Who doesn't love to find the next best chocolate chip recipe? Or a salsa that uses up all the tomatoes and zucchini taking over your garden? This program model is written for a generic recipe swap, but you can tailor it to a specific theme to make it more interesting or to meet certain programming goals. If you find the program proves popular, you could do a new theme each month or each week. Check out the textbox 4.3 for a list of ideas!

TEXTBOX 4.3

Recipe Swap Theme Ideas

- Healthy Eats
- Super Salads
- Marvelous Muffin Recipes
- Meatless Meals
- Road Trip Munchies
- 5 Ingredients or Less
- Best Breakfasts
- Smoothies and Shakes
- Creative Cookies
- Cooking for Kids
- Best Budget Meals
- Meal Prep Favorites
- Gluten-Free Recipes
- Best Slow Cooker and Instant Pot Recipes
- Air Fryer Favorites

- Canning and Preserves
- Family Favorites
- Appealing Appetizers
- Best Snacks for Sharing
- Box Lunch Ideas
- Winter Warming Recipes
- Holiday Recipes[12]

Advance Planning

Step 1. First, you need to decide whether to offer this online or in person. There are obvious drawbacks or benefits to each option, which are discussed more in the "Helpful Advice" section. You may want to read that first before continuing with the prep steps if you are undecided.

Step 2. Pick an online platform or location, plus a date and time. For an online event where people can add posts in their own time, it might last a whole week or more. If you are going for a holiday theme, don't plan it too close to the holiday as people will be busy. For example, hold a Christmas cookie-themed recipe swap in late November or early December, not the week before Christmas.

Step 3. Decide who on your team is going to run or moderate the program—it generally helps to pick someone passionate about food. If you are going with a digital format, make sure it is someone who is comfortable with the technology (or willing to learn!).

Step 4. Decide on a theme and prepare your marketing materials. How are you going to get the word out? Print media (posters, calendars, newsletters, etc.), email newsletter, website, Facebook, Twitter, Instagram, and other social media platforms are all good options (see figure 4.3 for a poster example). Don't forget to share with local groups who may be interested, such as book clubs, church groups, homeschooling associations, 4H clubs, the YMCA, and so on. If you are in an academic institution, nab a spot on campus radio to discuss or share with the student association. A little promo video on YouTube that can be shared on social media to hype up the event might also be worth your time. A video of you preparing and/or cooking a simple dish can really grab some attention.

Step 5. Book the room if you are doing it as an in-person event. If you have a kitchen or room with a sink, that is helpful if you are doing a taste-testing component to make clean-up easier, or to warm foods in an oven (if that complies with policy). Decide how you are going to organize the room (tables for placing food or recipes to swap, for example). If you are doing an online event, research which platform will be the most accessible for your target demographic and go ahead and create the interface for it (i.e., set up the Zoom or WebEx meeting, prepare the Facebook group, decide on the hashtag[s], write the code for the new webpage, or set up a blog space).

Step 6. Go over what materials you are going to need (see "Materials Required" section). This will vary greatly depending on the delivery format you choose. If you are making a full-on, bring-your-own-dish-to-share in-person recipe swap,

Figure 4.3   Recipe swap promotional poster. *Source*: Brendan Helmuth.

you are going to need to prepare a dish to share (unless the library isn't contributing, only hosting). If you are only swapping recipes, you may just need some index cards for people to write out recipes on or access to a photocopier. If you are doing it online, there are no physical materials needed, except maybe a camera to take pictures of a personal recipe you might be sharing and, obviously, your computer.

Step 7. Decide how you are going to control access to the program. If this is an in-person event, do you require pre-registration? Can people just show up with food to share? If doing an online Zoom-style event, how many people are you going to allow to join? Will everyone get a turn to share their recipe and talk about it? Who is going to provide tech support while you moderate? Who is going to moderate a group page, like a Facebook group? What are the rules for posting? If you are going to curate a recipe gallery on a webpage or blog, what format do people need to submit their recipes in? Will you accept video? What quality photos do you require for uploading? See the "Helpful Advice" section that follows for more prep-work brainstorming.

Step 8. If you are doing an in-person event and plan to take photos or video, you may (depending on your library's privacy policy) wish to prepare photo or video release waivers.

Materials Required

- Blank index cards (if using)
- Photo/video release forms (if using)
- Camera (for in-person event)
- Prepared dish for sharing (if you are picking this option)
- Napkins, cutlery, and dishes for in-person event (depending on the theme chosen—you aren't going to need forks for a cookie swap)
- Tablecloths (if using)
- Evaluation forms (if using)
- Dish soap and sponge/cloth (unless you use disposable items)
- Access to a photocopier (for in-person)

Budget Details

$0-$50+. This can be a very low (or no) budget event, based on what method you choose and how elaborate your delivery is. An online event using free software can cost nothing, or an in-person program with print marketing, disposable dishes, and fancy tablecloths could cost a lot more. Our in-person dessert recipe swap cost nothing, really, other than toner and paper. Patrons brought their recipes on cards, which we photocopied for them to hand out. They brought samples of the recipes to share. We used paper napkins for the desserts.

Day-of-Event

Step 1. If doing an in-person event, prepare the room (set up tables, prepare handouts, etc.). If doing an online event, prepare the platform space and make sure all technology is ready to go. Check your audio and video and make sure all cables are plugged in. If you work in a busy environment where you may be interrupted, make sure to let your coworkers (or, if working from home, your housemates) know that you need an hour (or more) of undisturbed time in your office.

Step 2. Prepare a display of materials for patrons to check out after the program (see "Literacy Tie-In" section for ideas) and/or create a digital resource guide to share recommended items. You can even make a special "Recipe Room" in your online catalog if your ILS interface allows for that. Have fun with it!

Step 3. Greet patrons as they join the event. Troubleshoot any online tech issues. Explain how the program is going to work. For an in-person event, perhaps everyone puts the dish they brought to share on the table and lays out the recipe card(s) next to the item. People can either copy the recipe by hand, you can photocopy it if that's feasible, or people can take a picture with their phone. If you are doing taste tests, dishes can be portioned out and placed on napkins or plates for sharing. For an online event, maybe everyone takes turns explaining their dish and posting a screenshot of the recipe in the chat for people to download.

Step 4. Make sure to have patrons sign the photo/video release waivers and take lots of pictures/video for an in-person event. You can live-tweet the event, if you'd like, and share the photos or video on Facebook or Instagram (or both!). If doing a non-live digital event where you are posting content patrons pre-sent you, make sure you are doing your updates regularly to keep your audience interested.

Step 5. Thank everyone for coming/joining the event. Hand out or email a link for an evaluation form, if using. Archive the online event, if feasible. Clean up from the in-person event. Eat the leftovers!

Literacy Tie-In

If your public library is anything like mine, you have an overabundance of cookbooks. If that's the case, finding materials for your display won't be a challenge, so maybe narrow in on the details. Based on your theme, try to find items that match. Don't be afraid to include DVDs of cooking shows, cooking magazines, or other food-themed items. Some libraries have food-related alternative collections they can tie in, like baking pans or appliances. This is where your reader advisory talents get to shine! There are thousands of cookbooks and food-related resources on the market, but here are some ideas to get you started.

Periodicals:

- *Bon Appetit*
- *Canadian Living*
- *Clean Eating*
- *Cook's Illustrated*
- *EatingWell*
- *Fine Cooking*
- *Food Network Magazine*
- *Food & Wine*
- *Martha Stewart Living*
- *The Pioneer Woman Magazine*
- *Saveur*
- *Southern Living*
- *Taste of Home*

Print, Electronic, or Audiobooks:

- *A Cookbook* by Matty Matheson
- *Flour Water Salt Yeast: The Fundamentals of Artisan Bread and Pizza* by Ken Forkish
- *Half Baked Harvest Cookbook: Recipes from My Barn in the Mountains* by Tieghan Gerard

- *Jamie's Friday Night Feast* by Jamie Oliver
- *Joy of Cooking: 2019 Edition Fully Revised and Updated* by Irma S. Rombauer, Marion Rombauer Becker, et al.
- *Mastering the Art of French Cooking,* vol. 1 by Julia Child, Louisette Bertholle, and Simone Breck
- *The Oh She Glows Cookbook: Vegan Recipes to Glow from the Inside Out* by Angela Liddon
- *Salt, Fat, Acid, Heat: Mastering the Elements of Good Cooking* by Samin Nosrat
- *The Silver Palate Cookbook* by Julee Rosson and Sheila Lukins
- *Solo: A Modern Cookbook for a Party of One* by Anita Lo
- *The Step-by-Step Instant Pot Cookbook: 100 Simple Recipes for Spectacular Results—with Photographs of Every Step* by Jeffrey Eisner
- *The Taste of Country Cooking* by Edna Lewis

DVDs:

- *Burnt* (2010)
- *Chef* (2014)
- *Julia Child: The French Chef* (2005)
- *Julia Child: The Way to Cook* (2009)
- *Julie & Julia* (2009)
- *Kitchen Confidential: The Complete Series* (2007)
- *No Reservations* (2008)
- *Ratatouille* (2007)

Helpful Advice

- If offering the program online, which platform will you choose? Will you get people to post recipes and photos/videos to Twitter or Instagram and tag your library and the program name? Will you form a Facebook group page for the program and have people post to that page? You probably don't want to allow people to post to your library's main page, right? Do you want to try out an online meet-up using Zoom or a similar free conferencing software and have people take turns presenting their recipe and showing what their finished product looks like from their kitchens? Do you want more control over the posts and more privacy for your patrons? Then maybe suggest people email you their recipes (properly sourced!) with photos, and then you can curate a gallery of the results on your library's website, blog, or social networking sites.
- Make sure your instructions to participants are extremely concise yet inviting. Your copy for a weeklong digital program could sound something like this: "Join the <insert library name here> for an online recipe swap the week of <insert date>! We'll be sharing our best Box Lunch Ideas for back-to-school! Any day from <insert dates> you are welcome to share your favorite family lunch ideas on our special Box Lunch Ideas Facebook group page <insert link>. In your post make sure you upload a photo of your meal, detailed instructions, and a link or mention of where you found the recipe (i.e., a cookbook, blog, TV show, Pinterest post, etc.). Enjoy trying other people's

recipes and see what your neighborhood families love best for their lunches. This is for adults too; we want to know what you love eating at work and your favorite ways to pack it!"

- The size of your audience may dictate which format you choose. If you think you are going to get inundated with hundreds of recipes, you may not want to choose the email-and-curate option. If you live in a small town as I do, it may be totally reasonable to host an in-person swap where the people who showed up and fed me cookies were also my neighbors.
- The demographic you are trying to reach will also dictate which platform you choose and what time or manner you hold the event. Aiming to target stay-at-home parents? Why not try a mid-morning Zoom event to share "Afterschool Snack Ideas" or "Favorite Family Dinners"? Aiming at young professionals? Why not an evening "Appealing Appetizers" meet-up, either in person or online? Have a large population of truckers or travelers in your neck of the woods? Why not share ideas for "Road Trip Munchies"?
- When publishing recipes online, there is the risk of copyright infringement, so unless the original recipe's author has given permission to share or you are providing the source (for example, you are sharing a link to a blog or website with the original recipe), I would avoid it. Ask patrons to share their original or family recipes or else cite the source.
- Check into your local food safety laws and your library's policies about serving food or sharing food. For example, in New Brunswick, Canada, we're not allowed to prepare food without a food safety certification (which some of my staff and board members have, myself included), and only certain foods brought in from offsite can be served. There may also be rules governing food temperature and food storage. For example, if someone is bringing in a meat casserole to share, it may have to be kept at a certain temperature or a rice dish cannot be left on a counter too long. There are hundreds of food safety aspects to consider (including washing dishes and choking hazards). You can avoid all this by simply sharing recipe ideas in person or online, without having food samples, but it is also less fun (and delicious). But food poisoning is *also* decidedly not fun, so choose wisely. Obviously, public health issues like pandemics will also dictate whether you should share food publicly.
- A digital recipe swap is a great alternative format during pandemic lockdowns or other times when the physical library is inaccessible. This format is also well-suited to those that work from home or work shiftwork and can't make it to the library during opening hours or have mobility or other transportation impediments. Digital programs are also great for those with social anxiety, sensory processing issues, or other barriers that prevent them from interacting in groups.
- If offering the program in person, will people bring in preprinted recipe cards to swap, or will you photocopy the recipe for them? Some people may prefer to just snap a photo with their phone. If handwritten, is it legible?
- If offering a taste-testing option, will you use disposable dishes/cutlery? This might be more sanitary and involve less washing but also be worse for the environment and cost more. Make sure you weigh the pros and cons.

- Consider offering a reward for most-liked recipe (digital version) or voting on best dish for an in-person taste-test-style swap. If you don't like the competitive element, it could just be a door prize every participant gets a chance to win. The prize could be a nice cookbook gleaned from the donation pile or a donated gift certificate from a local restaurant or kitchenware store that sponsors the event. Don't be afraid to seek partners for sponsoring even a fairly low-budget program like this—it may build a relationship that could be very beneficial for a future programming event!
- Think about recruiting volunteers to help you run the program (and participate). You can find great support from local farmer's market food vendors, students or instructors from a local culinary institution, or a high school home economics class. There are also many people in the community who love to cook in their spare time and are quite talented—don't be shy to put a call out on your social media platforms or ask that patron who is always bringing in delicious treats to share with staff—they might be flattered to be asked to help! (See figure 4.4.)

Figure 4.4 The author and her neighbor, Ellen Helmuth, at a recipe swap. *Source*: Brendan Helmuth.

Further Food and Drink Ideas

- Pop Up Juice Bar—If you can get access to a juicer and some donated (or purchased) fruits and veggies, you can create a juice bar! Patrons can learn about how fresh fruit and vegetable juice contains many more nutrients (and no added sugar and preservatives!) than the bottles they buy at the grocery store. Then they can use their library cards to check out a recipe book to take home and try making their own juice or smoothies. We set up our program to correspond with a weekly onsite yoga class so participants could get a healthy drink on their way to or from class. We created a menu with a few different varieties to try and employed some (kitchen safety-certified) volunteers in our staff kitchen (see figures 4.5 and 4.6)

Figure 4.5   Pop Up Juice Bar Menu. *Source*: Brendan Helmuth.

- Cookbook Book Club—Instead of holding a regular book club program, why not try a version where every month, participants read a different cookbook and try recipes from it? For an in-person event (if this meets your food policies), patrons could even bring in recipe samples to share. This program could also be run online as a monthly Zoom event. You can find a great example of a cookbook club in Salt Lake City by reading this blog post from Programming Librarian: https://programminglibrarian.org/programs /cook-book-club.[13]
- Grocery Budgeting Basics—Host a workshop on how to create a weekly or monthly grocery budget. You can invite a local financial planner to join the conversation or host a tour of your local grocer to show where the healthiest options are located and how to stretch those food dollars while still eating well. Take a cue from Ellsworth Public Library in Maine and even do it online! Find out more at the Programming Librarian blog: https://programminglibrarian .org/programs/cooking-matters%C2%AE-pop-grocery-store-tour-online.[14]
- Learn to Be Self-Sufficient—Host various food and drink programs that encourage patrons to grow, prepare, or preserve their own goods. Teach the classes yourself or recruit knowledgeable volunteers. These events can be easily converted to online versions by hosting Zoom programs or posting a recorded video on social media. Here are some program titles to get you started: "Make Your Own Condiments" (mustard, ketchup, mayo, salad dressing); "Brew Your Own Beer"; "Make Your Own Yogurt"; "Grow Your Own Salad"; "Grow Your Own Sprouts"; "Bake Your Own Bread"; "Grow

Figure 4.6 Pop Up Juice Bar Participants. *Source*: Jenn Carson.

Your Own Mushrooms"; "Harvest Local" (wild fruits, nuts, greens, etc.). Don't forget to make a fabulous book display or online booklist to go with your program and increase those circulation stats!

Whether you are planning an amazing cooking contest or a simple recipe exchange, there are plenty of innovative ways to get the adults in your community excited about food and nutrition. Great programs don't have to be expensive, fancy, or even in person! Use your amazing librarian skills and the tips in this chapter to create safe, fun, well-attended food and drink events. Just remember: if you are serving alcohol, apply for a liquor license well in advance or you'll end up making everyone Shirley Temples!

Notes

1. "Let's Move: America's Move to Raise a Healthier Generation of Kids," *Let's Move* online, accessed March 1, 2022, https://letsmove.obamawhitehouse.archives.gov/.

2. Office of Disease Prevention and Health Promotion, "Food Insecurity," *Healthy People*, https://www.healthypeople.gov/2020/topics-objectives/topic/social-determinants-health/interventions-resources/food-insecurity.

3. Louise C. Ivers and Kimberly A. Cullen, "Food Insecurity: Special Considerations for Women," *The American Journal of Clinical Nutrition* 94, no. 6 (2011): 1740S–1744S.

4. Craig Gundersen and James P. Ziliak, "Food Insecurity and Health Outcomes," *Health Affairs* 34, no. 11 (2015): 1830–39.

5. Tracie McMillian, "The New Face of Hunger," *National Geographic Magazine* online, accessed March 1, 2022, https://www.nationalgeographic.com/foodfeatures/hunger/.

6. Government of Canada, "Household food insecurity, 2017/2018," *Statistics Canada*, June 24, 2020, https://www150.statcan.gc.ca/n1/pub/82-625-x/2020001/article/00001-eng.htm.

7. Noah Lenstra, *Let's Move in Libraries*, accessed March 1, 2022, https://letsmovelibraries.org/.

8. Email message to author, 2020.

9. Noah Lenstra and Christine D'Arpa, "Food Justice in the Public Library: Information, Resources, and Meals," *The International Journal of Information, Diversity, & Inclusion (IJIDI)* 3, no. 4, (2019), https://jps.library.utoronto.ca/index.php/ijidi/article/view/33010.

10. Jenn Carson, *Get Your Community Moving: Physical Literacy Programs for All Ages* (Chicago: ALA Editions, 2018).

11. BPA stands for bisphenol A, a chemical that can leach into food and water. According to multiple studies, the possible health effects of BPA can affect the brain and prostate gland of fetuses, infants, and children, and it can also affect their behavior. There is also some research that links BPA exposure with increased blood pressure and other health issues in adults.

12. You can get more specific here, depending on your clientele. Some ideas: Diwali, Thanksgiving, Halloween, Easter, Christmas, Fourth of July (or Canada Day, or whatever your national holiday is), Hanukkah, New Year's Day, Chinese New Year, Eid al-Fitr, and Bodhi Day.

13. Elizabeth Hanby, "Program Model: Cook the Book Club," *Programming Librarian*, March 25, 2020, https://programminglibrarian.org/programs/cook-book-club.

14. Abby Morrow, "Program Model: Cooking Matters® Pop-up Grocery Store Tour: Online!," *Programming Librarian*, June 4, 2020, https://programminglibrarian.org/programs/cooking-matters%C2%AE-pop-grocery-store-tour-online.

5

✢

Arts and Crafts Programs

When you stop the average person on the street to mention a "craft program at the library," undoubtedly the first image they are going to conjure is either preschoolers up to their elbows in glitter glue or white-haired ladies hunched over a fussy tole painting project. While both of those programs may be happening at your branch on any given day of the week, the reality is that injecting some refreshingly edgy art programming or crowd-pleasing crafts into your calendar (and budget) isn't impossible. Especially if you draw on the magic of community partnerships with local arts organizations and talented volunteers.

Believe it or not, libraries all over the world are bringing world-class cultural programming to their libraries. Many branches are now hosting artist and writer-in-residence programs, and some, like the Vancouver Public Library in British Columbia, Canada, are even hosting Indigenous Storyteller in Residence programs.[1] New libraries are being built with huge gallery spaces, and other libraries are finding ways to accommodate art installations in tiny spaces with even smaller budgets. A number of years ago we created the Lorna Delong Children's Gallery in memory of a prominent library member and volunteer, with nothing more than some anchors, a length of wire, some clothespins, and a sign on an unused wall space behind our children's stacks (see figure 5.1). It didn't cost more than a hundred dollars but is regularly enjoyed by hundreds of parents and children every year as they get to see the colorful displays of artwork made during storytime, during our annual Summer Reading Club, our Afterschool Maker Club, and many other programs. Similar spaces have been carved out in libraries for the work of adult patrons, even using something as simple and temporary as a few wooden easels set up in a lobby or a community bulletin board temporarily hijacked to display quilt squares or beginner watercolors. Seeing their work on display helps library patrons experience place attachment (feeling grounded in their town and building) and makes them more likely to want to continue supporting the library in the future.[2] This also works for staff. When I was just beginning my library career as a part-time clerk at the Kennebecasis Public Library in

Figure 5.1   The author and her son at the grand opening of the Lorna Delong Children's Gallery.
Source: Brendan Helmuth.

Quispamsis, New Brunswick, I submitted an application to the gallery committee to display my bookbinding projects for a month, which was accepted. I was so proud coming into work to see my books in the glass cabinet in the lobby and got a little thrill whenever a patron would stop to admire them and make encouraging comments (see figure 5.2). It also drew more interest to bookbinding in general, and soon patrons were asking if I would offer bookmaking and book-repairing classes, which I did, and we also created displays of bookbinding-related materials. I encouraged other artist friends of mine to submit applications, and soon the cabinet and wall spaces were filled with their lovely creations as well. This drew more interest from the artistic community—knowing we had an available space where they could showcase their work—and in turn, brought in the artists' friends, families, and admirers.

Certainly, there are a number of cautions when hosting arts and crafts programming that we need to go over before diving into the program models. For one

Figure 5.2   One of the author's handmade books. *Source*: Jenn Carson.

thing, we must be sensitive about cultural appropriation. There is a significant difference between appreciation and appropriation.[3] Whether painting a window display or teaching a craft activity at storytime, don't take the iconography of another culture and use it for purposes other than what it was intended by the original culture, such as making dreamcatchers to decorate people's houses. This is not only insensitive but can be insulting and offensive. When in doubt, focus on appreciating cultures and giving space to that. I was once teaching at a sports conference in Arizona where the organizers wanted to put an "Indian" in a stereotypical feather headdress on the conference T-shirt. The conference theme itself had nothing to do with Indigenous culture, and the T-shirt wasn't being designed by someone from a First Nation. I objected on account of it not representing either the conference or the state of Arizona. People involved insisted there were lots of Native Americans in Arizona and so it fit the conference location. I wasn't disputing the presence and importance of Indigenous culture in the state. My point was that there are currently over twenty groups/tribes of recognized First Nation people in Arizona who all have vastly different cultures, dress, and languages. Before including a stereotypical image of a First Nation person, we should ask first "why?" and "what is the context?" and, more importantly, make sure the people we are representing feel comfortable with the image we are using. There isn't just one "First Nation" culture any more than there is one "Asian" culture. In the end, the conference removed the large-nosed, tanned-skin man with the feather headdress from the shirt and replaced him with a cactus. Much less cringe.

Avoid the embarrassment of teaching a program for which you are unqualified or don't have the proper equipment. For example, you wouldn't host a metalsmithing class without proper eye protection or offer guitar lessons if you weren't an already accomplished musician. I'm a fibre artist—and was raised by a British immigrant fibre artist—and so I'm totally qualified to bust out my knitting needles and create some Fair Isle mittens or fisherman cables.[4] But I'm not about to start teaching workshops that involve Indigenous art when I can reach out to my Wolastoqey friends who will happily share their expertise to create shakers out of deer hide or wampum belts out of quahog and whelk shells (see figures 5.3 and 5.4). I also make pots. I come from an Anglo-Saxon background, and my people made (flat-bottomed) pottery—which differs from the pointed-bottomed pottery that is indigenous to this land we now call Canada that my people colonized—so if I was going to teach a pottery class, I would teach the pottery that comes from my people. Maybe I would bring in a guest teacher from a First Nation to teach

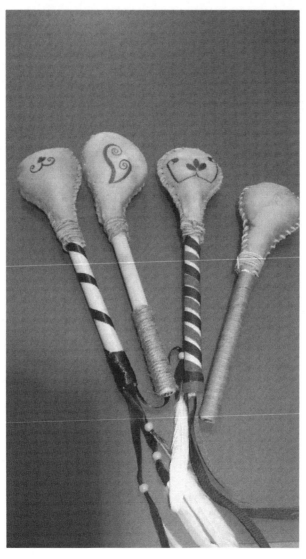

Figure 5.3   Shakers made with deerhide. *Source*: Jenn Carson.

Figure 5.4 Wampum Belt Sculpture. *Source*: Brendan Helmuth.

their style or would show examples to create appreciation, but I wouldn't teach it, because it is not my heritage, and I don't feel I have the right. I especially don't have the right to sell that style of pottery as my own. This is the difference between appreciation and appropriation.

I realize not everyone everywhere has access to people from the cultures from which they wish to share art or information. In that case, be honest and sensitive about it. If I'm teaching a sewing class, for example, on how to make a kimono-inspired bathrobe, you can be sure I'll discuss the difference between my pattern and an authentic Japanese kimono, as well as the garment's history and controversy.[5] Likewise, when dressing up for programs, please remember the catchphrase: *Culture is not a costume.* The difference between appreciation and appropriation is participation and consent.[6] If you have to ask yourself or someone else, "Is it okay for me to wear this _____ (headdress, veil, outfit, etc.)?" then the answer is probably "Nope." The deciding factor usually comes down to: What are you wearing it for? For example, if you are wearing a *gi* (from the Japanese *keikogi*, which means "training wear") to teach a class on martial arts such as karate or jiujitsu and you've studied under a long linage of professors and mentors from that culture, that's cool. That's the appropriate uniform for your chosen art form. Or if you are wearing a veil and hip scarf to participate in a belly dance class where you are dancing to traditional music and following an ancient pattern of dance moves taught by an expert—also fine. But don't "dress up" like this for, say, Halloween, Thanksgiving (no Pilgrims and Indians!), or a costume party at your library.[7] It's tacky and offensive. Someone else's cultural identity shouldn't be your party clothes.

Also, for safety purposes, know you and your volunteers or hired help's limits. I'm pretty handy around a sewing machine or pottery wheel, but I know nothing about glass blowing. You shouldn't hire teachers or have volunteers run a program without the necessary background checks. Besides their basic criminal record check, have references from the person who offers to teach a ballet class after school, and *actually call* the references to make sure the teacher in question has the experience they claim. If something goes wrong, it will not only reflect badly on you and your library, but it could also even be a liability issue. So, make sure you have any patrons who are engaging in risky physical activity (such as carving with sharp knives, felting with barbed needles, or dipping a partner in ballroom dance class) complete a liability waiver or holds harmless form.

Before you start expanding your art program offerings, I'd like you to go out and take a walk around the neighborhood surrounding your library. Are there any museums, galleries, artist-run spaces, concert venues, dance halls, or clay cafés nearby? Before you pump out a calendar full of craft nights, dance classes, and art openings, stop into these (often independent or nonprofit) businesses and check out what *their* calendars of events look like. You don't want to be offering a free beginner salsa class on the same afternoon as the local dance hall who is struggling to keep the lights on, and you don't want to be competing for an audience at your songwriters' circle if the bar next door is holding the same sort of event every Thursday night. If you are busy and overworked, why are you teaching the afterschool kids how to make their own sticker layouts in Canva (a graphic design platform) when there are a bunch of twenty-something artists at the low-rent studio loft a block away who would love to show off their skills for a reasonable fee?

I learned this hard lesson firsthand in the fall of 2019 when I offered a rug hooking class at the library. I thought I did everything right. I bought adorable snowmen and Santa kits for our holiday craft program (so people who didn't celebrate Christmas could choose an alternative) from a local indie art supply shop. I checked that none of the other cultural institutions nearby were offering a similar program. The artist-run gallery across the street had offered a rug hooking class from an out-of-town expert six months prior, but it had been a $95 two-day affair—much more extensive and expensive than my free two-and-a-half-hour intro lesson on a chilly Saturday afternoon. None of the current artists at the gallery were—*ahem*—hookers, and I felt like I had enough experience to offer the class, which several of my elderly patrons had been asking after for months. I sought funding to pay for the supplies through the Board, who had collected donations for art-related programming. So, I got to work hooking a handsome little snowman to use as an example and made a Facebook event and sign-up sheet. And then a war broke out. Well, an art war.

First, I got an angry phone call and then a visit from a concerned patron who wasn't convinced I was a "real artist" and didn't feel I had the qualifications to be teaching the workshop. Next, I got wind from my Board's Chair that a letter had been sent to him from the artist-run gallery asking us to cease and desist with all art programming as it was cutting into their bottom line and taking work away from the artists in their collective. Then one of the artists in the group, who also happens to be one of my yoga students and a regular library patron (and has taught art workshops at the library before), wrote a letter in response saying that the gallery had no right to get involved in the library's operations and that such an inflammatory reaction was not representative of all the gallery's members. I quickly called a bunch of separate meetings: with the concerned citizen, with the inflamed gallery owner, and with my Board.

I explained to all involved that the library doesn't charge for classes because we have a mandate to keep programs as accessible as possible to everyone in our community and that we were offering the class during the daytime on a

Saturday (their classes were usually on a weeknight) to try to attract underserved populations (low-income seniors, stay-at-home parents, and teens). I also explained that the cost of the class was being covered by funds raised by our Board and donated by patrons for exactly this purpose, to offer free art programs for adults and children. I also explained how I had an extensive art background, both as an instructor and exhibiting artist, and that what I would be teaching was an introduction-only class and wasn't remotely comparable to the more advanced class the gallery had offered and that I was more than qualified to teach it.

My meeting with the concerned citizen ended with her being satisfied with my explanation. The gallery owner apologized profusely for the confusion after I met with him. He didn't realize all the things the library did for the community or what our intentions were and said that he could see now some of the artists had overreacted and he had responded rashly to their concerns. I said I understood that he was only protecting his business and its clients and that in the future more open communication between our two organizations would help prevent this from happening. We resolved to alert each other to our upcoming programming schedules to make sure we weren't offering similar workshops at the same time, and we restated our intentions not to take business away from each other but instead to encourage the people of Woodstock to have more interest in the arts, which would benefit both of us. I encouraged him to continue bringing his gallery posters to the library, which we would share on our bulletin board and help promote their services. He said he would work more actively to promote the library to gallery and café visitors. He teared up and asked if it was okay for us to have a hug (this was pre-COVID), which was unconventional but not offensive to me, so I agreed. We both left the meeting on good terms and continue to have a flourishing partnership. He has become the leader of our ukulele group that meets once a week and always stops by my office to say "hi" during his visits. Our rug hooking workshop ended up full (with a waitlist!). We have plans to host another one once the pandemic subsides (since it isn't something I can teach easily without close contact).

I don't offer these cautions to shy you away from offering cultural programming, only to help guide you from my years of experience (and mistakes!). When done properly and safely, creating visual, musical, and kinetic art in your library's space is a beautiful and very rewarding thing indeed. And it will draw people from all walks of life who are curious and inspired by these remarkable gifts being shared in the community.

Program Model: Library Performance Art Series

While "Library Performance Art Series" isn't a sexy name for a program, I want you to take that with a grain of salt. It is merely a stand-in until you find a fab name for your own program, based on its content. Here are some real-life examples: The Boulder Library Concert Series, The Sunday Concert Series (this name is used at various locations), Discomfort Lab (a performance art series in Calgary, Alberta), Acrobatics with Li Liu (Boston, Massachusetts), and Chestermere Public Library Musical Theatre Program (they put on *Mama Mia!*). During the COVID pandemic, the Kitchener Public Library teamed up with Wilfrid Laurier

University's department of music to showcase talented student performers in their Music in the Lounge Series.[8] Classical music was played in the library's lounge and broadcast over Facebook Live for free for people to enjoy at home. Here in Woodstock, we offer a "Rhythm and Flow" yoga class that involves me teaching yoga while a local musician plays live music (during the pandemic, we did it online). The name of your particular program and its content will be entirely dependent on what sort of performing art you want to showcase (or what you get funding for). If it is mixed media, you can simply name it something generic like "The _____ Library Performing Arts Program." Either way, I'm sure it will be wonderful—so let's get started!

Advance Planning

Step 1. First you need to figure out what sort of performing arts program you want to host. Depending on the size of your town/city, the choices may be narrow or endless. What types of entertainment groups or performance artists do you have in your community? Is there a school that teaches dance—perhaps traditional Indigenous varieties native to your area, modern dance, or ballet? What about community-led group dancing programs like ballroom, ceilidh, or swing? Would the instructors or members be interested in coming to give a demonstration? What about contacting local music teachers to see if their students would like to perform a concert? (See figure 5.5.) Or booking a quartet or live rock band (depending on your venue size and location)? What about other performing arts such as acrobatics/circus art (think Cirque de Soleil on a smaller scale), community theater, opera, mime, puppetry, magic, illusion, or spoken word. *Vagina Monologues* (performed sometime between February and April to go along with V-Day) will usually draw a good crowd.[9] Before you reach out to any potential performers, make a list of possibilities, and then move on to Steps 2 and 3 before making phone calls. The performers will have a lot of questions, and you'll need to have (some of) the answers. Make sure you've got the logistics on your end at least partially figured out so you'll sound professional and serious about their involvement. The next phone call or meeting after the first one is when you can deal with the nitty-gritty. I'll talk more about this in Step 4.

Step 2. Location. Location. Location. Who or what you choose to display at the library is going to be entirely dependent on your space. An opera isn't going to work well in a tiny prison library, but a short performance of spoken word poetry might. Or a digital concert delivered via Zoom or Facebook live from a larger offsite venue. Maybe you are lucky enough to have an outdoor pavilion or bandstand on your grounds, or maybe even a dedicated music park (complete with instrument installations!) next to your library, like the one at Sherman Public Library in Texas.[10] Do you have a large auditorium or concert hall in the building or on campus that could be put to use? Are you at a cramped inner-city branch or one-room rural library? Never fear; perhaps you can find a local theater or park where patrons could gather to watch the performance as an outreach program. Also, try to think of your space as being more fluid than it may have been originally designed. If you are like me and your one activity room has giant support posts in the middle of it, can you move a concert or

Figure 5.5   Teen jazz band performing at the library. *Source*: Brendan Helmuth.

dance troupe upstairs to the stacks by setting up folding chairs and moving all the tables? Can you have a fashion show down the lobby stairs or hold a parade or mini-Tintamarre down a long corridor?[11] A flash mob on the lawn and side-walk? Where there's a will, there's a way!

Step 3. Decide if this is going to be a one-time performance or a themed series. When will you host it? How often? If you are going the digital route, will it be live-streamed? If so, will the streaming be recorded and hosted on a site, such as YouTube, for people to check it out at a later date?

Step 4. This is the stage of the game where it is probably a good idea to start reaching out to your possible performer list and see who is ready, willing, and able to perform in the location and during the time period you are considering. Once you've got a rough idea of your performance, you can move on to the details of the following steps. You may want to iron those out first, before you contact potential performers, but in my experience, starting with a general "Are you interested?" conversation and then following up with more details (pay, copyright, equipment, set up/tear down, and other logistics) at a later date is easier. It becomes more of a partnership, a collaboration. You'll feel less like a bookie—taking bets on who will show up—and more like an event manager (which is what you are).

Step 5. Decide how you will record the statistics for this event. If it is in a theater or room with chairs, that is easy: just count the empty seats and subtract from the total. If it is digital, will you count the number of views? The number of likes or shares? If it is in person but in an open space, such as a park or bandstand where people might just walk by and not pull up a chair and stay for the entire performance, will you just make a best estimate? If it is both live and recorded, will you combine the total real-time audience with later viewers? And for digital content, how often will you record the number of views (which will continue to change)—daily, weekly, monthly, quarterly, yearly? Or for a set period while it is posted and then after you will remove the content? Figuring out how you will keep track of your statistics will help narrow down your delivery model(s) to something manageable. Do this before you get any further in the planning process. It will also impress your Board and administration—these types of metrics are often what you need to get the go-ahead for future, more elaborate projects.

Step 6. Set your budget. Plan accordingly. See "Budget Details" section for more thoughts on this.

Step 7. How will people register for your event? Will you sell or give away tickets ahead of time? Can people just drop in until the room is at capacity? If it is an outdoor event, or offsite, how will you register people in advance? Do they call or email the library to sign-up or the venue? If you need to create a sign-up sheet, now is the time to prepare and tell your staff about it.

Step 8. Research performance rights for the material you (or others) will be presenting. You may need to pay fees for licensing certain songs, plays, or pieces to be performed. These may be different for in-person versus online performances. In the case of a traveling theater troupe or musical act, this may already be covered by them, but you should still ask. If not, it will be your responsibility. You can get started by checking out the websites of the American Association of Community Theatre (https://aact.org/obtaining -rights), SOCAN (https://www.socan.com/what-socan-does/licensing/), the Canadian Musician Reproduction Rights Agency (https://www.cmrra.ca/), or others.[12]

You'll also need to keep in mind copyright regulations for event attendees. This is another discussion to have with your performers. Are people allowed to photograph or record the event? If not, how will you police that? Does the library have written permission to share recordings or photographs of the event online? This is where you need to write up and sign a photo and video waiver. You may also wish to write out a memorandum of understanding (MOU) detailing the library and the performers' responsibilities and obligations.

Step 9. Once you've finalized the location, you may need to sign a room/venue rental agreement (if offsite) or book the room (onsite). You may need to pay a deposit. You don't want to go to all this bother only to find you don't have a place to have your stars perform. Now is also the time to book any rental equipment you'll need (see "Materials Required" section).

Step 10. Organize the staff and volunteers needed to pull off the event. Appoint someone as the volunteer coordinator if it is a program (such as a multi-day event) that requires a lot of logistical planning of who needs to be where at what time doing what. Have them create a little chart, including contingency plans if someone calls in sick. You don't want to be the stage manager *and* the event planner. That is too much, and you will hate your job. Set yourself up for success by delegating. Trust me on this one.

Step 11. Where I live (east coast of Canada), you need to pick storm days for events (an alternative date/time to host the program in the event of a blizzard/

power outage/ice storm/hurricane or all of the above). Book the room and per-formers for your regular date AND storm date. If that's not possible, you may need to offer them a kill fee in the event of the performance being canceled. But you can negotiate this in your MOU as discussed in Step 8.

Step 12. By now you should have all the details gathered in order to announce your event to the public: date(s), time, location, performers, registration info, and a way they can access further information. This should be made into some form of shareable document like a cool graphic for social media. An event page can be created on Facebook to allow you to see how many are interested. A PDF poster could be created and printed and posted on bulletin boards around town and the library. A press release to local radio stations, newspapers, weeklies, and websites is a good idea. Share on your library's print and digital calendars, as well as your municipality's calendar and webpage. Don't forget about email or print newsletters. Make sure your performers have access to your marketing material to share with their friends, family, and other fans—especially if they have a strong social media presence.

Step 13. Gather the materials you need prior to the big day. See the list that follows for possibilities. It isn't exhaustive, but it will get you started. The materials will vary wildly depending on what sort of art is being practiced in what sort of venue.

Materials Required:

- Sign up sheets or tickets for the event and/or a digital event page to track attendees
- Liability waivers for the performers (if they are doing something physical, like dance or acrobatics) and any possible participants
- Sound or light equipment, as needed
- Stage props or backgrounds, as needed
- Folding chairs for seniors and those in need for an outside program
- Refreshments and their supplies, as required
- A camera on a tripod if you plan on filming or photographing the event
- You may also wish to rent or use a separate mic to record the audio
- A phone or laptop with a good camera if you plan on making it a Facebook Live event, or using some other live streaming platform
- Feedback forms, if using

Budget Details

$0–$100+. Realistically, what is your *total* budget? As in, what can you offer your performers *and* pay for everything else? Technically, you could pull this off for nothing (I have). But please, please, please don't *expect* people to perform for free. I mean, some of them might and will offer to, especially students. But if there is any way possible for you to offer them some sort of stipend or gift, please make every effort to do so. The performing arts are pathetically underpaid and suffer from often horrible working conditions (outside of the Hollywood glitterati, of course). If there is no money in your budget, consider asking your Friends of the

Library group or Board to fundraise on your behalf; or else look into arts grants, of which there are plenty. Grant Connect is a good place to start. If you are unsure of what to pay your performers, ask them what their rate is, and trust they won't swindle you. Or look up the average salary for that working group online. For example, I usually pay musicians $30 to $60/hour, depending on the complexity of the task and their amount of experience (and my available funding). I also get a local student orchestra to play at the library every year for free as it gives them a nice venue and experience, but I feed them (and the guests). Is it possible to do this program totally for free, with volunteer performers? Can you pull it off as an online-only shindig? Absolutely. Is it also possible to spend $10,000 or more doing a multi-month performance series with top-notch artists and fancy sets and lighting? You bet. You make the call based on your budget, capacity, and your intended audience.

Don't forget to also include the cost for printing tickets, posters, programs, and other materials (unless you are doing it all online). Will you be buying refreshments and everything that goes with it (cups, napkins, etc.)? Do you need to rent any sound or light equipment (mic, amp, musical instruments, stage lighting, etc.)? If it is a theatrical production, are the performers providing all the props and sets? If it is after-hours or off-site, will you need to pay for extra janitorial services? Do you need to pay a room or venue rental fee (or performance fee if in a municipal park or other outside location)? Check your local bylaws.

Something else to consider in budgeting: Will you charge admission? This is one way to offset the cost of hiring performers but may go against your accessibility policies. We're not supposed to charge for onsite events if at all possible, but I once partnered with Woodstock First Nation to bring award-winning Indigenous artist Jeremy Dutcher to Woodstock for a sold-out concert at our local high school auditorium (we didn't have enough seating capacity at the library). Elders from both nearby First Nations were invited and received free tickets and a bus ride to the venue, and we sold tickets to the public at the library and in various locations around town. We kept the cost of the ticket prices reasonable ($25). The proceeds went directly to the musician. I also bought a copy of his CD to add to our music collection so people who couldn't attend the event could still enjoy his music for free.

Day-of-Event

Step 1. Rally your volunteers or staff members and go over who is doing what. If this is a big production, you will want to designate an event coordinator in advance to help organize everyone.

Step 2. Arrange the room/stage or another venue to prepare for your performers' arrival. Set up audio-visual equipment.

Step 3. Greet the talent when they arrive. If you have prepared a green room or practice space or other setups, let them know where it is. Make sure any liability waivers and photo/video releases are signed.

Step 4. Go over any last-minute tweaks to the AV equipment and make sure your recording technology is working perfectly.

Step 5. Set up refreshments, if you are providing them.

Step 6. Greet your patrons as they arrive. Usher them to their seats. Make sure exits and bathrooms are clearly marked (this is super important if you are off-site and people aren't familiar with the location). Make sure people sign video/photo release waivers or hold harmless forms, if needed by patrons.

Step 7. Once it is go-time, make sure your recording equipment is on (if using) and welcome everyone to the event. Go over housekeeping details (no flash photography, location of exits/bathrooms, thank your sponsors, etc.).

Step 8. Sit back and enjoy the show, jumping in when you need to assist offstage with anything (sound tweaks, light dimming, etc.).

Step 9. Thank everyone for coming after the final applause. If the show will be recorded and posted later, make sure to share the details. Again, thank your sponsors. Distribute evaluation forms if using (or mention the link to an online survey for a digital performance or recommend people "like" or "share" the event).

Step 10. Help the performers tear down the set/stage as needed. Put away chairs and other items. Clean up refreshments. Pat yourselves on the back!

Literacy Tie-In

If you'd like, prepare an eye-catching display to correspond with the event (this can also be done on digital platforms for e-books!). Choose books, films, and periodicals that have to do with dance, music, and other performing arts. Try to find something that would appeal to different types of patrons—punk, classical, heavy metal, modern dance, and so on. What follows is a short list of some diverse materials you could use for a performance-friendly display to get you started!

Periodicals:

- *Acoustic Guitar Magazine*
- *American Songwriter*
- *American Theatre*
- *Billboard*
- *Classical Music*
- *Dance Current*
- *Dance Magazine*
- *Inside Arts*
- *Native Max Magazine*
- *Playbill*
- *Revolver Magazine*
- *Rolling Stone*
- *The Source*
- *Vibe*

Print or audiobooks:

- *The Art of Movement* by Ken Browar and Deborah Ory
- *Born to Dance: Celebrating the Wonder of Childhood* by Jordan Matter
- *Dancers among Us* by Jordan Matter

- *Life in Motion: An Unlikely Ballerina* by Misty Copeland
- *Performance* by Diana Taylor
- *Performance Now: Live Art in the Twenty-First Century* by RoseLee Goldberg
- *Raising the Barre: Big Dreams, False Starts, and My Midlife Quest to Dance the Nutcracker* by Lauren Kessler
- *Theatre* by David Mamet
- *This Is Your Brain on Music: The Science of a Human Obsession* by Daniel J. Levitin

DVDs:

- *Bigger Than the Sky* (2005)
- *Billy Elliot* (2003)
- *Bohemian Rhapsody* (2018)
- *Center Stage* (2001)
- *Cremaster 1* (1996)
- *Dance with Me* (1999)
- *Footloose* (1984)
- *Green Book* (2018)
- *Judy* (2019)
- *Les Misérables* (2012)
- *Lord of the Dance: Dangerous Games* (2016)
- *Mad Hot Ballroom* (2005)
- *Marina Abramovic: The Artist Is Present* (2012)
- *One Last Dance* (2005)
- *The Phantom of the Opera* (2005)
- *Punk's Not Dead* (2007)
- *Save the Last Dance* (2001)
- *The Sound of Music: 50th Anniversary Edition* (2015)
- *A Star is Born* (2018)
- *Straight Outta Compton* (2015)

Helpful Advice

- This may seem obvious, but please tell your staff—especially those that answer phones, run social media accounts, or work the front desk—about the event prior to advertising it. You know what annoys patrons? Calling to sign up for something your staff doesn't seem to know anything about. You know what annoys employees? Having people call asking about an event they know nothing about. Communicate. Your staff members are your best allies for spreading the word about your programs.
- Don't overlook your staff and volunteers as possible performers. My own staff and volunteers have performed musical numbers or dance routines or given poetry readings over the years (usually on a volunteer basis or during their working day). And don't forget their kids (or yours). My son plays the cello, and he performs at multiple events at our library every year—solo and with other youth orchestra or quartet members. Is this free child labor?

Figure 5.6 Staff member Kate Waller and her husband Bob performing at the library. *Source:* Brendan Helmuth.

Maybe! It's also an excellent way for him to get experience with the pressures of live performance in a pretty low-key environment (with a built-in fan base!). I'm also lucky to have musical friends and staff members! (See figure 5.6.)

- Check to make sure your insurance covers physical performance in your space. If a dancer or acrobat got hurt performing, you don't want to be sued or find out you don't have the proper insurance coverage. I recommend having all performers sign a liability waiver (or hold harmless forms) the day of the performance. Sometimes library volunteers and staff are covered under these policies but hired guests aren't. Some performers will have their own personal liability insurance; it is always good to ask.

- Consider how you will solicit feedback from audience members. If running a digital event, are "likes" and "shares" enough? Do you want to link to an online survey? You can use free software like Survey Monkey for this. In a live performance, do you want to invite the audience to complete a short paper survey at the end? Make sure it is no more than three questions (for example: What did you like about this performance? What didn't you like? Would you recommend this program to a friend?). You can also invite them with just an open textbox to share their impression of the performance.

- The program isn't over once the performers walk off stage (or grass, or floor, or wherever you are hosting it) if you plan on recording the event to share later. Now comes the hard part of editing the video and audio (you could also just post it unedited, but it won't look very professional). This will be to prepare a file to upload to YouTube or some other video-hosting platform. Make sure you assign this task to someone who knows what they are doing.

You can get really fancy with this and add subtitles for the hearing-impaired and/or translate it into multiple languages if you live in a bilingual area (I sometimes have my yoga videos dubbed in French, for example). There are many different video or audio editing programs available to download (most have free versions), such as Movie Maker, iMovie, or GarageBand.

- If this is an ongoing program series with multiple dates and performers booked, you may need to consider having a backup act in case someone cancels.

Program Model: Trashion Show

Looking for a fun, low-stress, low-budget program that will attract a twenty-to-thirty-something crowd? Or maybe something geared toward teens and their parents? Want to use up a bunch of craft supplies and empty your recycling bin? Itching to do something creative? Well, this is the program for you! Gather all the

Figure 5.7   Hats can be made out of anything, including newspaper. *Source*: Ebony Scott.

(clean) trash you can find, put out a bunch of books about fashion or run videos for inspiration, cue a dance-y playlist, plug in the glue guns, roll out the red carpet (or butcher paper, or whatever)—and you've got yourself a Trashion Show! (See figure 5.7.)

Advance Planning

Step 1. Decide how you'd like to carry out the program. You need a big enough space to work on the wearable items with room for tables, chairs, electrical outlets, and so on and also a space to use as a catwalk. Here's where you can start to be creative. The catwalk doesn't have to be traditional metal staging, and it doesn't have to be a Hollywood red carpet. (See figure 5.9.) You can line chairs up along a reading room or roll out some butcher paper or hallway runners. You can use a staircase, and the audience can watch from the sides, top, and bottom. You can have people strut down your open stacks. Go outside and make it a parade! You can even move the whole program online and have people make their outfits at home and show off their wares on-screen through Zoom or Facebook Live. On campus you could use a theater or foyer or bandstand. You can also take this program offsite for outreach opportunities to a local community hall, church, theater, or art gallery. The possibilities are endless!

Step 2. Once you've picked a space and delivery method, choose a date and book it. If you are picking an offsite venue, you might need to plan in advance and check their calendar of events.

Step 3. Narrow down your audience. In an academic setting, will this be for students and/or staff? For a certain age demographic in a public library? Are there going to be number restrictions based on space and supplies? Keep in mind if you do this outdoors or digitally, you can probably have greater numbers. Do you want this to be an intergenerational program? I know this is a book about adult programs, but many of your adult patrons have families, and sometimes the only way they can come to the library is if their kids come too. (See figure 5.8.) Of all the programs in this book, this one is ideally suited to include all ages (depending on whether you are using glue guns or sewing machines). It also really appeals to young, hip twenty-somethings (just don't call them that). And don't discount older adults; they like to strut their stuff too and are often experienced seamstresses/tailors!

Step 4. Gather your materials (see "Required Materials" section for a detailed inventory). Think of any trash or recyclables that could be repurposed for clothing or accessories. We used discarded books, bags of tangled yarn, plastic and paper grocery sacks, newspapers, wrapping paper and bows. You could throw in scrap fabric, unplayable DVDs and CDs, discarded cables and cords, paper bags and boxes, beads and sequins, unclaimed items from the lost and found bin, or any other bits and bobs from your junk drawers (or, if you are like my library, junk closets). Try to guess how patrons might expect to work with these items in advance so you can make sure to have the proper tools on hand. Will you need fasteners? Glue guns? Needle and thread? String? Duct tape? Glue sticks? A stapler? A sewing machine? Anything you don't have on hand, plan to bring in for the big event. Make sure you aren't buying too much stuff though; the point is to use up what you already have. If you are doing a

Figure 5.8   Trashion Show designers and models. *Source*: Ebony Scott.

digital version, prepare a list of suggested materials and tools for participants to gather at home.

Step 5. Advertise your event by creating an eye-catching poster and post on social media. You could even film a little video preview of a staff member modeling a Trashion piece they created to build interest. You can use Canva or another free online software to help with graphics. Make a Facebook event and promote on Twitter and Instagram, or other platforms frequented by your target audience. A print poster on local bulletin boards might catch eyes. A public service announcement on a local radio station might also reach people outside your frequent attendees.

Step 6. If you are going digital, make sure to test out the technology ahead of time and book the meeting and send invites. For in-person and digital programs, you'll need some way to track attendance and registration. For an in-person program, you don't want to run out of supplies (or space), and for a digital program, you'll need to be mindful of how many can comfortably join the program and have the allotted time to show off their creations. In the case of an online event, I would put the call out early to have makers create their outfits ahead of time (give them at least two weeks) and then hold the online event for the Trashion Show portion only. It might be awkward to just have an open Zoom meeting with everyone watching each other craft. In real life, you can allot a certain amount of time to the creation of the garments (an hour is good, these don't need to be overly complicated, unless you are doing this with fashion students or something) and then—depending on your numbers—at least ten to twenty minutes for the show itself.

Figure 5.9   It's easy to make a runway out of chairs between the stacks. *Source*: Ebony Scott.

Step 7. Fashion shows are as much about the music as the clothes. Now is the time to create a killer playlist. Something upbeat and dance-y for the creation time and then something strut-worthy for the runway. Be mindful of any copyright/SOCAN laws if you are recording (in-person or online) or plan to broadcast at a later date. I highly recommend including the Canadian 80s classic of Fashion-Television's iconic theme song, which is what we used on our runway.[13]

Step 8. Decide the tone you want to set for the affair. Is this just about having fun and making some outrageous outfits, or would you like to open a larger discussion about the environmental impacts of the fashion industry and/or the personal consequences of fast fashion in our own lives? Would you like to invite discussion on the Maker Movement (DIY subculture focused on making things from scratch rather than buying existing products) and talk about the loss (and potential revival) of hands-on skills? Or do you just want to make stuff and have fun? Both are a valid choice! Sometimes it is fun to get a discussion going while you work.

There is a list of suggested resources in the "Literacy Tie-In" section to help you learn more about these topics, but here are some questions you could use to get the discussion started while people create their outfits (in person) or after the (digital or in-person) show. You may want to keep the conversation on the more personal realm (as in how our culture affects the patron personally) rather than in a larger global way (which can quickly get political and heated—not always a bad thing but maybe not the vibe you wanted). I've included questions that touch on all these areas; discard any that don't work for you. They are purposely open-ended to invite dialogue, not produce "right" answers. People also shouldn't feel pressured to answer any particular question (this isn't an interview or quiz!), as there might be a feeling of shame associated with being seen as not owning "enough" or the "right sort" of clothing. Omit any questions from the discussion that you feel might create shame-based reactions in your group.

1. How do you feel about the clothes you own? Do you have enough? Too much?
2. Where do you normally get your clothes: second-hand shops, online, retail shops, outlets, hand-me-downs, and so on?
3. Do you know how to repair garments? Sew a button? Mend a seam? Patch a hole? Hem your own pants?
4. Did anyone make clothing for you as a child? As an adult? How did it feel to wear something handmade just for you?
5. What do you think are the environmental consequences of the fashion industry? How do you think it compares to the automotive or oil or coal industries?
6. Where does your clothing go when you no longer wear it?
7. Do you keep clothing with sentimental value, and what do you do with it?
8. How much time do you think you spend cleaning, folding, organizing, repairing, or otherwise caring for your clothing and the clothing of other people in your house?
9. How do you feel about fashion that is made for an elite audience, such as runway or couture items worn by models and celebrities, versus the fast fashion available at big box stores and popular retailers? Would you wear the items on the runway if they were given to you?
10. How do you feel about the shoes that you own? Do you feel you own enough? What do you use them for?
11. What materials are the majority of your clothes and shoes made out of? Do you think in the future we will invent new fabrics, or will we go back to using more natural, renewable sources, like linen, fur, cotton, wool, leather, or hemp?
12. How do you feel about wearing items made from animal products? How do you feel about other people wearing them?
13. Does your family-of-origin or religious background include certain styles of dress that you engage in?
14. How do you feel about seeing traditional cultural dress used in the fashion industry (for example, Native headdresses being worn on the catwalk, or Celtic knots decorating a bra)?

15. What makes you buy a certain item of clothing? The price? The fit? Whether it is trendy? Its usefulness?

16. How much time a month would you spend shopping for clothing and accessories, including browsing online?

Step 9. Create some evaluation forms to hand out at the end of the program if you'd like feedback. If doing a digital version, send out a link to a quick survey at the end.

Materials Required

- Music and something to play it on
- Your list of discussion questions (if using)—ideally in your head, not on paper/your phone
- Recyclables and other treasures pulled from the trash such as: string, cardboard, plastic bags, CDs/DVDs, toilet paper tubes, wrapping paper, old cards and envelopes, discarded books, chip bags (washed), cans and bottles (rinsed), pop tabs, beads, old cables and cords, unused craft supplies, broken toys and board games or puzzles with missing pieces, scrap fabric, pipe cleaners, buttons, elastic, sequins, newspapers and magazines, old clothing and shoes, and so on. (See figure 5.10.)
- Fasteners and buttons
- Glue guns and glue sticks
- Needles and thread
- Duct tape or fabric tape
- A stapler and staples
- A sewing machine (if you have one on hand)
- Scissors, utility knives, cutting mats
- Hole punch (can be used for threading yarn or cables through cardboard or paper)
- Carpet, string lights, or battery-operated tealights to line the runway
- A camera and photo/video release forms (if using)
- Display of related materials (see "Literacy Tie-In" section for ideas)
- A computer and online conferencing software (if hosting a digital event)
- A microphone and portable sound system if you are having a large event and need to be heard over a crowd to introduce the "stars" on your catwalk
- A full-length mirror or access to a bathroom so patrons can check out their progress as they work and to prepare for their big moment on stage
- Evaluation forms (if using)

Budget Details

$0–$20+. Ideally a Trashion Show should cost you nothing . . . since that is really the whole point. You want to make something fabulous out of nothing, out of garbage, out of leftovers! I understand that you may need to rent a venue space. You may also want a few supplies that you don't already have on hand to get it all together, such as some duct tape, glue sticks, or a pack of sewing needles—most of these things can be found cheaply at a dollar store or people may be willing to donate!

Figure 5.10 Supplies for Trashion Show outfit building. *Source*: Ebony Scott.

What is even better, in my experience, is just forcing yourself to rely on whatever you have on hand. Don't have a needle and thread or sewing machine? Oh well. Use a hole punch and hand-thread yarn through old Pokémon cards to join them up and make a belt! Don't have any yarn? Use an old cable from the junk drawer that's been around since 1984 and you've long-since forgotten its use. Don't have any feathers to decorate your hat made out of cardboard? Use leftover craft pom-poms or balled-up pieces of newspaper. The most exciting part of the whole event will be watching how incredibly creative your participants will be coming up with their outfits! Take lots of pictures. Have lots of laughs. Trust the process. Fun doesn't have to cost a dime. This is process-oriented art, not product-oriented consumerism.

Day-of-Event

Step 1. If this is a digital event, run through your tech first to make sure everything is working before go time. For an in-person event, check your sound system/music and lighting (if using), and gather your supplies.

Step 2. Print off any photo/video release forms and make sure your camera is working. Have some pens handy too.

Step 3. Set up the room where the outfit-building will take place. I like to set out tables with supplies on the edges of the space and a central table of tools (scissors, fasteners, glue, etc.) in the middle for everyone to share. Then, if you have the capacity, some worktables for the assembly process (if you are short on space or tables, this will need to combine with the trash-supply tables). Many people will stand while they work but have seating options for those that need/want it. Put out your full-length mirror, if using. Set up your catwalk, photo booth, circulation material display, and any other required stations (like maybe a water table if you'd like to put out some cups and a pitcher of water for refreshment).

Step 4. Welcome your guests as they arrive and check them against the registration form (if using). Have them complete their photo/video release form and collect these in a confidential folder.

Step 5. Once everyone arrives, show them where the bathrooms and exits are located. Explain the layout of the room and how the event will proceed. People can either work in teams to create a look for their elected model to wear on the runway, or everyone can make their own item to wear (you may not have the time or supplies to make a complete outfit). Decide this ahead of time so no one is fighting over the piles of garbage or stressing out—this is supposed to be fun! Tell them they have a time limit for the creation portion (thirty to sixty minutes is good) and set the clock/timer (if using). Explain that afterward there will be a short fashion show to share their talent with the rest of the group (and the public, if you are hosting the runway outdoors or in a central location or holding it at a venue where you've invited an audience). If you are hosting a digital event where patrons share their made-at-home creations, skip this step and the one below and head right into the Trashion Show.

Step 6. Time to get creative! Turn up the motivating music and walk around to the tables to see if anyone needs help. If people are working alone, offer to be their mannequin to try on the item so they can see it from all angles. Remind people to use the in-room mirror or visit the bathroom mirror to check their progress (or you can take photos or video of each other to show/share). Open up dialogue using some of the recommended discussion questions to start conversations with participants. If you are hosting a digital event where patrons share their made-at-home creations on-screen, have the (optional) discussion after everyone has a turn presenting.

Step 7. Once your creative time is up, assemble participants in order that they will proceed down the catwalk. If this is a more formal event, you will have to announce to the audience that the show is about to begin (friends, family, and curious onlookers will enjoy watching this, and I really recommend inviting people; it creates a fun buzz for the models too!). Blast your runway theme music and have your patrons strut their stuff down the catwalk. If you are MC-ing, you can announce what each participant is wearing and what they made it out of. This portion of the event will go by quickly, as people often speed walk out of nervousness.

If this is a digital event, give each participant a set time (two to three minutes is good, depending on the size of your group) to share their outfit by modeling it (encourage them to play music!) and then explaining how they made it. After everyone has shared is a good time to open up the floor to discussion about their experiences of the event and also about the fast-fashion industry in general.

Step 8. Wrap up and say your goodbyes. People can take home their creations or you can send them off to be recycled. Hand out evaluation forms (or send a link) if you are looking for feedback.

Step 9. Tear down the room and runway and celebrate your accomplishment!

Literacy Tie-In

Having a fun display of books and other materials about fashion, garment construction, and environmentalism in the textile industry is a great way to increase circulation and promote further learning to your participants (and anyone else who walks by the display). Or, perhaps you are looking to beef up your collection by including more books about "refashion" or conscious shopping? Well, this is a great list to get you started! For a digital event, why not make a curated collection in your online catalog or share a bibliography via PowerPoint slides? Here is a sample of titles, and there are many more on the market.

Periodicals:

- *Burda Style*
- *Fantastic Man*
- *Fashion*
- *GQ*
- *InStyle*
- *Make Magazine*
- *Men's Fashion*
- *MIIT: Men in This Town*
- *Ottobre Design*
- *Peppermint*
- *The Rake*
- *Resurgence and Ecologist*
- *Selvedge*
- *Simply Sewing*
- *Taproot*
- *Threads*
- *Vogue*
- *Vogue Patterns*

Print or audiobooks:

- *50 Nifty Thrifty Upcycled Fashions: Sew Something from Nothing* by Cynthia Anderson

- *Clothing Poverty: The Hidden World of Fast Fashion and Second-Hand Clothes* by Andrew Brooks
- *The Conscious Closet: The Revolutionary Guide to Looking Good while Doing Good* by Elizabeth L. Cline
- *The Dirty Side of the Garment Industry: Fast Fashion and Its Negative Impact on Environment and Society* by Nikolay Anguelov
- *The End of Fashion: How Marketing Changed the Clothing Business Forever* by Teri Agins
- *Fashionopolis: The Price of Fast Fashion and the Future of Clothes* by Dana Thomas
- *Fix Your Clothes: The Sustainable Magic of Mending, Patching, and Darning* by Raleigh Briggs
- *How to Break Up with Fast Fashion: A Guilt-Free Guide to Changing the Way You Shop for Good* by Lauren Bravo
- *Make Garbage Great: The Terracycle Family Guide to a Zero-Waste Lifestyle* by Tom Szaky
- *Make It, Own It, Love It: The Essential Guide to Sewing, Altering and Customizing* by Matt Chapple
- *Mend & Patch: A Handbook to Repairing Clothes and Textiles* by Kerstin Neumüller
- *Overdressed: The Shockingly High Cost of Cheap Fashion* by Elizabeth L. Cline
- *The Refashion Handbook: Refit, Redesign, Remake for Every Body* by Beth Huntington
- *ReFashioned: Cutting-Edge Clothing from Upcycled Materials* by Sass Brown
- *ReSew: Turn Thrift-Store Finds into Fabulous Designs* by Jenny Wilding Cardon
- *Routledge Handbook of Sustainability and Fashion* by Kate Fletcher and Mathilda Tham
- *Sewing Green: 25 Projects Made with Repurposed & Organic Materials Plus Tips & Resources for Earth-Friendly Stitching* by Betz White
- *Stylish Remakes: Upcycle Your Old T's, Sweats and Flannels into Trendy Street Fashion Pieces* by Violette Room
- *The Sustainable Fashion Handbook* by Sandy Black
- *To Die for: Is Fashion Wearing Out the World?* by Lucy Siegle
- *Trash to Treasure: 90 Crafts That Will Reuse Old Junk to Make New & Usable Treasures!* by Kitty Moore
- *Wardrobe Crisis: How We Went from Sunday Best to Fast Fashion* by Clare Press
- *Wayward Threads: Techniques and Ideas for Upcycling Unloved or Discarded Garments* by Lorri Ann Scott
- *Wear No Evil: How to Change the World with Your Wardrobe* by Greta Eagan
- *Wear, Repair, Repurpose: A Maker's Guide to Mending and Upcycling Clothes* by Lily Fulop

DVDs:

- *Coco Before Chanel* (2009)
- *The Devil Wears Prada* (2006)
- *Doir and I* (2014)
- *The Dressmaker* (2015)

- *Funny Face* (1957)
- *Gospel According to André* (2017)
- *Iris* (2014)
- *RiverBlue* (2017)
- *The September Issue* (2009)
- *The True Cost* (2015)
- *Unzipped* (1995)
- *Zoolander* (2001)

Helpful Advice

- It's great to hold this event near Earth Day (April 22) or as a foil to Fashion Week.[14]
- Don't bother with white glue. It takes way too long to dry and is really hard to get out of your hair. You do not want to make a hat or crown using white glue. Trust me.
- I like to keep some fashion magazines out for inspiration in case someone is struggling. You could also play a loop of runway footage from YouTube on a wall projector if you have the space and equipment.
- No clue what to make? Look under "trashion show ideas" on Pinterest to get you started.
- I don't recommend having your list of discussion questions printed off to read from (or worse, photocopied and handed around). That's *way* too much like school, or some sort of planned psychological experiment. It's awkward. Instead, just memorize a few of the questions or topics to keep in the back of your mind and throw them into the discussion casually as you are making outfits during the first phase of the program. Or bring them up at the end of the digital event, after everyone's shared their creations. Or ignore them entirely. The idea of the questions is to just get patrons thinking about clothing and fashion in a broader way (and hopefully point them toward borrowing an item from your awesome display or online curated collection to indulge their curiosity).
- If you don't have room for a catwalk, set up a photo booth and take snaps of the participants modeling their creations and send the photos to them after the program (they can include their email on the photo release waiver).
- Consider inviting the media—this is truly a feel-good event with an important environmental message.
- Make sure your catwalk is safe and your patrons aren't wearing anything that could compromise their health. No walking on platform shoes made out of wobbly old books or pop cans on a three-foot-high stage. No plastic bags across faces. No cutting off circulation (plastic cording or duct tape can get horrendously tight quickly)! Yes, you may have to explain this to adults, not just kids. Give everyone a chance to practice their strut and turn at the end of the runway (even if you just do this "backstage" in your crafting room before the main event).

Further Arts & Crafts Program Ideas

- Art Battle—Put out a call to local artists to come create a spontaneous painting on a certain time and day. Invite the public to watch them work on the clock (usually set for twenty minutes). You provide the canvas, water, mixing palette (can be as simple as repurposed Styrofoam), and acrylic paint (artists bring their own brushes). When the twenty minutes are up, the audience votes on which two paintings are the best. Then those two artists create a second painting in a final showdown. Artists must register ahead of time. If you get a large number of people interested (and you have the space and budget), you can also have two groups painting for the first round and take the four winners from those rounds (two each) to compete against each other in round two (two separate competitions), and then have the final showdown between the winner of each from round two. Paintings can be auctioned off after the battle to raise money for the library. You can also give part of the proceeds from the auction to the artists (40 to 50 percent is nice). More info can be found on https://artbattle.com/artist-faq/.[15]
- Holiday Card Decorating—Lots of people (like me!) forget to make or buy holiday cards until . . . the day before the holiday. Let's help forgetful people out! This program can be done at any time of the year, just pick an upcoming holiday (Valentine's, Christmas, Easter, Diwali, Chinese New Year, Mother's Day, Father's Day, etc.). This is an excellent way to use up extra craft supplies and involves low involvement and planning from staff. Just set a time and date for the program, put out supplies, put on holiday-appropriate music (if so desired), and let people create. They can also make gift tags (have a hole-punch handy!), bookmarks, or wrapping paper (with stamps, crayons, paper tape, markers, etc.). You just need a staff member or volunteer around to help show patrons how to use equipment safely, such as large paper cutter, punch outs, glue gun, or to refresh the supplies as needed.
- Coloring Group—Buy some adult coloring books, high-quality pencil crayons and gel pens, and provide an electric pencil sharpener and invite patrons to relax. You can even do this as a passive program by setting up an adult coloring table somewhere in the library with a sign inviting people to join. Soothing music and free tea or coffee are also a nice touch. Our library offers this program once a week, and it is very popular, especially with seniors. (See figure 5.11.)
- Knitting/Crochet Group—This is similar to the coloring group, but instead, we provide yarn and needles/hooks and have a weekly reservation in our activity room for fiber-friendly people to gather and chat while they make things. Sometimes we offer lessons or workshops, but often, this is just a space to create and be with others who share their interests. (See figure 5.12.)
- Traditional Craft Workshops—Have an expert in a traditional craft come and teach an introductory workshop. Some ideas that have worked well in our community: drum-making or shaker-making (using deer hides and bear grease) taught by First Nation elders; *kolam* (also known as *rangoli*), which are intricate shapes drawn using rice flour from the southern Indian tradition; Japanese origami; British or Nordic styles of paper quilling; Japanese stab

Figure 5.11   Adult Coloring Program at the library. *Source*: Jenn Carson.

binding (handmade books); sock or slipper knitting (such as *skóleistar* from the Faroe Islands); making *dandiya* sticks and learning the accompanying dance, to name a few. These classes can be taught in person or online (just make sure participants know in advance what materials they will need). (See figure 5.13.)

- Tile Art — Decorating tiles using permanent markers and rubbing alcohol is the easiest program for adults who are scared to make art. You can't screw it up—it is supposed to look "drippy" and abstract! Patrons get to take home a pretty tile to use as a coaster, trivet, or decoration. White tiles are cheap, and markers are plentiful. This is a perfect low-stress, low-budget program. For more details, you can read a blog post I wrote for the American Library Association's Programming Librarian website: https://programminglibrarian.org/blog/tile-art-creative-program-all-ages.[16] (See figure 5.14.)

- Learn It in an Hour!—Host various one-hour-long classes (either in person or online) to introduce people to simple, foundational creative tasks, such as: drawing and shading an apple or orange; darning socks; sewing on a button; patching a garment; hemming pants; editing a photo; making a small embroidery sampler of basic stitches; making a pom-pom; learning basic macrame knots; crocheting a dishcloth; sewing a pincushion; making homemade chocolate, learning a dance move, cursive writing or calligraphy basics, and so on. The possibilities are endless!

- Rock Painting—There's a very popular movement where people paint rocks, often with inspiring messages, and hide them for people to find. We've held rock painting (and hiding!) sessions at the library, and it is really engaging for all ages. This could also work well as an outreach or online program. For more details, you can read a blog post I wrote about it for the American

Figure 5.12 We have a love of yarn at the library. *Source*: Ebony Scott.

Library Association's Programming Librarian website: https://program minglibrarian.org/blog/libraries-rock.[17] (See figure 5.15.)

- Music Groups—Offer a place for local amateur musicians to meet and practice songs together. We offer a weekly space for a ukulele group, and it is very popular. We host them in a meeting room next to the circulation desk and away from the study rooms and quiet reading areas. A bonus is the staff gets to enjoy a little live music while they work (some appreciate this less than others). It could be any instrument: acoustic guitar enthusiasts, harp players, or banjo lovers. Even a small singing group (a whole choir might be a bit much) would work. And you might want to draw the line at drummers or trumpet players, unless you've got a soundproof room available! (See figure 5.16.)
- Treasure Boxes—Do you collect boxes or have a hard time throwing them away—especially if they are small, well-made, and potentially useful? Me too. In fact, I bet a lot of your adult patrons suffer from the same affliction. Why not make a fun program to celebrate our collective neuroses? Plus, it's

Figure 5.13 **Traditional weaving on a lap loom at the library.** *Source*: Brendan Helmuth.

Figure 5.14 **Tile art.** *Source*: Kate Waller.

eco- and budget-friendly! Have patrons bring along a special box they've been saving and together transform it into a treasure box for keepsakes! Decorate with washi (paper) tape, Japanese paper, stickers, paint, glitter glue (ugh, if you must; I *abhor* glitter!), buttons, or other craft supplies you've got lying around. See figure 5.17 for an example of an old hair straightener box I transformed with some Japanese paper, a nice button, and string. Makes a great gift or storage box for photos and other things you can't seem to throw away!

- Fall Leaf Garland—A great way to use up old newspapers and scrap paper lying around the library is to make a fall garland by tracing fall leaves (or using a template if you live in a climate without them) and painting them. Once they dry, you cut out the shapes and hang on a string. Kids and grown-ups love this program equally, and it is easily taught online as well as in person. For more details, you can read a blog post I wrote about it for the American Library Association's Programming Librarian website: https:// programminglibrarian.org/blog/eco-friendly-fall-garland.[18]

Figure 5.15 Rock painting display at the library. *Source*: Jenn Carson.

Figure 5.16   Uke Group members playing at a Christmas concert. *Source*: Brendan Helmuth.

Figure 5.17   Box made by the author. *Source*: Jenn Carson.

Figure 5.18 The author and a patron with their rug hooking creations following a workshop.
Source: Kate Waller.

- Take-Home Craft Kits — During the pandemic, my staff created many craft kits that included basic supplies and instructions for patrons to complete at home since we couldn't offer onsite programming for awhile. They can be geared toward kids, adults, or families. We even made kits specifically for adults from a care home that had cognitive disabilities and really enjoyed making things. They would come back each week with their support person to pick up new kits and tell us what they made. These have proven so popular we will continue them long after the pandemic ends!

Whether you are planning a grand cultural extravaganza or a simple make 'n' take craft night, there are plenty of fun ways to get the adults in your community feeling creative. (See figure 5.18.) As we've learned in this chapter, it doesn't have to be expensive, complicated, or even in person! Use your amazing librarian imagination and sensitivity to come up with an easy-to-follow, culturally appropriate, successful event. I can't wait to hear all about it on social media—don't forget to take lots of pictures!

Notes

1. "Indigenous Storyteller in Residence," *Vancouver Public Library* online, accessed March 3, 2022, https://www.vpl.ca/storyteller.

2. Melody Warnick, *This Is Where You Belong: Finding Home Wherever You Are* (New York: Penguin, 2017).

3. Much of my understanding of appropriation versus appreciation comes from talking with my First Nation friends and colleagues, including Shane Perley-Dutcher, who gave an excellent talk on the subject at the 2021 Wild Child Symposium (online) on March 13, 2021.

4. For a fascinating list of the endangered (and extinct) crafts of the United Kingdom, please visit Heritage Crafts online: https://heritagecrafts.org.uk/redlist/categories-of-risk/.

5. For an excellent rundown on why wearing a kimono is loaded with backstory, please read Sara Tatyana Bernstein and Elise Chatelain, "The Dress Code: Is the Kimono Trend Cultural Appropriation?," *Dismantle* online, accessed March 3, 2022, https://www.dismantlemag.com/2019/07/22/dress-code-kimono-cultural-appropriation/.

6. For a fascinating video on wearing costumes from different cultures on Halloween, please watch Rosanna Deerchild, *Cultural Appropriation vs. Appreciation*, CBC Radio, video, October 27, 2016, 3:46, https://youtu.be/vfAp_G735r0.

7. If you've been living under a Plymouth-sized rock and still think it's okay to dress up like this at Thanksgiving, please educate yourself by reading David J. Silverman, "The Vicious Reality behind the Thanksgiving Myth," *New York Times* online, November 27, 2019, https://www.nytimes.com/2019/11/27/opinion/thanksgiving-history-racism.html.

8. CBC News, "Laurier, Kitchener Public Library Collaborate to Offer Free Virtual Concerts," *CBC* online, last modified November 5, 2020, https://www.cbc.ca/news/canada/kitchener-waterloo/laurier-kitchener-public-library-virtual-concert-series-1.5790659?fbclid=IwAR3uFRSH_ouWSLxaEjTs0A3yLZnnvxg6OxWdFTza5mul6E1BvxJZQT6P87A.

9. "About V-Day," V-Day online, accessed March 3, 2022, https://www.vday.org/about-v-day/.

10. Michael Hutchins, "Library Park Brings Music Outdoors," *Herald Democrat* online, last modified October 14, 2020, https://www.heralddemocrat.com/story/news/2020/10/14/sherman-showcases-native-texas-plant-life-new-library-music-park/3656001001/.

11. A Tintamarre is an Acadian tradition where people march down the streets of their community using makeshift noisemakers and waving flags to celebrate their French heritage. It is a very common practice in the province of New Brunswick where I live. You can learn more by reading Dominique Millette, "Tintamarre," *The Canadian Encyclopedia* online, last modified July 15, 2015, https://www.thecanadianencyclopedia.ca/en/article/tintamarre.

12. "Performance Rights Organisation," *Wikipedia*, accessed January 20, 2022, https://en.wikipedia.org/wiki/Performance_rights_organisation.

13. The song is "Obsession" by the group Animotion. You can find the music video on YouTube. You will not regret it. Animotion, "Obsession," *AnimotionVEVO*, video (1985), June 11, 2010, 4:01, https://youtu.be/hIs5StN8J-0.

14. You can find a list of the latest/nearest Fashion Week to your hometown by Googling "Fashion Week" and the current year. That should give you a list of upcoming dates. Keep in mind there is usually a Fashion Week for each season.

15. "Art Battle Artist Frequently Asked Questions and Competition Rules," Art Battle, accessed March 3, 2022, https://artbattle.com/artist-faq/.

16. Jenn Carson, "Blog: Tile Art: A Creative Program for All Ages," *Programming Librarian*, December 8, 2018, https://programminglibrarian.org/blog/tile-art-creative-program-all-ages.

17. Jenn Carson, "Blog: Libraries Rock," *Programming Librarian*, August 7, 2019, https://programminglibrarian.org/blog/libraries-rock.

18. Jenn Carson, "Blog: Eco-Friendly Fall Garland," *Programming Librarian*, September 18, 2019, https://programminglibrarian.org/blog/eco-friendly-fall-garland.

6

✦

Books and Writing Programs

Adult programs at the library on the subject of literature may not seem like a radical idea, and I'd forgive you for thinking you'd just skip right over this chapter with a "been there/done that" attitude. I probably would too. I mean, the title of this entire tome is *Beyond Books*, right? What librarian worth his or her salt hasn't formed a hundred book clubs, agonized over the itineraries of many authors' tours, and shooed overzealous amateur poets offstage as the evening drew to a close so the weary staff (and sometimes audience) could go home? But I'm going to challenge you to think outside the stacks over the next dozen or so pages.

More than just throwing more program ideas at you (and I will do that too, I promise), I hope to get you thinking about the way that we look at books. Yes, books are altered wood pulp and ink that convey the ideas of their authors and illustrators, but they are also fascinating objects, in and of themselves. Well-crafted stories also build worlds, worlds that are sometimes so powerful and enticing people would rather spend their time there instead of in their humdrum daily life. Take, for example, the world of Jane Austen. Not just the eighteenth century in which she lived but also the tight, domestic spaces in which her novels were written. The romance, intrigue, scathing insight into popular culture of the time, and her wry observations of family dynamics are elements that millions of people all over the world identify with. There are costume balls, fashion shows, tea parties, trivia nights, cocktail hours, films, fan fiction, museums and exhibits, walking tours, and even entire festivals that all revolve around the life and writing of just one woman that lived over 250 years ago. What's to stop you from picking any author in your collection and making an event out of their work and life? Dress up like a Neil Gaiman character and recite your favorite lines. Host an Agatha Christie-style whodunnit murder mystery night. Have a sci-fi writers' week where you have a different event each day. Even better, why not highlight a local author? (See figure 6.1.) Have them come in and lead a writing workshop, or be a writer-in-residence, or do a reading. And don't forget the illustrators! Bring

Figure 6.1   Author visit online. *Source:* Jenn Carson.

in a graphic artist to teach people how to draw a simple cartoon. Have a graphic designer teach people about layout and font choice. People are really interested in self-publishing, so why not have a class on that from someone who's had success at it? One workshop I like to teach is aimed right at authors themselves: I offer a class on how writers can approach libraries for potential program opportunities or get their books on the shelves. What seems simple to us on the inside can seem intimidating or downright impossible from the outside. Pandemics or other barriers (like budget constraints) don't need to stop you. Many events, like book talks, author interviews, trivia nights, and writing circles, can all happen online!

One habit I've established is having a really good working relationship with local publishers and bookstores. While it might seem counterintuitive to affiliate with a bookshop (aren't we their competition?), they are a treasure-trove of partnership possibilities. For one, you should buy books from your local independent bookstore instead of large distributors (if you are allowed), which will earn their respect and love. Second, if you are offering an author tour and the author isn't supplying copies of books for buying/signing, bookshops can provide that (or if you have an anti-selling policy at your branch, you can refer patrons to the bookshop to get their copy to bring to be signed prior to the event). You can chat with booksellers about what subjects people are browsing and asking for, to help with collection development. You can source copies of out-of-print editions their clients may be looking for or help them with research projects. You can help promote their events on your bulletin boards. They can help promote yours. Perhaps they'd be willing to stick your newsletter in their shopping bags? Or put up posters for your events? They can give you free promotional bookmarks for your patrons to grab at the circulation desk.

Similar partnership opportunities exist with local publishers. We have an excellent working relationship with our free community newspaper. We carry copies of their paper for patrons to pick up at the library and, in turn, they regularly feature library programs and news highlights in their articles. I also regularly contribute book reviews and book-related articles to other provincially based periodicals, like travel and art magazines. We have a book publisher's office (Chapel Street Editions) three blocks from the library, and we keep a standing order to purchase two copies of everything they print: one for our archives and one for the circulating collection. We have similar arrangements with other publishers in our province. In turn, they often hold book launches and author talks at our branch, and we participate in annual literary festivals and conferences together. We've also collaborated on book art and local history exhibits. We even send local authors looking for a publisher their way, and we promote their books at our library with displays and word-of-mouth. It truly is a symbiotic partnership, as one of their employees also works part-time at the library and another sits on our Board. Some may argue this is nepotism, but in a small town where every local dollar spent directly puts food on a neighbor's table, supporting our small businesses as well as international book conglomerates further invests community members in our library and contributes to our strategic goal of promoting and investing in local artists and authors.

Now that I've got you all fired up with ideas, let's flesh a few of those out with some in-depth program models. I've included suggestions for further literacy tie-ins to help increase those circulation statistics. There will also be a list of ideas at the end of the chapter you can run with. You can follow the same planning format I've used with my program models or make up your own!

Program Model: Pop-Up Poetry Reading

Poetry readings can sometimes be dull, angsty affairs. And I'm a published poet, so I've fidgeted through a lot of them over the last two or three decades. Everyone waiting nervously on uncomfortable chairs for their chance on stage, barely listening to the other performers. Someone's delivering a ten-minute epic about wandering through their backyard searching for blackberry bushes. The emcee stumbling through awkward jokes and mispronounced names. And yet, they can also be glorious: full of daring invention, much-needed camaraderie, and a chance to get introverted writers out of the house and sharing their work. I'll never forget an event I attended at a coffee shop where a young woman, still in college, got up and performed a brilliant piece she'd just written at her table about being afraid to get up and read poetry. All the poets in the audience cheered, buoyed by the shared vulnerability of her honest reflection. We knew *exactly* how she felt. She confessed to me afterward that it was the push she needed to get writing. And isn't that what we're in the business of in libraries—inspiring readers and writers?

The beauty of a Pop-Up Poetry Reading is that it can be done anytime, any-where, and feeds on that nervous energy of the crowd and channels it into some-thing fun (instead of a panic attack). The idea is that you take materials, such as paper, pens, old-fashioned typewriters, whiteboards and markers, chalkboards and chalk, magnetic poetry, and so on, and you put them out for people to try

Celebrate National Poetry Month
at the L.P. Fisher Public Library's

Poetry Night

Thursday, April 13 from 6:30-8:00

Listen to local poets
read their works and
read one of your own.

There will be a poetry
experiment station on
hand for spontaneous
writing fun!

For more information call the library at 325.4777
www.facebook.com/L.P.Fisher.Library

Figure 6.2 **Poetry Night poster.** *Source*: Brendan Helmuth.

their hand at writing. (See figure 6.2.) It can be poems, prose, limericks, whatever; the point is just to get their juices flowing. I like to set up a room with a type-writer or two at the back (who can resist that *clack-clack* of the keys!?), with reams of paper and pens and pencils for those who'd prefer them, and a display table or bulletin board and push pins. Make sure to have a recycle bin handy for the rejects! People can then tack their work up for display (anonymously or signed) or else tuck them in their pockets to share later (or not). Sometimes having magnetic poetry sets can force people to use the existing words, and that gives them more structure to get started rather than facing the terror of a blank page!

As people are milling around the writing desks, you can also have out snacks and coffee and tea (or get a liquor license and some wine and you might get some *really* spicy work on display!). Having something to sip and nibble on while they think up their spontaneous creation really helps. Then, after everyone has had time to try their hand at writing something, you can have an informal reading from anyone who volunteers. People can also bring work in advance to read if they'd prefer. And it never hurts to have a few short poems by famous authors tucked aside to get the ball rolling—preferably something witty and not-too-serious, to match the mood of the event. And the best part is there is no pressure. No one has to get up in front of a crowd; they can just watch from the audience. Poetry, believe it or not, can be fun. We don't *always* need to agonize over every comma.

Advance Planning

Step 1. Reach out to your local writing groups or poets you know and get a feel for when a good time would be to hold the event. Weekday or weekend evenings, or even weekend afternoons, have worked well for us. Keep in mind many people are parents and are struggling to work and wrangle kids into bed and don't have a ton of free time. A Saturday or Sunday afternoon from 2 to 4 p.m. might work well, or an evening from 7 to 9 p.m. (if you are open that late). What about holding the event as part of National Poetry Month (April) or World Poetry Day (March 21)?

Step 2. Be discerning about the location. What is your goal here? If you are looking to attract new members, maybe try something offsite, like holding it at a bar, park bandstand, coffee shop, or even a yoga studio or bookstore (yes, you *can* partner with bookshops; they are not the enemy!). As long as you can schlep a few supplies there, you are free to go to unusual places (provided you have the blessing of your administration). Poetry doesn't take much space, which is part of its beauty. If you are aiming to be as accessible as possible, why not go online? People can still write spontaneous poems and share them, people can mill around the chat box, can connect and share—all without leaving the house! If these aren't options for you, or you'd like to be more traditional (nothing wrong with that!), hold the event at your library. Perhaps in a closed room if you are concerned people may feel intimidated sharing out in public. Or perhaps right in the stacks, next to the poetry section. Or maybe loud and proud in the lobby on a makeshift stage? Again, focus on your goal for the program and your intended audience, and go from there. Just make sure to book the space well in advance.

Step 3. Do a budget check. Look under the "Budget Details" section for possible expenses. This event can be done for pretty much zero dollars, if you use supplies you already have, don't need to pay a booking fee to rent space, don't offer refreshments, or just go online.

Step 4. Source your materials. See "Materials Required" list for possibilities. Think about how fancy you want to get with supplies. I really like putting out typewriters for people to use. It is an authentic way to get into the writing spirit. They can often be found in decent working condition (try them first!) at yard sales, second-hand shops, or languishing in office storage closets or relatives' basements. The hardest thing is usually finding replacement ink tape. This can be sourced online or at office supply stores. Having crisp paper and an abundance of pretty writing pens and pencils is essential. Nobody wants to use a dried-up Bic when the muse is whispering in their ear. Don't forget to apply for a liquor license in advance if you plan to serve fancy beverages. Otherwise, tea/coffee, water, and juice are usually easy enough to procure. You may also want to serve snacks, depending on your library's food policy.

Step 5. Think about your room set-up and plan accordingly. Will you need a mic and amp? A stage? A bar or snack table? Chairs? Tables or desks? What software will you be using if doing the program online? Make sure you have a working webcam and mic. Test everything ahead of time. DO NOT wait until five minutes before the program starts—trust me.

Step 6. How many people are you expecting to attend? Do you have the (in-person or online) capacity? Will you be requiring advance registration or is this a drop-in event? In my experience, it is always a good idea to secure the commitment of at least a handful of professional or amateur poets that you know will come. Ask them to be prepared to do a little writing onsite but also bring a few pieces with them to share. They will usually be flattered and happy to oblige. Take it a step further and ask one to emcee or "headline" the event, offering a small honorarium if you can afford it. Investing in your writing community shows you are serious about supporting local authors and having a published author lead the event lends an air of credibility. If you are worried this may scare new writers away, ensure that the more seasoned poets are willing to contribute something spur-of-the-moment. You want everyone to know it is okay to be vulnerable. And that getting good at writing poetry takes not only more than talent but also concerted effort and practice. Let this be a lighthearted celebration of an often too-serious pastime. Spoken-word or improv poets are often the best to invite because they love this sort of atmosphere already and know how to inspire others to have fun with it. This advice applies equally to online events.

Step 7. Will you be taking photos or video? Then you are going to need to have participants sign a photo/video release waiver. You may also want to add a stipulation about copyright on there if you'll be sharing any audio/video of people reading their work. Something to the effect of, "All rights remain with the author but that you have permission to share on social media (list platforms) and won't be held accountable if others share the post, alter the video, etc."

Step 8. This is an excellent opportunity to make a display to show off your poetry collection (see my suggestions under the "Literacy Tie-In" section). Make sure to highlight local authors and publishers. Don't forget about literary magazines! And spoken-word CDs, if you have them. If you are doing the program offsite, take a small display of items with you for people to peruse. It may entice them into the branch to check out items at a later date, or bring along a portable check-out terminal, if you have one. If you are hosting the program online, provide a link to a curated list in your virtual catalog.

Step 9. What's the best way to market your event to potential writers, poetry lovers, and reclusive authors? This is where having a good relationship with your local bookshops and publishers comes in handy. Prepare an eye-catching poster to put up in their shops and ask them to spread the word to the literary company they keep about your event. Put up the poster in coffee shops, bars, coworking spaces, and in the study rooms and cubicles of your own library. Pretty much anywhere you think your local booklovers might be hanging out. A lot of writers listen to talk radio while they work, and putting out a free PSA on your local stations might reach their ears. Creating a Facebook event for the program, as well as sharing the poster on social media, as well as in newsletters (paper and digital), will also give the event a wider reach. In my experience, Twitter is where authors spend the most time, so make sure to tweet about the event and tag local writers. And don't forget word of mouth! When your circulation staff notices someone checking out poetry books, they can mention the event, or make an announcement at your book clubs, author talks, book launches, and writing circles. You can also tie into larger events like National Poetry Month (April) or World Poetry Day (March 21) in order to garner attention with their familiar names, hashtags, and logos.

Step 10. For online programs, don't forget to email out the Zoom links and clear instructions to everyone who registers (unless you are just providing a general link to the event that anyone can join). For an in-person event, make sure the format of the event is clearly outlined, so people know what to expect.

Step 11. Prepare short evaluation forms (everyone already has pens!) or a quick survey link (lots of free software like Survey Monkey to be found online) to gather feedback, if you'd like.

Materials Required

- If online, you'll need conferencing software, like Zoom, and hardware, like a webcam
- A mic and amp (unless it's a really small room/group)
- A stage or cleared area for the readers
- Chairs
- Table or bar area for snacks and drinks
- Coffee, tea, and other beverages or snacks
- Napkins, cups, plates, spoons, stir sticks, etc.
- Typewriters and ink reels (if using)
- Writing desks or tables
- Pens, pencils, and lots of paper
- Recycle bin for the rejects
- A basket of fidget spinners or other tactile objects (see "Helpful Advice" section for why)
- Photo/video release and copyright waivers
- A bulletin board for people to display their creations
- A magnetic poetry set and something metal to stick it to
- Evaluation forms, if using

Budget Details

$0–$100+. This event is potentially really easy on the budget. If done online or by simply supplying paper and pens you already have on hand and no refreshments, you can get away without really spending anything. If you can borrow some typewriters from friends, family, or an old supply closet—even better! You may have to buy some ink rolls, which will cost you about $15 each. Or you can re-ink old ribbons yourself if you have a lot of time on your hands and don't mind getting messy.[1] If you are going to get a liquor license to serve wine or beer (here in New Brunswick, this costs $50 Canadian), source someone to provide alcohol. Also, if you provide other beverages and foodstuffs, you can expect to see your budget climb into the hundreds. But your attendance may also increase exponentially. If you take the simpler option of just having tea and coffee for a small crowd, that shouldn't cost more than $30. A few fidget items can be found at the dollar store or in your craft supply closet. A used bulletin board can be found cheaply or for about $20 new. A magnetic poetry set is about $15. A white-board is going to cost about the same, or more, than a cork bulletin board. You can also just use old card catalog cards or recipe cards and tape them up. Use your imagination to stay within your budget.

Day-of-Event

Step 1. If you are having your Pop-Up Poetry Reading online, you'll need to test out the equipment and log in about fifteen to twenty minutes early to greet your guests and any special authors you may have asked to join. If possible, it's best to have two people on the call: one who can greet people and explain the software functions and another who can monitor the chat and provide tech support to patrons and speakers. Obviously, an online event is going to look a lot different than an in-person one, so you can skip most of the other steps that follow. At starting time, you'll introduce your guest speakers (if you have any) or just open the virtual floor to let people read their work. If there is some reluctance, you can jump in with a poem of your own, a fun nursery rhyme or limerick, or perhaps a famous poem you really like. Everyone who wants to read gets a turn, but you may need to set time limits or some chatty speakers will monopolize the whole event. Five minutes per person is usually good. You probably don't want the event to last more than an hour, as that is about most people's sit-still-on-Zoom limit without needing bathroom breaks or a good stretch.

Step 2. For an in-person event, make sure your poetry display is well-stocked, or set it up if you haven't done that already. Share the link to the curated online collection via email or chat with your online participants. Set up the bulletin or magnetic board to display poetry, if using.

Step 3. For an in-person event, set up the room (including the bar area, if using) and put out your supplies. Brew your coffee and tea about twenty minutes prior to the start of the event—unless you want it really strong!

Step 4. Prepare and post directional signage for the room, such as "Coffee/Tea Station," "Experimental Poetry—Try It Yourself," or "Pin Your Poems Here."

Step 5. Print off the waivers. Locate a staff member or volunteer at the door with a clipboard and pens to greet participants and have them sign the forms and explain the process for the event. Have them show people where the writing stations are and let them know what time the reading will start.

Step 6. After giving people plenty of time to try their hands at writing something (at least twenty to thirty minutes) and have a drink or snack and mill around, then you can get up on stage in front of the room and announce that the reading will commence. If you are emceeing, you can launch right in; if not, introduce your emcee or guest speaker. Here's where having a poem handy to read and break the ice really helps if you don't have a professional author prepared to do that.

Step 7. Invite people to come up one at a time to share what they wrote during the free time at the beginning or else share something they brought along. If there are a lot of people or you are short on time, allocate five minutes per person or less.

Step 8. At the end of the event, thank everyone for coming and invite them to take their creations home. Pass out evaluation forms, if using. For online events you can share a link to a quick survey for feedback. Don't forget to file your photo/video waivers!

Step 9. Put some fun shots up on social media. Bask in the glow of how enjoyable poetry readings can be when you don't take yourself too seriously.

Literacy Tie-In

If you'd like, prepare a display to correspond with the pop-up event (this can also be done on digital platforms for e-books!). Choose books, CDs, films, and periodicals that have to do with poets and poetry. Try to find something that would appeal to everyone. You could even curate a list of poetry podcasts (a quick internet search will give you a bunch of them). Below are some suggestions of well-known titles you might already have in your collection to get you started. Make sure to include as many local authors and publishers as possible!

Periodicals:

- *American Poetry Magazine*
- *The American Poetry Review*
- *Arc Poetry Magazine*
- *Brick*
- *Canadian Poetry*
- *The Fiddlehead*
- *Matrix*
- *The New Yorker*
- *The Paris Review*
- *Ploughshares*
- *Poetry London*
- *Poets & Writers Magazine*
- *PRISM International*
- *Quill & Quire*
- *The Sun Magazine*

Print or audiobooks:

- *Beowulf: A New Translation* by Maria Dahvana Headley
- *The Collected Poems of Dylan Thomas* by Dylan Thomas
- *Devotions: The Selected Poems of Mary Oliver* by Mary Oliver
- *Essential Bukowski* by Charles Bukowski
- *Felon* by Reginald Dwayne Betts
- *Inward* by Yung Pueblo
- *Milk and Honey* by Rupi Kaur
- *Night Sky with Exit Wounds* by Ocean Vuong
- *The Oxford Shakespeare: The Complete Sonnets and Poems* by William Shakespeare
- *Our Numbered Days* by Neil Hilborn
- *Poems and Songs* by Leonard Cohen

- *The Poetry of Strangers: What I Learned Traveling America with a Typewriter* by Brian Sonia-Wallace
- *The Prophet* by Khalil Gibran
- *The Selected Poetry of Rainer Maria Rilke* by Rainer Maria Rilke

DVDs:

- *Barfly* (1987)
- *Before Night Falls* (2000)
- *Bright Star* (2009)
- *Dead Poets Society* (1989)
- *The Edge of Love* (2008)
- *Howl* (2010)
- *Kill Your Darlings* (2013)
- *Neruda* (2016)
- *Paterson* (2016)
- *Poetic Justice* (2003)
- *A Quiet Passion* (2016)
- *Quills* (2000)
- *Sylvia* (2003)
- *Total Eclipse* (1995)
- *Wilde* (1998)
- *Wild Nights with Emily* (2019)
- *William Shakespeare's Romeo + Juliet* (1996)

Helpful Advice

- If you have a regular poetry-writing group that gathers in your library, or you are looking for a fun challenge, why not host several of these events over the course of the year and have different themes, such as: Rhyming Couplets Only!; Haikus and You; Dirty Nature Poems; Vegetable Verse; Dr. Seuss Style; Epic Journeys in 100 Words or Less; Oh Noetry! Intentionally Bad Poetry!; Angry Rant Readings; Elegant Shopping Lists; and so on. The possibilities are endless, and it gives everyone a chance to stretch their writing muscles in a genre or subject they don't normally write in.
- This event could work really well with college students taking English Literature or Creative Writing. If you are an academic librarian, reach out to your English or Fine Arts Department. You could even run it as part of a contest with the student newspaper or university's literary magazine (if you have one). A few pieces from each Pop-Up Poetry Reading could be published in the periodical. Just be careful it doesn't make for an overly competitive atmosphere—this is supposed to be fun, after all.
- Have a basket of fidget spinners or other tactile objects like stress balls, pipe cleaners, pompoms, or elastics for nervous writers to play with while they wait their turn. Leave these on the table by the paper and typewriters with a note encouraging people to take one and explain what they are for. If you make sure they are inexpensive items you already have on hand (like

pompoms or elastics), then you don't need to worry about people pocketing them. Many writers have issues with anxiety (especially social anxiety) or other neurological issues (like attention deficits) and offering these items both validates their feelings (reading your work in public can be scary!) and offers a temporary solution to help calm their nerves. Most people list public speaking as their number one fear—even more than death or spiders!

- In your promotion of the event, make sure to describe the process so people know what to expect. But also make sure to stress that participation is optional, so you don't scare anyone away. What you are hoping for is a nice mix of appreciative audience members and impulsive artists who will enjoy entertaining others with their whimsical words.
- Get creative with spontaneous wordplay. Bulletin boards, cork boards, chalkboards, giant Post-it notes, whiteboards, those big pads of paper on an easel, magnets on a bunch of cookie sheets to hold slips of paper in place or those little magnetic poetry pieces . . . the possibilities are only limited by your imagination (and budget). Pens, pencils, markers, crayons, typewriters, tablets, and even Etch A Sketches allow you to get creative with your marking implements. This is supposed to be fun and appeal to a wide range of people. By including multiple modalities, you'll also be more accessible to those that struggle with more conventional writing formats.
- Don't be afraid to get creative with the location of your Pop-Up Poetry Reading and experiment with the format. This doesn't require a lot of planning. One boring day in July, you could just set up a little table with a typewriter in the parking lot, library's front lawn, or in the lobby and just invite passersby to try their hand at writing something, anything they like. You do not have to hold a formal reading; participants could just tack up their work on a board for others to read (if they wanted to share) or take it with them. Maybe instead of a reading you could have an audio track of a famous poet playing in the background for inspiration and to get attention.
- Why not make this a passive program and just set up the supplies somewhere in view of the circulation or reference desk and put out some signage inviting patrons to try their hand at writing something? You may have to check in periodically to replenish supplies and to discourage vandalism.
- Think about holding these events around holidays. Do it around Valentine's Day and encourage people to write a love poem (or anti-love poem). Around Christmas and Hanukkah, people could write poems to their family members or friends as gifts. Mother's and Father's Day could be cause for poems dedicated to parents (for better or worse!). New Year or Chinese New Year could invoke poems about upcoming dreams and wishes for the future. Halloween poems could be spooky mystery tales told over candlelight.

Further Books and Writing Ideas

- Cursive Writing—Handwriting classes aren't just for kids! With days and nights spent typing and texting, when was the last time you sent a handwritten card to someone? When was the last time you used cursive? (Signatures don't count.) Learning how to recognize cursive letters allows people to read historical documents and handwritten letters from their grandparents and ancestors. Many middle-aged adults who learned cursive as children are keen to keep these abilities alive or rekindle them entirely. Young adults who only received instruction in basic printing after the cursive curriculum was removed will be fascinated to learn this basic skill. I recommend buying simple workbooks that can easily be found on Amazon or by printing worksheets from the internet. (See figure 6.3.) This can be a stand-alone class to whet their appetites or a series of classes culminating in a project, such as composing a letter or copying a poem. You can learn more about classes I've taught on cursive writing by visiting my Programming Librarian blog.[2]

- Calligraphy Classes—Take your handwriting classes to the next level by teaching calligraphy. Play on the huge interest in historical fiction and period drama television shows and movies to encourage patrons to try their hand at old-fashioned lettering. You can find lined calligraphy pads at the office or art supply shop (or online) for practicing with. Purchase some fancy cardstock for the final project to make it really special. We like using the basic Speedball calligraphy nibs and pouring liquid ink into small wells (those tiny white paint trays from the dollar store work great). If you don't have anyone on staff who knows how to teach calligraphy, look for an enthusiastic volunteer in your community. If not, follow along with some videos on YouTube—there's plenty to choose from!

- Bookbinding Workshops—Think reading books are great? What about making them? Entice crafters to your library to try their hand at a simple stab binding or accordion-folded book (see figure 6.4 for an example). I happen

Figure 6.3 Cursive Writing. *Source:* Jenn Carson.

Figure 6.4   Accordian-style bound book. *Source*: Jenn Carson.

to be a fairly decent bookmaker, so I teach these myself at the library, but I encourage you to reach out to your local bookbinding guild chapter (yes, these exist!) and find an artist to teach a class.[3] The nice thing about simple bindings is they don't require a lot of fancy equipment (or skills!). In fact, this program can be run using repurposed Davey board from discarded hardback books as long as the covers aren't warped. You can also use this board to make really cool boxes (see figure 6.5).

- Make Fancy Bookmarks—Who doesn't love bookmarks? I mean, realistically, we know most people (guilty!) just grab the closest thing and shove it in their book (a coaster, toilet paper, a gum wrapper, etc.)—or worse, dog-ear the page—but everyone loves the *idea* of a bookmark, and they make great (inexpensive) gifts for the reader in your life. This is where you can have a lot of fun and get creative with stuff you already have lying around the library. Got adult coloring books gathering dust? Make bookmarks out of them! Got lots of discarded hardcovers of the classics? Repurpose the fabric or leather book spines by gluing them to cardstock or Davey board wrapped in nice paper. Bonus points if the hardbacks have pretty gold lettering or an illustration. Got some washi (paper) tape and balls of yarn lying around? Use it on some cardstock to make a whimsical bookmark with a fancy tassel! These ideas are easily translatable to a passive program. Just leave out the supplies in your Maker Space or another suitable location with an infographic for instructions. This also makes an excellent curbside pick-up kit.
- Record Your Own Audiobook—Hold a workshop for writers to teach them how to record and share audio versions of their self-published works. You can go over different types of recording and editing software, how to edit, how

Figure 6.5 Box made using discarded materials. *Source*: Jenn Carson.

to add sound effects or music (respecting copyright laws), and how to set up the proper space for recording (sound dampening is essential!). You can also discuss different hosting platforms and how to generate income from downloads or streaming services. If this is beyond your scope of knowledge, reach out to a local sound engineer to teach the class or a college student studying the topic. This is an excellent program to deliver in an online format.

- How Writers Can Work with Libraries—I teach a popular workshop on how writers can work with libraries to get their books on the shelves (and circulating), host author talks and book launches, and teach workshops to the community. Reach out to your local writing club or college's English department for a willing and eager audience. Many authors don't have the first clue about how librarians can be their biggest allies when it comes to book promotion. Explain the mystifying world of libraries, e-books, and circulation stats to the people writing the content of our livelihood! Invite local publishers to attend as well and let the networking opportunities abound.

- Trivia Night—One surefire program to get adults into your library (sans kiddos) is to have a trivia night centering on a popular book/TV series. *Downton Abbey* is a hit in almost any location (see figure 6.6).[4] Other popular choices are the *Outlander* series of books and episodes, the *Games of Thrones* books and TV show, Jane Austen books and movies, the *Olive Kitteridge* books and mini-series, the *Dr. Who* books and TV shows, and *Harry Potter*, of course (though people have *very strong feelings* about J. K. Rowling, so be warned!). Prizes and food are essential. Bonus points if everyone comes in costumes. For a more detailed rundown of how to hold a trivia night, even in a tiny library, visit the Programming Librarian website.[5]

Figure 6.6 *Downton Abbey* **Trivia Night participants.** *Source*: Jenn Carson.

- Digital Storytelling—Don't be afraid to try your hand at running online literary programs. People are spending a lot more time online these days and
  are interested in learning more about how to be creative using new software
  for old formats. Oral and visual storytelling have been around for as long
  as humans have, and capturing this magic digitally has never been easier.
  Whether it's a budding poet who wants to illustrate their love poem to their
  sweetheart, or a parent who'd like to create an adorable bedtime story for
  their children to watch on a tablet while they are traveling for work, you'll
  find many adults who are interested in learning more about this exciting
  medium. For a step-by-step guide on how to create a digital story, please visit
  my Programming Librarian blog post on the topic.[6] You'll even get to watch
  a story I created with my own boys many years ago about a wayward carrot
  and a cranky old pickle!

Whether you are planning a year-long series of author talks or an easy book-
mark-making curbside pick-up kit, there are plenty of fun ways to get the adults

in your community excited about books beyond just reading them. As we've learned in this chapter, when you connect local authors, publishers, and curious strangers, magic happens! When writers in your community feel supported and loved by their local library, the creativity and joy they express will be returned to you many times over. Behind almost every writer is the story of at least one library or librarian who made a difference in their lives, often at an early age. And as we learned in the Pop-Up Poetry Reading Program model, books and writing don't always have to be taken seriously. Share the joy of the written word with your patrons and they'll be coming back for more—and bringing their kids and friends too!

Notes

1. Find out how to re-ink old typewriter ribbons with these online instructions: RequiemScrc (screen name), "How to Re-ink a Typewriter Ribbon," *Instructables*, accessed March 18, 2022, https://www.instructables.com/How-to-Re-ink-a-Typewriter-Ribbon/.

2. Jenn Carson, "Blog: Cursive Writing Course," *Programming Librarian*, July 19, 2018, https://programminglibrarian.org/blog/cursive-writing-course.

3. In Canada, we belong to the Canadian Bookbinders and Book Artists Guild (https://www.cbbag.ca), and in the United States, you'll want to contact the Guild of Book Workers (https://guildofbookworkers.org).

4. Rachel Breen, "Program Model: *Downton Abbey* Episode Viewing and Afternoon Tea," *Programming Librarian*, February 1, 2016, https://programminglibrarian.org/programs/downton-abbey-episode-viewing-and-afternoon-tea.

5. Chelsea Price, "Blog: Trivia Night at a Tiny Library: It Can Be Done!," *Programming Librarian*, June 26, 2019, https://programminglibrarian.org/blog/trivia-night-tiny-library-it-can-be-done.

6. Jenn Carson, "Blog: Digital Storytelling in 6 Steps," *Programming Librarian*, March 31, 2020, https://programminglibrarian.org/blog/digital-storytelling-6-steps.

7

✙

Technology and Media Programs

It continues to shock and appall me at how little libraries are associated with technology, despite the fact we are steeped in it, and, frankly, at this point, we couldn't function without it. I recently received a phone call from a local school principal who, for whatever reason, had a giant inventory of books in her currently non-functioning school library, and she wanted to know if I would be able to come over and organize them for her. She had gotten my name from someone in the community who knew I was a librarian. I asked her what they were currently using for ILS (integrated library system) software. She didn't know. She went on to describe a piece of equipment made by Honeywell. I explained that it was a scanner, which was hardware, not software. I told her it was used to scan the barcodes on the books, which input the data about the book into the software program but that someone needed to first enter all that data into the system, creating MARC records with call numbers to correspond to that item ID. I asked her if the library employed a librarian. It did not. A technician or other trained staff member? It did not. At present, it didn't even have any volunteers, but she was hoping to get some (I think this is where she thought I came in). I (as gently as possible) explained that these volunteers would need to have some sort of consistent system for organizing these books and tracking who was borrowing them, assuming she wanted the teachers and students to actually use them consistently. Oh yes, she very much wanted them in use. She said she just didn't realize it would be so complicated and was hoping someone could just "come over and put them on the shelves." I did everything in my power to calmly explain that the reason librarians have master's degrees is because the organization of data and metadata is not something easily undertaken by a casual volunteer with no experience. I suggested she reach out to the school district to find out what ILS software they were currently subscribing to and to see if they were able to hire a librarian and at least one technician to run the library. I explained getting their library up and running was going to take considerable effort and time. I had visited their school before, and the library was a beautiful space, but I just didn't realize at the time of my quick peek in the window that it wasn't actually being run as a library and was more of a random book-reading room. I wished her well.

I tell this story (and I'm sure you have your own) to illustrate the point that the average adult in your community (even those in possession of a wannabe library) vastly underestimates not only how many unique services the library provides (as discussed in previous chapters) but also just how much information management skills it takes to run a library. And this was an elementary school principal; she was not lacking in education or experience with the research process (I should hope!). She had certainly used a library before. On the flip side, we also all know those patrons who think we are magic IT gurus and assume we can divine passwords out of thin air or jump-start a dead device without a charger. When we think about offering adult programs centered on learning about different media and technology, I think we need to aim for somewhere in the middle. We don't need to turn every patron into a librarian-in-training (we all know the job pool is crowded enough these days), but we also don't want everyone so dependent on us that they can't search the catalog or watch their grandkids on TikTok without our help. Plus, learning about new programs and sharing that knowledge is fun and it is a great way to attract a wider demographic to the library. Perhaps those that think the library really is like a giant reading room will be pleasantly surprised when they find out they can come here to learn how to capitalize on their phone's picture-taking abilities or become the internet's most revered YouTuber.

Most of the media we consume these days is online, or at least on-screen, and this chapter will give you a jump-start on ideas about how to use screens and technology to engage your patrons, both inperson and in the web-o-sphere. As the platforms and devices we use are constantly upgrading and changing, this gives the library world a built-in service mission to strengthen our community's media literacy by offering tutorials and programs to get our users comfortable with whatever comes next. And the good news is we get to learn right along with them!

Program Model: Learn Stop-Motion Animation[1]

This is an engaging workshop to teach adults how to set up and create a simple stop-motion animation. The minimum time required is three hours, preferably with extra space left at the end as the participants often work at different paces. A full day would be even better. This is a labor-intensive program, as the instructor will guide the participants through all the steps of creation and should be led by a staff or volunteer that already has some experience with stop-motion (and lots of patience!). Significant one-on-one work is essential. This program can be very rewarding, especially for the creative, detail-oriented patron. Offering this program may attract a perhaps more introverted and tech-savvy demographic than your other adult programming. Try it and find out!

A note on materials (a handy list of needed items is provided in the "Materials Required" section) and set-up: Any camera will work for this program, but a smartphone or tablet allows image capture directly within a stop-motion

Figure 7.1   Stop Motion Animation. *Source*: Julia Chandler/Libraries Taskforce.

application. A traditional camera requires the extra step of importing the images into your chosen software. Most apps are able to do this so it's not a huge barrier, but it takes more time and is a challenge to fit within the average allotted space of a program. If going this route, a daylong workshop with access to multiple desktop terminals would be ideal. If you happen to have a media lab or maker space with multiple devices available, that would be the best place to set up. The big advantage to using a phone or tablet is the ability to preview your animation while making it. Since most people have a suitable phone or tablet, a program built around these devices is more accessible. (See figure 7.1 for a suitable set up in a library.) If you recommend an app in advance, patrons can come with it already downloaded to save time. The advantage to using a traditional camera is being able to produce higher quality images and having a choice of focal lengths by using interchangeable lenses. It will be up to you if you want to aim for quality or accessibility (or try to have some hybrid of both). Unless you happen to have a big budget or a lot of extra devices on hand, participants will need to supply their own. Audio should also be something that is either optional, to be done at home afterward, or to be added at a later date (maybe in a "Part 2" version of the workshop). The great thing about this program is it is customizable. You can make it as simple or as complex as you'd like, as challenging or accessible as you desire. If you'd like to focus on the literary component, spend more time writing scripts and storyboarding before you film. Fine-tune the format to fit your own comfort level, the needs of your clients, or your time limits. Let's get started!

Advance Planning

Step 1. The first important step will be determining who is going to run this program. Do you have a tech-savvy and creative staff member who would jump at the chance to do this? If not, do you have someone willing to take the time (and ensure they are given the time during their workday) to learn about the software, do some test runs, and gather the necessary supplies? If not, do you have a competent community volunteer? Are you able to reach out to a student from your local art college or high school that would be excited to share their skills? Once you secure this individual, you can move on in the planning process.

Step 2. You need to budget for at least a half-day for this workshop, especially if you plan on having a larger group (more than five participants). If you are hoping to add sound, or would like to use DSLR cameras, lenses, and complicated lighting, I would suggest a full-day event. Or make it a two-parter. Decide on the time and date. Evenings and weekends would allow for the broadest range of participants, but daytime may draw a different crowd entirely.

Step 3. Figure out your audience and where to situate them. The program is somewhat portable, so it could be taken offsite to community centers, student art commons, or conferences—wherever you are prepared to lug supplies. This would be an excellent program to offer to other library staff for professional development. It also works really well in an academic setting to give students and staff a break from exams and have fun making something unique. It can also be modified as an intergenerational program for families, with the kids building the sets and the parents helping with the details (though, often, the kids will be more adept with the software and devices than their elders!). Book the room/media lab or any offsite locations you plan to use well in advance.

Step 4. Prepare a registration process (hard-copy sign-up sheet at the circulation desk, Facebook event, etc.) and decide on your preprogram requirements. What devices will patrons need to bring? What software should they have preloaded (if any)? Do you want people to work solo or in pairs? Do they need to have a minimum skill level to join? If people don't have access to a device, will you provide them? How many people/devices can you reasonably accommodate/provide? Should people come prepared with a mini-script or at least a story idea in advance? How long should each script/video be? You don't want some participants showing up with a ten-page, incredibly detailed screenplay with storyboards and others just winging it, do you? (Maybe!) How do you want this to go? Do you want everyone to work at their own pace, or do you expect all participants to leave with a similarly finished product? Is this more about learning the process of stop-motion, or creating a certain product? Is your instructor included in this conversation (they should be!). The facilitator will set the tone for the class and need to communicate the expectations (adjusting as necessary) for the group. Making sure you've contemplated these questions and have a good framework for how the workshop should proceed in advance will help things run more smoothly on the day. It will also help patrons from showing up unprepared and feeling discouraged.

Step 5. I highly suggest testing a few stop-motion apps in advance to see which one will work best for what you intend to create. Most software listed in the textbox 7.1 is free or has a free trial to let people test it out. It's best to try them

ahead of time because some require in-app purchases to access certain components, and you'll likely want to avoid those. Watch tutorials to become comfortable with all the features and functions of your chosen app. You may decide to
switch after testing one out. The software we use is called Stop Motion Studio.
It is available on the widest selection of operating systems. It offers a free trial
and appears to be the most popular, gauging from online reviews, but there
are many others to try out. To make instructions easier during class, everyone
should be using the same app.

TEXTBOX 7.1

Stop Motion Software:

1. Clayframes (Android only)
   Free trial available, learn more at: https://sites.google.com/site
   /mrlightbox/home/clayframes
2. Frameographer (iOS only)
   This product costs US $4.99 and can be found at: https://apps.apple
   .com/us/app/frameographer/id503347879
3. I Can Animate (for Windows and macOS)
   Link to free trial option: https://www.kudlian.net/products
   /icananimatev2/download.html
4. iMotion (iOS only)
   Free (with optional in-app purchases): https://apps.apple.com/ca/app
   /imotion/id421365625
5. iStopMotion (for macOS and iOS)
   Available with a free trial at: https://boinx.com/istopmotion-create
   -stop-motion-animation/
6. Lapse It: Time Lapse & Stop Motion Camera (for iOS and Android)
   Free (with optional in-app purchases): http://www.lapseit.com/faq/
7. PicPac (Android)
   Has a free trial but contain ads, and you have to pay for many features:
   https://picpac.tv/
8. Stop Motion Studio (for iOS, macOS, Android, and Windows)
   This is the software we prefer. Link to free trial option: https://www
   .cateater.com/try.html
9. Zing StikBot Studio 2.0 (Android, macOS, and iOS)
   Free and designed to be used with their licensed StikBot figurines but
   can be adapted to any action figure, like LEGO mini-figs or posable dolls.
   Link to download: https://play.google.com/store/apps/details?id=com
   .zingglobal.stikbot2&hl=en_CA&gl=US

Step 6. Decide whether you'd like to include an audio component. The audio part
is optional for anyone who has an animation that needs a voice-over. It should
be done after shooting and recorded as a lip sync while watching the animation.
Most apps include the ability to add audio to your movie. Some include sound

effects and music as well as allowing you to import audio from your device. Some apps allow you to record audio directly in the program. If you are using a DSLR camera to take stills, the audio will need to be added after you compile everything. Adding audio is an optional step but helps make the animations feel more complete. Be aware of copyright issues when importing music. Any audio provided within the apps is fine to use as it is already licensed for this. If you plan to use audio from outside the app, research and test this now. Remember: if you use anything copyrighted from outside the app, you can't share it publicly (sorry, no Beyoncé to spice up your animation), unless you've purchased licensing rights. You can easily find copyright-free music online to download. Some of it isn't even terrible. Free Music Archive is a really great source for free indie music you can use in your videos.[2]

Step 7. Gather your necessary supplies (see "Materials Required" section for more details). What are participants going to use to tell their stories? Are you going to do some storyboarding first? Do you want everyone working in the same medium (like modeling clay, for example)? How much artistic experience and input are you expecting from people? It takes a lot more skill to make your own posable figures than to use some existing toys or dolls. What are you going to use for backgrounds? Will you make full-on dioramas, or will you just have a common drop cloth background everyone can use? Most importantly: How much time do you have? The more options you give and the more freedom to create and experiment, the more time you will need.

Step 8. Secure funding to pay for the program (see "Budget Details" section for specifics). STEM grants or funding to teach seniors or low-income/high-risk/ underserved populations about technology may be available. Be aware that this may alter the demographic you will be advertising to, so it is best to figure this out in advance.

Step 9. Create your own short stop-motion movie ahead of time, using the chosen software and supplies. It will serve as a teaching tool for participants and also help you advertise the program. It doesn't have to be very long; one or two minutes is great!

Step 10. Let people know about your program and how they should go about registering. Make sure to include all the preprogram requirements (device needed, charging cords, software needed, materials provided, any story-creation work to be done in advance, etc.) in your copy so participants come prepared and also understand what they are signing up for. You can include the program in your print and online calendars and newsletters, as a Facebook event, or on a poster to be put up around town or campus. Share your short stop-motion video on Facebook, YouTube, and Instagram to show potential attendees what can be done. And don't forget word of mouth! I also suggest making a nice display of stop-motion movies and books (examples are listed in the "Literacy Tie-In" section) surrounding a poster advertising the event to interest passersby at your library.

Step 11. Prepare video/photo release waivers and any feedback forms you may require.

Step 12. Test all lighting and audio equipment well in advance of the day to make sure it is working. Don't forget to charge batteries!

Step 13. Install and test software on all devices being provided by the library for participant use. Make sure they are well charged in advance of the program. Taking photos uses lots of power. Some phones and tablets may need to be hooked up to power sources all the time as their batteries just won't last. Gather the necessary power bars and extension cords and make sure you have access to outlets.

Materials Required

- Oil-based modeling clay (it won't dry out), such as Van Aken brand
- Posable figures (such as dolls, LEGO minifigs, action figures, art mannequins, etc.)
- Connectable building toys (for building sets and props)
- Any movable or shapable objects of appropriate size (such as toy cars, plastic fruit and vegetables, model trees and fake flowers, doll furniture, etc.)
- Dioramas or dollhouses for settings and backgrounds (shoeboxes with one side cut off work well)
- A drop cloth or other plain backgrounds, such as a blank wall or table turned on edge
- One smartphone, tablet, or camera per participant (may be supplied by patrons)
- Extension cords and/or power bars and power banks
- All necessary charging cables and dongles
- A tabletop tripod or full-size tripod (at least one per camera)
- Smartphone or tablet holders (one per device)
- Lighting (not necessary but nice to have; see "Budget Details" and "Helpful Advice" sections for more information)
- Photo/video release forms if you will be sharing on social media
- Stop-motion software (this will need to be preloaded on existing devices or done through the library's Wi-Fi once patrons arrive for the program)
- Paper, pens, pencils, and markers for storyboarding[3]
- Large monitor or projector for sharing work and illustrating examples of technique (including a laptop or other device to plug into this)
- Clay wire cutter or dental floss (if using clay)
- Evaluation forms (if using)

Budget Details

$0–$100+. If participants bring their own devices, you use free software, and also use existing toys, props, and lighting from the library, you could essentially pull this program off for nothing. If you plan on providing oil-based modeling clay, that can run between US $13 to $15 per two-pound block. It is cheapest to buy in bulk. You can cut up the blocks into smaller pieces using a clay wire cutter, which runs about US $5 to $10, or use my cheap hack: dental floss wrapped around two pencils. If you want multiple colors, you will need to buy a fair amount and hack them up into chunks for each person. Another option is to buy a multi-color pack for each participant, but this can get pricey and the quantities are smaller.

Van Aken Claytoon Modeling Clay comes in a one-pound pack that contains four complimentary colors and is about US $5 each. You can also buy each four-ounce color separately at about US $1 per pack.

There are different types of lighting that could be used, beyond existing tabletop lamps and overhead lights you might already have. What you might want to buy are mainly marketed as LED video conferencing or webcam lights. They are widely available on Amazon and Best Buy, as well as at office supply stores. Some plug in, and some are battery-powered. Be sure to check how long the batteries last. It would be good to have multiple backups of the battery powered ones if the battery life will be less than the length of the shooting session. The less expensive lights will have the shortest battery life. See the textbox 7.2 for suggested models of various lights from our resident camera expert, Brendan Helmuth (keeping in mind new models come out all the time). But remember, if you are short on money, any clamp-on or portable desk light will work as well. Even though these lights aren't that costly, it could get expensive to purchase enough to have them for each setup. The benefit is they can be reused in the future for many other programs, or for taking photos in the library.

TEXTBOX 7.2

Camera-Mounted Light

Digipower–Insta-Fame Dimmable 50 LED Super Bright Video Light with 3X Light Diffusers and Smartphone Mount—US $20.00 for one

Tabletop Light

Emart 60 LED Continuous Portable Photography Lighting Kit for Table Top Photo Video Studio Light Lamp with Color Filters—Two Packs; US $32.00 for two

Tripod-Mounted Light

Foxin 88 LED Dimmable 5600K USB LED Video Light Led Panel Lights Studio Lighting with Adjustable Tripod Stand/Color Filters, Studio Light/Lighting for Video Recording—US $60.00 for two

---

Day-of-Event

Step 1. Prepare the program space in advance. Create a separate place for each person to set up, with all the materials laid out.

Step 2. Test all equipment and batteries to make sure everything is working.

Step 3. Welcome participants as they arrive and have them complete their waivers and show them to a workstation. Ensure they have the proper software downloaded, or that they are familiar with the device you are lending them. Divide into pairs, if you are working in teams.

Step 4. Once everyone has arrived, go around the room and have each person introduce themselves and announce their favorite stop-motion movie or TV show. Don't spend too much time on intros; you have a lot of work to accomplish!

Step 5. Give an introduction describing the fundamentals of the workshop, a walkthrough of how to use the app, and what you expect to accomplish in the program. This is a good time to show everyone your sample video and give them a few moments to play around with the software and ask any questions.

Step 6. Encourage everyone to make a storyboard and shot lists. Assess one-on-one and troubleshoot any issues (such as an unrealistic number of shots).

Step 7. Have them start creating their scenes using the materials provided. Go around and provide help if they get stuck for ideas or need technical assistance. They can start filming their shots as soon as they are ready.

Step 8. Let participants work at their own pace. For the inexperienced, it can be helpful to make multiple short animations (ten to thirty seconds) to see how it goes before attempting something longer and more complex. If people are getting bogged down with an overcomplicated storyline that requires too much rearranging of scenes and figures, remind them this isn't a full-length Hollywood film and to just think of it as a short, animated story, like those hand-drawn flipbooks. Have them take their character from point A to point B and then add some narration, if they'd like. It doesn't need to win an Oscar.

Step 9. If participants want to add audio, they will need access to a quiet space to record (unless they are using preloaded music or sound effects from the app). A bathroom or closet should work fine. Help them with this step, as needed (maybe don't go in a closet with them, that could be weird).

Step 10. As the animations are finished, have participants upload them to a designated shared storage space, such as a Google Drive folder, or on a library laptop set up to a projector.

Step 11. Have a mini-film festival to show off your work! If there is time leftover, make more animations!

Step 12. Thank everyone for coming. Remind them about posting and copyright laws. Have them complete evaluation forms, if using.

Step 13. Clean up. Celebrate a job well done! Post images and videos to social media, with permission.

Literacy Tie-In

If you'd like, prepare a display to correspond with the program (this can also be done on digital platforms for e-books and catalog links). Choose items that have to do with all sorts of animation to get people's attention, but especially DVDs from studios that use Claymation or other forms of stop-motion animation. There are even live-action movies that use stop-motion (like the *RoboCop* series). Below are some suggestions of different movies and how-to books (and a few periodicals, if you happen to subscribe) to get your display started. Include a little clay figurine and a poster about the upcoming program to entice the curious and creative!

Periodicals:

- *3D Artist Magazine*
- *Animation Magazine*
- *ImagineFX*
- *Make: Magazine*
- *Movie Maker Magazine*
- *Sight & Sound*

Print or audiobooks:

- *The Advanced Art of Stop-Motion Animation* by Ken Priebe
- *The Art of Aardman: The Makers of Wallace & Gromit, Chicken Run, and More* by Peter Lord and David Sproxton
- *Cracking Animation* by Peter Lord and Brian Silbey
- *The Making of Fantastic Mr. Fox* by Wes Anderson
- *Stop-Motion Animation: Frame by Frame Film-Making with Puppets and Models* by Barry Purves
- *Stop-Motion Armature Machining: A Construction Manual* by Tom Brierton
- *Stop Motion: Craft Skills for Model Animation* by Susannah Shaw
- *Stop Motion Movie Making for Poor People* by David D'Champ
- *Stop-Motion Puppet Sculpting: A Manual of Foam Injection, Build-Up, and Finishing Techniques* by Tom Brierton

DVDs:

- *Anomalisa* (2015)
- *The Boxtrolls* (2014)
- *Chicken Run* (2000)
- *Coraline* (2009)
- *Corpse Bride* (2005)
- *The Empire Strikes Back* (1980)
- *Fantastic Mr. Fox* (2009)
- *Frankenweenie* (2012)
- *James and the Giant Peach* (1996)
- *Kubo and the Two Strings* (2016)
- *The LEGO Movie* (2014)
- *The Little Prince* (2016)
- *Mary and Max* (2009)
- *The Nightmare before Christmas* (1993)
- *ParaNorman* (2012)
- *RoboCop* (1987)
- *RoboCop 2* (1990)
- *Shaun the Sheep* (2015)
- *Starship Troopers* (1997)
- *The Terminator* (1984)
- *Wallace and Gromit: The Curse of the Were-Rabbit* (2005)

Helpful Advice

- If you are using any trademarked toys or items in your recordings (LEGO, action heroes, Barbies, Hot Wheels, etc.), remind participants that it is essential to check the copyright rules and even request permission from the parent company if they plan to share the videos publicly. The same rules will apply if you are sharing any video or stills made during the class on the library's platforms. Any animation using LEGO or other trademarked products is likely to be considered fair use because of the transformative nature of the items, but it would depend on the intent of the video. Is it for entertainment or education? If it could be construed as having commercial intent (such as primarily for making money or trying to sell something, such as toys) that could be considered copyright infringement. It is best not to show any logos. Again, to be safe, you can always check with the parent company before posting.
- Remind your patrons: You *must not share* videos publicly if they contain any copyrighted music. If they go home and throw in some random old U2 song and post their video to YouTube or Facebook, it's going to get flagged and taken down or at least muted.
- If you will be sharing patrons' projects on social media, make sure to have their written permission with a confirmation that they maintain copyright but that you have permission to publish for a limited period. This can be included in a subsection of the photo/video release waiver.
- This program could be done outdoors (at least partially), setting scenes in parks, library gardens, or on picnic tables and rock walls. Figures wading through the tall grass like trees would be delightful! But you'd have to be mindful of the weather (and rapidly changing light), as well as not catching other people in your shots if the area was busy.
- Some participants will need more attention than others, especially those with lower digital literacy skills. If you are able to have an assistant, that is a plus. Some participants will be able to help each other, but some will rely solely on you (and your staff/volunteers).
- Keep the numbers for this program small, especially if you have limited tripods and workstations (and are teaching it alone). You will want no more than five patrons per instructor.
- Small tabletop tripods can sometimes be found cheap at the Dollar Store or online in bulk. Not all tripods will fit all devices, but you can have a mix of tripods, tablet stands, and phone holders to keep things steady.
- When people register for the event, record what type of device they will be bringing. Make sure it is a device they are already comfortable with. This will help you gather materials in advance. For example, if everyone is bringing a smartphone or tablet, you won't need any camera tripods.
- An email reminder before the event with a list of things they need to bring is an excellent idea.
- Since everyone will be working on devices and presuming you have access to Wi-Fi, why not make your evaluation forms digital through something like Survey Monkey? Just email them the link from the email they gave you when they registered.

- There are lots of online stop-motion tutorials, but if you are looking for a good one that focuses on how to teach the subject, we recommend learning about the basics of stop motion animation with Joe Vena. This can be found on YouTube.[4]
- You will need to decide how fancy you want to get with the lights. Generally, an overhead room light is fine. It provides an even light with minimal, diffuse shadows. Any other type of light (an articulated desk lamp, for example) could be used for dramatic effect. As mentioned in the "Budget Details" section, inexpensive studio lights can be purchased for less than $50 but are not necessary. If used, look up general instructions for configuring studio lights on the internet. If you happen to already have some lights on hand, or patrons want to bring their own, at least you'll be prepared with some extra knowledge. Stop Motion Central is a great website with tips on how to best light your animation.[5]
- To avoid harsh shadows, prop a sheet of lightweight white paper between the light and the subject. This will create a diffuse light that wraps around the subject creating a softer look. This can also be achieved by turning the light away from the subject and reflecting it off a white surface like a wall or a piece of foam core aimed at the subject.
- Don't worry about not having all the answers. Try to keep the class process-oriented instead of project-oriented. If you don't finish the video in the allotted time, that's okay! Patrons can always continue working on it at home if they brought their own device. The best way to learn is through teaching and doing!

Further Technology and Media Program Ideas

- Nerd Out Night—STEM programs aren't just for juvenile patrons. If you have a collection of fun STEM robots or build-it kits like Sphero, Cubelets, LEGO Mindstorms, Ozobots, Snap Circuits, Cubetto, or LittleBits kits, why not put them out and invite your adult patrons to play with them? (See figure 7.2.) You can stand by to help decipher instructions, look for small pieces that roll under tables, and be a general cheerleader/troubleshooter. Between our busy work and child-/elder-care schedules, few adults take the time to just play with no other agenda. You might find your patrons leap at the chance to try. If you need a hook to get them in the door, you can market this program to older adults as a way to increase brain plasticity and improve memory (because solving puzzles and playing games does this!).[6] Or you can entice parents, grandparents, aunts, and uncles to come try out the toys with the intention of seeing if they might make fun presents for the children in their lives. A "try-before-you-buy" sort of idea. You can do it prior to Christmas, if you think that would entice more people. But once they get in the room and start making those robots move and lighting up those circuit boards, they'll get lost in the bliss of pure play! As a bonus, this program won't cost you a thing if you already have the kits anyway.
- Brick Builders Club for Grown-Ups—Similar to the previous program, a lot of adult folks really love playing with LEGOs but don't have the time (we

call it "Brick Builders" to avoid any trademark issues) or the budget—brick kits are expensive! If you happen to have a stash of bricks already on hand, why not bring them out some evening, put on some tunes, and invite adult patrons to play! If you find there's a good response, you could start having theme nights (Pirates! Architectural Wonders of the World! Build Your Own Bathroom! Baby Animals! Labyrinths! etc.) and post creation selfies on social media. This may especially appeal to Gen-Xers and older Millennials nostalgic for long-gone weekends and summer vacations spent building imaginary worlds in childhood bedrooms and basements. (See figure 7.3.)

- Social Media Isn't Scary—We regularly offer social media tutorials aimed at lower-literacy adults that would like to know how to use social media but don't know where to start (and are sometimes embarrassed to ask). These folks don't always have access to devices, the internet, or people who can help them navigate the web, and they feel left out when their friends and family are sharing things on social media they don't know how to access. You can try offering group classes, if you have a media center or people have their own devices. Or try one-on-one programs where you can help people directly on their own phone, tablet, or laptop using your library's Wi-Fi. Be prepared to take written notes to help them remember passwords and steps (having preplanned, easy-to-follow guides you can print off ahead of time really helps). I recommend only introducing one platform at a time. If it's easier for staff, you can offer different sites on different days. For example: Facebook on Mondays, TikTok on Tuesdays, Instagram on Wednesdays, Twitter on Thursdays, Goodreads on Fridays, Snapchat on Saturdays, and

Figure 7.2   Cubetto, the adorable screen-free wooden robot. *Source*: Jenn Carson.

Figure 7.3   Brick creation built by an adult patron. *Source*: Jenn Carson.

YouTube on Sundays. Or whatever works for your audience and schedule. Pick whichever apps would most appeal to your patrons. Don't forget about Reddit, Pinterest, Tumblr, Discord, WhatsApp, and many more. Or maybe make a list of which platforms you offer help with, offer fifteen-minute tutorials, and have patrons sign up to whichever one meets their needs. There are lots of ways to customize this program to help the most people increase their digital literacy.

- So, You Got a New _____ for Christmas?—Every new year, we like to offer our services to help adult patrons figure out the new devices they got over the holidays. We advise them to call in and book a time with a reference staff member (or volunteer) who will sit down and show them how to use their new Kobo, iPad, cell phone, digital camera, or whatever. It's a great program to pair volunteering teens after school with elderly patrons that don't know how to navigate the digital world (yet!).
- Digital Photography 101—It's often shocking to realize how many people are walking around with *very* expensive cameras around their necks with no real idea of how to use their features and functions. I can guarantee you there are a number of patrons at your library that own top-of-the-line cameras and are basically using them to point-and-shoot. Recruit a volunteer or eager staff member to teach basic introduction to a digital photography course that will let patrons bring in their cameras (without shame!) and learn how to use them properly. This can also be taught online, and a list of digital resources can easily be shared.
- Online Chess Club—Have patrons meet up online through a conferencing platform to introduce themselves. Every week (or however often you

Figure 7.4   Chess set at the library. *Source*: Brendan Helmuth.

plan to meet), go over one new chess strategy together. Then log in to online chess games (everyone using the same app) with easily identifiable handles and play each other. Not all programs have to be in person. But, of course, you can be an overachiever *and also* have an in-person chess club like we do! (See figure 7.4.)

As we've seen in this chapter, getting our adult community members better acquainted with technology and/or more interested in creative media doesn't need to be cumbersome, expensive, or patronizing. Library staff know full well how much technology plays into our work every day at the library, now we just need to convince patrons that we have the skills and enthusiasm to make it fun! Let them know we are here to help beyond resetting passwords and navigating Google searches. As more and more new games, toys, and software get released, we can make it our mission to test them out and help the masses navigate our digital landscape with ease and joy.

Notes

1. This program was created and delivered by library clerk Brendan Helmuth. His advice was invaluable in my writing of this chapter, and some lines were lifted directly from his notes, with his permission.

2. "Tribe of Noise," *Free Music Archive*, accessed 12 January 2022, https://freemusicar-chive.org/.

3. You can also print storyboard templates for participants to use, and these can easily be found on the internet to download for free. For example, visit https://boords.com/storyboard-template.

4. Artrageous with Nate, "How Do You Create Stop Motion Animation?" *YouTube*, November 8, 2017, https://youtu.be/nHyc0GAfjJg.

5. "Stop Motion Lighting Tips," *Stop Motion Central*, July 6, 2018, https://www.stopmotioncentral.com/stop-motion-lighting-tips/.

6. Gary Small, "Mind Games: A Mental Workout to Help Keep Your Brain Sharp," *The Guardian* online, October 13, 2018, https://www.theguardian.com/lifeandstyle/2018/oct/13/mental-exercises-to-keep-your-brain-sharp.

8

✛

Health and Wellness Programs

When we think of health and wellness programming, our first thoughts might not be related to libraries. Have libraries historically been a repository of medical information and research? Yes, of course. Even outside the academy, the general public will often look for books or websites to do with their health (or lack thereof) at their local community branch or ask reference librarians to parse medical journals to find relevant information for them to take home. Doctors sometimes send patients to the library to gather books and other resources about their condition (or a loved one's condition). But when we think of health and wellness, we probably first visualize a spa, health club, gym, yoga studio, medical clinic, meditation retreat, or maybe even a hospital. The reality is, as I've discussed extensively in other publications, libraries are often perfectly positioned to reach underserved community members who otherwise have little access to health-care or wellness programs.[1] Especially ones that are free. The social and economic determinants of health strongly affect whether or not we will lead healthy lives and be able to access quality care. This is true even in countries like Canada, which has (some) universal health-care programs (Canadians still pay for many services, like prescriptions, eye care, dental, etc.). The main determinants of health, according to the Government of Canada's website, include:

1. Income and social status
2. Employment and working conditions
3. Education and literacy
4. Childhood experiences
5. Physical environments
6. Social supports and coping skills
7. Healthy behaviors
8. Access to health services
9. Biology and genetic endowment
10. Gender

11. Culture
12. Race and experience of racism[2]

We don't have the space here to get into how *all* these factors influence your patrons' health and well-being, but let's unpack a few of them that will be relevant to the programs I'm going to suggest in this chapter.

Your physical environment, for example, can radically affect your health. If you live in a remote, northern climate, you will have less access to fresh fruits and vegetables. The same applies if you live in a food desert (a rural or urban location where you don't have easy access to a well-stocked grocery store and instead must rely on convenience stores, take-out, or infrequent shopping trips to collect goods).[3] Your location can also affect your ability to source medical care or health programs. Rural locations make it difficult to reach a doctor or hospital, or even an ambulance in an emergency, as well as the difficulty to attend fitness programs or go to the gym. Likewise, your financial situation can limit your ability to access those same programs and services. If you cannot afford health care (or a health-care plan), or gym memberships, or equipment, such as a yoga mat or snowshoes, it makes it nearly impossible to participate in these services or activities. This leads to worsening health and a continuous cycle of decline unless some intervention or healing takes place. Add a disability (mental or physical) or discrimination on top of this (or, often, sadly, both) and it becomes nearly impossible to improve your conditions. Lack of education concerning health topics and lower literacy levels compounds the issue even further, so we end up with an entire segment of the population that cannot access services, doesn't even know where to start if they could, and has very real emotional, intellectual, and physical barriers to seeking those services in the first place. Throw a large heaping of culturally induced shame on the fire and you can begin to understand why so many people are in poor health and are incapacitated to seek help. Hopefully this insight gives us more compassion for their plight.

Now, if I haven't depressed you too much, let's brainstorm some ways libraries can tackle this giant issue (while fully acknowledging that it is a *systemic problem* far beyond our capacity to rectify and that many of our own staff and volunteers are affected daily by these barriers to health and wellness, which is why I advocate in other places for addressing these issues internally as an organization as well).[4] I'm not proposing we can save everyone, or prop up a broken system that takes advantage of the caregiving nature of most library employees. I'm proposing we do what we can, within our means, with the tools and skills we possess (or can outsource through partners). We can't fix the ill-health of our entire communities or take down the capitalist framework that says only the wealthy should afford quality care, but we can make a difference by helping one patron at a time. I've seen it firsthand in my own library and in my own life. Let's get moving!

A Word About Consent and Liability

In all health-and-wellness-related programming, the importance of safety and verbal or nonverbal consent should be at the forefront of everyone's minds. First off, a liability waiver (also known as a "hold harmless agreement") should be signed by anyone taking part in a movement-based program (or their parent/

legal guardian on their behalf) where there is risk of accident or injury at the library—or offsite for outreach programs.[5] You want to make sure participants understand that there is risk involved (however small) with their chosen activity.

Secondly, it is always important to check in with patrons during the program to make sure they continue to feel comfortable or allow them to check in with you, as needed. I like to use something called the "Thumbs-Up Approach."[6] You can use this technique during any class at any time, but it is especially important to consider when teaching at-risk populations, such as veterans, women, members of the LGBTQ+ community, First Nation populations, and others that have a likelihood of suffering from the negative consequences of violence and systemic abuse that arises in our culture. I use this in any program where a patron (of any age) is likely to be triggered, such as a grief group, a yoga or martial arts class, a mental-health training, or meditation session. I like to tell participants at the start of class that when they need to leave the room for any reason to please give a "thumbs-up" on their way out the door. They should hold it high over their head so anyone can see. That way, if an instructor sees someone grabbing their stuff and leaving class early or running off, we know that they are just needing the bathroom, or have to leave early to pick up their kids, or need to take a breather by themselves. It's a good way to check on the pulse of the class. They don't need to tell you why they are leaving; they just need to let you know everything is okay with the visual confirmation of a thumbs-up.

If, on the other hand, someone leaves the room or storms off and doesn't give a thumbs-up, that's an indication to me, or any of the other trauma-informed instructors, that we need to follow that person. They are indicating they are *not okay* and may be experiencing a flashback, panic attack, general anxiety, rage, embarrassment, overwhelm, or a physical injury. We will follow that person and stay with them while they process what is happening, or intervene and deliver mental or physical first aid, as is necessary. Being trained, we know how to do this in a way that is safe for them and ourselves. It is very important to have at least one staff member trained in mental health first aid and non-violent intervention. Mental health first aid knowledge is just as important in public service roles as knowing CPR or how to apply a Band-Aid. In fact, I advocate that it is essential and have all my staff trained in trauma-informed approaches.

A third point to remember is not everyone likes to be touched (for myriad reasons), and some of these health and wellness programs may involve physical interaction between patrons or between a patron and a facilitator. You could assume everyone would speak up about their level of comfort, but some patrons may be too shy or anxious to do this. When I give adjustments during yoga classes, I try to either ask each person individually if they would like to be touched, or I hand out consent cards (see figure 8.1). These paper cards are given out at the beginning of class, and people can put them at the front of the mat indicating whether they would like adjustments. This makes it more private and gives the student a feeling of autonomy. They can also change their mind at any point during the class by flipping the card over. This option could also be included on the liability waiver, asking individuals if they consent to being touched during the program, but you'd have to keep track of who indicated what, and my memory can't be trusted for that, especially in a large group where I don't know everyone's name.

Figure 8.1 Yoga consent card. *Source*: Brendan Helmuth.

It is important to make people feel okay for not participating the way everyone else might be. For example, if you were hosting a ballroom dance class, and someone didn't feel comfortable being touched, they could practice the steps alone without a partner. Even if you feel awkward and don't know what to do or say, it is better to ask questions and make accommodations so that patrons feel safe and understood rather than risking causing harm that could have been avoided.

Finally, make sure you are holding space for patrons with cognitive or physical disabilities. If someone shows up to your run club or dance class and presents with a disability and you aren't sure how to help them, openly admit you don't have all the answers. Ask the patron how you can best accommodate them in your program. They know their disability better than anyone else. They may not want any accommodations at all, but let them tell you that—don't make assumptions. And remember, many disabilities—like MS (multiple sclerosis), the complications of lyme disease, or autism spectrum disorders (ASD), for example—are often invisible. Clearly outline at the beginning of the class what is going to happen step-by-step. Remember to speak your instructions in class slowly and clearly, as those with processing or overstimulation issues may experience cognitive overload if they are trying to learn new steps or techniques quickly, and also trying to contend with being touched by a stranger or being in a new location or group dynamic. Above all else, be compassionate and kind. We want to increase people's wellness by attending our programs, not create more stress in their lives.

Program Model: Go Fly a Kite!

What's a healthy, easily accessible program that gets people outdoors and learning a new skill together? Kite flying! Adorable, right? But what about those who want to take it to the extreme? Why not kite fighting! Yes, really. You can build eco-friendly kites pretty easily and then fight them! *Muwahahaha*!!! (That's my evil librarian cackle.) Or, you know, let them dance peacefully on the breeze in a field of flowers. Whatever floats your boat. Attract adults from all demographics to this program: those that come to fly kites quietly as a form of meditation and communing with nature, those that want to find a simple, easily portable activity to do with their children or grandchildren, or those who want to start a rad and highly competitive new hobby! (See figure 8.2.) And don't think this program can only be done in rural libraries or on a campus with a park and a soccer field. Kite flying (and fighting) is extremely popular in some of the most densely populated cities in the world, such as Rio de Janeiro in Brazil.[7]

This program model contains multiple components and options. It's basically a big daylong (or weeklong) kite extravaganza. If you don't have the budget/resources/time/interest to make it such a big event, pull out the components that work for you and leave the rest. The kite festival would ideally be held on a warm day with a slight breeze and access to a large, untread field, but we all know we can't control the weather or every aspect of our environment. I will offer options for how to modify the program's elements to suit your situation, and I'm sure you are creative enough to come up with some of your own ideas, too. The basic structure of the program model is:

1. Establishing a kite-lending library (using a community partner, if possible).
2. Launching said library with kite-flying and cake. Fun!

Figure 8.2 Young families enjoy kite flying together. *Source*: Ebony Scott.

3. Holding kite-making workshops. These can be simple paper kites or more robust fabric kites made from materials like nylon. You can even use garbage bags!

4. Organizing a kite-fighting tournament (this can be as competitive or as relaxed as you'd like).

Advance Planning

Step 1. This first step requires sourcing kites to start your kite library. If you don't plan on having a dedicated collection for circulation but would like some kites to use during programs, this section may also be of interest. If you are only planning to make kites from scratch for your program, you might want to skip ahead, but there are still some interesting details in this step.

If you follow my work, you will know I'm always on the lookout for new materials to add to our alternative collections to help support physical literacy. At my library, we have yoga mats, snowshoes, hiking poles, climbing structures, a weaving wall, a dress-up center, Hula-Hoops, tumbling mats and

Figure 8.3   Kite cabinet designed by Leland Wong-Daugherty. *Source*: Greg Campbell.

tunnels, skateboards, helmets and protective gears, and board games and puzzles that challenge fine-motor skills. But even with my experience, I was concerned about where I was going to get a bunch of good quality but reasonably priced kites. Then my friend, Leland Wong-Daugherty, creator of Little Cloud Kites, approached me about the possibility of having some kite programming at the library, and a fabulous community partnership was born.[8]

Dreams do come true, folks. Leland generously donated six organic-cotton, wood-framed kites, complete with quivers (a shoulder bag for carrying the kite) and wooden spools with hemp string. It is really important to have a quiver or else the kites get easily tangled and the pieces get mixed up. Together we designed a laminated instruction card to include with each kit. Luckily, Leland is an artist and woodworker, so he designed a catchy logo for our collection, illustrated the cards, and built an eye-catching cabinet in which to store them in (see figure 8.3). I had the instruction card translated into French, as we live in a bilingual province. Kite-flying instructions can be found in Sidebar 8.3.

If you have the budget, I highly recommend ordering your kites from Little Cloud Kites.[9] They start at about CAN $99 (no, I don't get any kickback for recommending them), and they come with a lifetime guarantee, including free repairs *and replacement* if you get them stuck in a tree![10] For real. They are handmade, and they are beautiful. And they support a young family. I am biased. Take a look at the textbox 8.1 to see lots of other great sources for kites you can find online or stop by your local kite shop, if you are lucky enough to have one.

TEXTBOX 8.1

Online Sources for Kite and Kite Accessories

1. Great Canadian Kite Company, based in Taber, Alberta, Canada. Excellent selection of brand-name kites for sport or relaxation. They offer classroom kite kits that can be ordered in packages of ten or twenty and can be built and decorated by hand, which would make an ideal ready-made program: https://www.canadiankitecompany.com/.
2. Into the Wind, based in Boulder, Colorado, United States. Stunt, fighting, single- or multi-line kites in various shapes and out of many different materials with a variety of price points. Free shipping over US $200: https://intothewind.com/kites.html.
3. The Kite Guys, based in Bentley, Alberta, Canada. Offers a variety of single-line kites and dual-line stunt kites. They also offer a "Kites in the Classroom" program that involves a 1.5-hour workshop presentation and includes a kite for all participants, which could be modified to be offered in libraries as long as they have a large activity room or gymnasium available (ideal for academic campuses): https://www.kiteguys.ca/.

4. Little Cloud Kites, based in Knowlesville, New Brunswick, Canada. An investment, as these are expensive but high-quality and ethically sourced. Lifetime guarantee, organic-cotton, artist-designed, handmade delta kites: www.littlecloudkites.com.
5. Pro Kites USA, a large, family-owned online retailer based in New Jersey, United States. Their website features a large variety of kite types with a flat US $4.99 shipping rate on all orders as of the time of this writing: https://www.prokitesusa.com/.

Step 2. Once you find a kite source, decide what type of kites you want to fly or what supplies you'll need to make them. This may depend on a lot of variables (budget, target age and skill level, what's available, etc.). See textbox 8.2 for a breakdown of the most popular types of kites on the market to help you make your decision easier, including some links for how to make your own. If you get really into kitemaking (why not form a club at the library!?) or just want to dive deep, I recommend nosing around on the American Kitefliers Association website, especially the webpage dedicated to free PDF kite downloads.[11]

TEXTBOX 8.2

Types of Kites[12]

1. Delta—These are some of the most popular kites and the ones we have in our collection. Shaped like a triangle, they are easy to launch and fly in only a slight breeze, making them perfect for beginners. They can be single- or double-stringed and sometimes have tails to make them more stable. (See figure 8.4.)
2. Diamond—The classic. When children draw kites, this is the shape they make. Another great option for beginners, these diamond-shaped kites have a crossbar that makes them stable in a variety of conditions and easy to launch. You can make them quickly and cheaply on your own using paper, freezer bags, or plastic sheets and some dowels and glue (see figure 8.5). You can find easy kite-making videos on YouTube.
3. Foil—These kites have no frame and look like parachutes. They are durable and suffer little damage when crashing, making them a good choice for beginners prone to kite accidents. They often have multiple lines, which requires a bit of dexterity to manage, so maybe not the best for young kids or those with limited hand mobility.
4. Box—These decorative, rectangular kites have four struts parallel to each other, wrapped with sails on either end. They often have ribbons and other flourishes, like wings on the side. They fall under the classification of "cellular kites." Because they have more complicated frames, they are heavier and require more wind to fly. Commercial versions are usually made from rip-stop nylon, but you can make your own out of newspaper

Figure 8.4 Delta kite. *Source*: Ebony Scott.

or construction paper and thin dowels. Beautiful but not the best for beginners. They make lovely decorations to display in the library too!

5. Sled—These kites look like a big scoop, similar to the front of a bulldozer but turned sideways. They have (at least) two vertical, parallel spars (sticks). Sometimes they have multiple chambers. Newer versions come with inflatable spars, making them almost crash-proof and really easy to store (they squish up small!).

6. Rokkaku—Six-sided fighter kites originating from Japan, these kites can be easily decorated because of the symmetry of the sails. Traditionally made using washi paper and bamboo spars, they are extremely lightweight but also prone to damage. They are great fun to make and battle with! Here's a video tutorial on how to make your own rokkakus at the library: https://www.youtube.com/watch?v=R3lraiZGID0.

7. Capucheta—These rectangular fighter kites come from Brazil. They are super easy to make and very environmentally and budget friendly—you can just use up old newspapers or wrapping paper! My children and their friends have built and decorated these in an afternoon and fought many battles! Equally fun for adults, trust me! You will only need paper, string, tape, and a toilet paper tube (for a spool). You can find directions and free printouts at *Little Cloud Kites* online.[13]

Figure 8.5 Handmade kites for fighting. *Source*: Kathryn Southan.

Step 3. Okay, before you go all out buying kite kits or scrounging up parts to make them, we need to talk about your budget. There is a detailed breakdown of item costs in the "Budget Details" section, but this is when you need to decide if you can finance this program in-house or if you'll need to start applying for grants. We received a wellness grant to help fund our program, as well as food donations from local businesses for the launch party. When searching on a grant database such as Grant Connect, look for keywords like wellness; sports; physical literacy; physical activity; exercise; health; nature; art; crafts; creativity; seniors (if that is your demographic); families (if that is your demographic); outdoors; play; mental health; mindfulness; environment; relaxation; or fitness.

Step 4. Once your funding is in place—and if you are buying ready-made kite kits—order them now; they may take a while to arrive. Or visit your local kite shop to purchase. I would do this even before you set a date for the event(s). Supplies can sometimes be limited, and shipping can be slow. You wouldn't want the stress of the day approaching and your kites not ready to go. If you are planning to build kites without a ready-made kit, make sure to gather all the needed supplies well in advance. You don't want to go looking for string the day of the program only to find your Children's Librarian used the last of it for a craft at storytime that morning.

Step 5. Make sure your timing is right for the launch. You are going to need decent weather. I'm not saying you can't fly a kite in a snowstorm, but do you really want to try? Kite flying is generally a warm-ish weather activity, and a light breeze is essential. I realize you can't always predict the weather, so this is why it is helpful to have all your supplies ready in advance, keep an eye on the forecast, and then plan the program only about a week or two in advance. It's always a good idea to pick a rain date, too, just in case the forecast is wrong.

Step 6. Decide on a location. Do you have a local ball field, park, beach, or wide-open space that would accommodate a bunch of kites and humans? Do you need to book that space in advance? Does the space have adequate parking, public transportation, or is within walking distance from a populated area? Think of your intended audience. If you are trying to reach working millennials in the suburbs, maybe a local state park would be a good meet-up; if you are trying to reach inner-city seniors that lack transportation, anything at a distance is not the right location. If you are at an academic library, is there a commons or football/soccer/baseball field or track that could be used? If you have a local park next to or near the library, check the city or town ordinances to make sure it allows for kite flying. Some municipalities have banned kites due to issues with electrical wires and trees.[14] The strings can wrap around equipment and harm wildlife.

At my library, we go down to the waterfront, which is a short walk (or ride, for those in wheelchairs) and about two blocks. It is accessible with some paved surface, some gravel surface, sidewalks, a grassy field, and a large dock right along the river; people can choose where they feel most comfortable flying. The water is fairly shallow, and we try to stay away from right at the water's edge if small children are in attendance so that there is a low drowning risk. There are no trees or telephone poles nearby. It is right next to our community college's campus and is very visible from the downtown market square, so it gathers lots of attention. Main Street runs along the waterfront, so people driving by can see our beautiful kites in the air. I make sure to bring a large banner (that sticks in the ground, so the wind won't blow it away) to alert everyone that it is a library-sponsored event. This is great free publicity!

Remember, if you are making your own kites to fly, you'll also need to book a space to assemble the kites pre-launch. I don't recommend doing this outdoors, especially if it is windy (which you want!), as paper, fabric, and string will blow all over the place and be a real pain!

Step 7. Once you have narrowed down a location, decide how many people the space (and your supplies) can accommodate. When we had our launch party, we used the six kites in our collection, plus we also encouraged participants to bring their own kites from home, and Leland brought kites from his business to share as well. I can't remember how many kites were in the air in total, but from looking at the pictures, at any one time, there were at least ten to twenty kites soaring high. Those who didn't have their own kites took turns sharing. This went surprisingly well, with no one hogging the kites too much. Everyone wanted to share the joy!

Step 8. Recruit volunteers and instructors for your program. Maybe you or someone on your staff feels competent in kite-building or kite-flying skills, but if not, look for a local volunteer kite enthusiast or else hire someone from your local kite club or kite shop. You could also explore having a recorded video or online teaching component as an alternative. Even if you aren't building kites from scratch, you will need someone in charge of the program and provide instructions on how to assemble and disassemble the kites, as well as how to fly them safely in a variety of conditions (see textbox 8.3). You'll want to have multiple volunteers or staff members on hand to help participants with launching their kites, making repairs or adjustments, untangling strings, and keeping everyone calm (as inevitably happens, lines will get crossed, and tempers may flare!). If you are having a tournament, you'll want an impartial judge (and maybe prizes?). Kiting is great at helping us be more mindful and patient!

TEXTBOX 8.3

How to Safely Fly a Kite

- Do not fly in crowded places. Watch out for people who are unaware you are flying kites. I have seen people walk right into low-hanging strings. This can be really dangerous. Especially watch out for children who may be mesmerized by the kite and not paying attention to the strings at all. You also don't want a kite to take a sudden downturn and land on someone's head (or vehicle!). Make sure you have *lots* of space.
- Don't fly kites around dogs, as some will chase them and chew them when they land or hurt themselves running into the strings. Dog walkers with long/multiple leashes are also a hazard. Be mindful of other animals as well, especially horses, that can be spooked by the noise and movement of kites.
- Don't fly too close to roads. You don't want your kite to land in the middle of traffic, and you don't want to distract the drivers. We fly in a location that runs along a busy main street, but it is 0.18 miles (or 0.29 kilometers) from the road, so there is no risk of the kites or participants being anywhere near the vehicles or pedestrians. The kites look like small diamonds and triangles in the sky from the intersection.
- Kites can be noisy and unpredictable, especially if the wind is high. You may want to warn patrons of this ahead of time, in case anyone has sensory issues that would make this experience uncomfortable. The noise can also spook children and animals.
- Don't fly near trees, telephone poles, or buildings.
- Be aware of nesting birds (who are not just in trees but also bushes and on the ground, especially near shorelines).
- Kite lines conduct electricity. Never use a metallic material or wire as a line. Keep your line dry. Don't fly in stormy weather. Always pick a rain date so you don't feel pressured to go out anyway.
- Don't fly within five miles of an airport.
- Gloves are recommended to prevent line burn on your hands.
- Clean up after yourself, and don't leave any trash behind.
- Don't attach anything other than your kite to its line, and don't tie your kite to something, like a stroller or park bench. Keep in control of your kite at

all times. Be especially mindful if you are sharing a kite with a partner and handing the spool back and forth.

- Be aware of your own kite-flying limitations. Don't fly a kite larger than you can handle or in conditions that are too windy. Do not take beginners out on a super windy day; but remember, you will need some breeze to launch. Ideally, about four-to-ten-mile-per-hour winds. You should be able to feel a light wind on your face and see flags and leaves rustling.
- Always double-check your line knots to make sure they are tight before launching.

Step 9. Once your kites arrive, you will need to decide if you are going to keep them as program props or if you want to catalog them as an alternative collection for circulation. As I mentioned earlier, having a quiver (a long, thin bag to store the kite; see figure 8.6) makes them much easier to organize (and process). Our kites are placed in their quivers and hung inside a custom-made cabinet with hooks to hang the bag handles. Inside the cabinet is a map of the region with pins marking good kite-flying locations. Inside each quiver, there is a quarter-page bilingual, laminated instruction sheet detailing how to assemble the kite and how to launch, fly, and land safely. We accompanied each description with a hand drawing done by Leland (you could also just use photographs), to make it more accessible for people with low literacy levels or for whom French or English isn't their first language. We are very lucky to have someone as talented and generous as Leland as a partner (see figure 8.7).

If you are going to make a MARC record for the kites, you'll need to figure out the dimensions of the kite poles and quiver, the number of pieces included, the value of the kite (for replacement if lost or damaged), the color (and any

Figure 8.6   Kite quivers in their cabinet with Jenn and Leland. *Source*: Jody McCleary.

Figure 8.7   Leland Wong-Daugherty, our kite creator and partner. *Source*: Ebony Scott.

other descriptive elements), and how long the lending period will be. Ours is three weeks, just like our books, which we chose so people could feel free to take them on vacation or to their cottage. You may wish to have a shorter lending period. We don't permit the kites to be placed on hold. Consider whether patrons can renew them. You'll also have to decide what is an acceptable amount of maintenance to be done by circulation staff. For example, do spools need to be returned perfectly wound and knot-free, or is this something staff don't mind helping with? Advice: ask them first! What are your criteria for replacement? Make sure you have that detailed in writing and explained to staff so they can share this information with patrons at checkout (so they know what they are responsible for!). Consider whether you want to add a liability waiver to the checkout process as well, just in case someone was to be injured from using the kite.

You will also need to store them somewhere safe. Kites are very fragile. We purposely chose not to put the (unlocked) cabinet in the Children's Department or anywhere out of sight of the main circulation desk because we didn't want the kites to be taken out and played with or, worse, stolen. If you aren't keeping them out on the floor, one of those long, shallow plastic tubs that fit under the bed to store rolls of gift wrap or clothing makes an ideal dust-free, easily stackable storage option.

You'll need to permanently identify the kites, whether you catalog them or not. We put laminated barcode ID tags on the quivers and wrote the last four digits of the ID number, as well as our library code and provincial signifier, on the dowels and spools with permanent marker. Another thing to consider is your climate and whether this collection will be available all year or only during certain months. Our kites are available from April thru November, since we are located in Eastern Canada.

Step 10. Now that you have this awesome kite collection and/or program planned, you must get the word out! Think about who you want to target with your announcements. Are you hoping to have families use this service? Twenty-somethings? Seniors? All of the above? If you have the budget, you can plan a broader marketing campaign to let the world know you've got kites to borrow (print, radio, and online boosted posts, for example), but if you are working from a more modest budget, you can still get the community interested in your kites. Using a free graphic design software like Canva, you can create a tile (a graphic plus text) to share on social media (such as Twitter, Instagram, and Facebook). You could also record a little promo video of a staffer flying or assembling one of your kites to post to your library's YouTube account that you can share. You can make print posters (also using a free program like Canva) to put up on local bulletin boards in high-traffic areas. Why not make a free public service announcement to your local radio or TV station to let them know that you'll be having free kites available to borrow (with a valid library card!) and/or an upcoming kite-flying program? I also recommend sending out a press release to news media that may want to report on the event or collection and to local organizations who could benefit from these services, such as adult group homes (kites are usually a big hit with adults living with cognitive disabilities), multicultural associations, student services on college campuses, recovery centers, nursing homes and assisted living facilities, parks and recreation services, churches, and various clubs. This book is focused on adult programming, but kites and kite programming are also great for children and can be marketed to schools, daycares and afterschool centers, and early learning service centers.

Step 11. Okay, so now that the kites are bought and paid for, all nicely organized, and you've decided on how, when, and where to launch your kite programming and to whom, what's left to do? Well, if you are going to have a big launch party and then go fly kites, you'll need someone to make a little speech and talk about the joys of kite flying, maybe plan to cut a ribbon in front of the cabinet (cheesy, but we did it, and it makes for a great photo op!), and get some cake or cupcakes or punch or kite-shaped cookies or something to munch on! We got a theme cake from our local grocery store (see figure 8.8). You might need some napkins and paper plates and things like that, which you'll need to gather in advance. If you aren't making a permanent alternative collection and a launch and are instead doing a make-'n'-take build-your-own kite program or just holding an event where people fly non-circulating kites, you might still want to think about food and drinks. People love free snacks, and sometimes the promise of munchies is about more than just enticing people; it helps calm nerves for the socially anxious. If you have something to sip or nibble on in a room full of strangers tying little knots in strings and about to do something they've never done before, the shelter of a soothing treat can go a long way. Also, food security is a real issue in many of our communities, and any program with free food accompanying it may help put food in bellies that would otherwise be empty. For the time-crunched, knowing they can show up at a program and have something to eat, when maybe they are just rushing to the program after work/school or from one of their many responsibilities, makes it more likely they will come. Since we're focusing on wellness in this chapter, think about

Figure 8.8   Kite cakes to celebrate the launch of our kite library. *Source*: Ebony Scott.

how you can use this program (and any library program) to meet multiple needs that will help balance the whole person. So, to recap: gather food/drink and launch supplies and plan a little speech (see "Materials Required" section to help keep all this organized).

Step 12. Prepare photo/video and liability waivers if you are using them. Create feedback forms or an online survey with a link you can send for follow-up.

Step 13. Test out your kites! Play with them. Get comfortable. Your enjoyment will be infectious. Take photos or videos to share on social media to entice people to come.

Step 14. Build a display of kite-related material in the library or create a bibliography in your online catalog that goes with the program (see "Literacy Tie-In" section for suggestions). Don't be afraid to put out children's books even if the program is for adults; parents, teachers, or other caregivers may wish to borrow them to share with young people.

Materials Required

This is a big list that encompasses everything needed for a simple kite-lending program to a full-on kite build and tournament. Just strike off the stuff you won't need.

- Supplies to build kites: thin (quarter-inch) wooden dowels, nylon fabric or newspaper or garbage bags, glue, string, toilet paper tubes or thicker dowels for spools, ribbons (if using), masking tape, rulers, pencils, scissors, a small handsaw if the dowels aren't pre-cut

- Ready-made kites and quivers
- Prizes and scorecard for tournament
- Cake, cupcakes, or other treats
- Water, juice, and other refreshments
- Napkins, plates, forks (if needed), hand sanitizer
- Ribbon for launch ceremony and scissors
- Storage cabinet or portable bin for kites
- Laminated instructions and maps of good kiting spots
- A first aid kit
- Gloves (cheap gardening gloves from a dollar store are fine)
- Camera and photo/video release waivers
- Liability waivers
- Registration forms (if using)
- A banner or sandwich board outdoors with the library's (and sponsor's) logo(s)
- For kite-building video tutorials, you'll need to have your library's audio-visual equipment (projector, laptop, speakers, mic, etc.)
- Tables and chairs for indoor kite-building
- A few chairs outdoors (for those with limited standing ability) during the flying
- Feedback forms (if using)

Budget Details

$20–$1,000+. Like most sporting activities, you can get as tricked out with premium gear as you want, or you can do it as cheaply as possible. If you plan to build kites with repurposed materials, you can probably pull this off for the cost of a few dowels ($10 to $15) and some snacks ($10 to $20). If you want to invest in a full-blown kite collection and you aren't as fortunate as we were to have a company donate the kites, you are going to have to go in search of funding upwards of $500 for at least a decent amount. A premium kite that will last through multiple seasons and patrons is going to run you at least $60 to $100 each. If you buy cheaper nylon and plastic-framed kites, expect them to break after one or two uses. If you have a proper storage cabinet built instead of using a plastic tote ($20), you are also going to need some serious coin ($200 to $300 and above), unless you can find a generous cabinet maker willing to donate one. You can ask people to bring their own gloves for flying, or you can buy a multi-pack of cheap gardening gloves in one-size-fits-most versions.

You will also need to factor in the cost (and time) for repairs. Kites require frequent tune-ups. Dowels snap in heavy winds, fabric frays and paper rips, strings break or become tangled beyond all reasonable untying skills, and pieces go lost and need replacement. Don't forget to factor this into your annual budget and keep some money aside for seasonal upkeep. As discussed in Step 3, there is a great deal of funding and partnership opportunities available, so don't be discouraged by the initial start-up costs. Reach out to your local kite dealers, and you might be surprised how willing they are to donate or offer significant discounts on older models or ones with slight defects in return for free advertising and the growth of the sport in your community (which leads to more potential sales for them!).

Day-of-Event

Step 1. Check the weather! Especially the wind! Sunshine isn't so important (in fact, it is better to have it overcast so the sun isn't shining in your eyes). If the skies aren't going to cooperate, now's your time to alert everyone to the rain date.

Step 2. Get out your registration list and send everyone a quick email or text reminder. If you have people on a waitlist and others have canceled at the last minute, now is the time to give them a ring.

Step 3. Gather all your important supplies for the day and go pick up the cake or treats from the bakery (clearly the most important thing!). Chill the drinks or brew the coffee.

Step 4. Set up the room where you are building the kites or doing the launch. For outdoors, make sure to set up a banner, tent, or sandwich board to make the group identifiable to late-comers and passersby. Also great for free advertising!

Step 5. Have all your paperwork ready to go, including: opening speech and introductions, instruction handouts, and liability and release waivers. Print off evaluation forms, if using. Don't forget pens! To simplify your life, prepare a follow-up email in advance you can send out swiftly after the event with things like your local kiting hotspot map, building or flying instructions, and a link to a feedback survey.

Step 6. Make sure your camera and any other equipment are charged and ready. Take a few test shots to check the light.

Step 7. Go over the game plan with staff, volunteers, and any outside partners, and make minor adjustments to the set-up or schedule as needed. For example, if the weather looks like it will only hold for a short period, maybe shorten the opening activities so you can get out there flying as soon as possible. Likewise, if it is currently bad but looks like it will improve, consider elongating the beginning of the program to allow time for the rain clouds to pass. A weather radar is your best friend for flying. These are easily found online through the National Weather Service (in the United States) or your local weather forecasting station.[15]

Step 8. Welcome guests as they arrive and have them fill out any necessary paperwork. Show them where to gather or where their workstations are (if building kites). Make your speeches, cut your ribbons, or otherwise get started! Walk/ roll to the kite-flying location if required.

Step 9. Build and fly (and fight!) all the kites. Have fun and be safe!

Step 10. Untangle and assist kiters as needed. Be mindful of offering just enough support that they are successful but not so much you are doing it for them. You want them to learn the skills so they can enjoy kite flying on their own. Troubleshoot any issues they may be having.

Step 11. Hand out prizes if you are planning on it. Podium shots are hilarious for social media if you really want to ham it up.

Step 12. Show participants how to carefully roll up the kites and store them in their quivers or storage box and note any repairs that may be needed.

Step 13. Thank everyone for coming, and encourage them to check out a kite to take home (if you have created a lending program) or to visit your local kite shop to get one of their own. Hand out kite flying or building instructions if you were providing them (or email a follow-up link or attachment). Hand out evaluation forms if using (or email a link to an online survey).

Step 14. Clean up and celebrate another awesome adult programming adventure! Recap what went well and what you'd do differently next time.

Literacy Tie-In

Here's an excellent opportunity to create a display of kite-related material for patrons to enjoy taking home after the program. Periodical archives can be a treasure trove of old kiting magazines. Don't be afraid to include materials for all ages, as people may now want to share their love of kiting with their whole family. A digital booklist to share online in your web catalog or on social media is also a great tie-in and keeps the party going! Pro tip: when doing searches, don't confuse kite flying with kite surfing (also known as kiteboarding). Also, it is not the same as paragliding or other inhabited kiting. Radically different sports! This is just a basic list—feel free to expand on it—the world of kiting is vast.

Periodicals:

- *KiteLife*
- *Kite Lines*
- *Kiting*[16]
- *Stunt Kite Quarterly*

Print or audiobooks:

- *The Art of the Japanese Kite* by Tal Streeter
- *Asian Kites: Asian Arts & Crafts for Creative Kids* by Wayne Hosking
- *Best Ever Paper Kites* by Norman Schmidt
- *The Best Winds* by Laura Williams
- *Big Book of Kites* by Jim Rowlands
- *Building Free and Recycled Kites* by Glenn Davison
- *Catch the Wind: All about Kites* by Gail Gibbons
- *Come Fight a Kite* by Dinesh Bahadur
- *The Complete Beginner's Guide to Making and Flying Kites* by Edward Dolan
- *The Complete Book of Kites and Kite Flying* by Will Yolen
- *The Complete World of Kites* by Bill Thomas
- *The Creative Book of Kites* by Sarah Kent
- *Days with Frog and Toad* by Arnold Lobel
- *Flying Kites at Night with Lights* by Glenn Davison
- *The Great Kite Book* by Norman Schmidt
- *Henry and the Kite Dragon* by Bruce Edward Hall
- *High Hopes for Addy* by Connie Porter
- *How Ben Franklin Stole the Lightning* by Rosalyn Schanzer

- *How to Fly a Kite* by Glenn Davison
- *Indoor Kite Flying* by Glenn Davison
- *Japanese Kite Prints* by John Stevenson
- *The Kite* by Masaaki Modegi
- *The Kite Festival* by Leyla Torres
- *The Kite Fighters* by Linda Sue Park
- *Kite Flying* by Grace Lin
- *Kite Making and Flying* by Harold Ridgeway
- *Kite Physics* by Glenn Davison
- *The Kite Rider* by Geraldine McCaughrean
- *The Kite Runner* by Khaled Hosseini
- *Kites for Everyone: How to Make and Fly Them* by Margret Greger
- *Kites in the Classroom* by Glenn Davison
- *Kites: Magic Wishes that Fly Up to the Sky* by Demi
- *Kites: The Science and the Wonder* by Toshio Ito and Hirotsugu Komura
- *Kites: Twelve Easy-To-Make High Fliers* by Norma Dixon
- *Kiteworks: Exploration in Kite Building and Flying* by Maxwell Eden
- *The Kite Workshop Handbook* by Glenn Davison
- *The Legend of the Kite* by Chen Jiang Hong
- *Magnificent Book of Kites* by Maxwell Eden
- *Making & Flying Stunt Kites & One-liners* by Wolfgang Schimmelpfennig
- *Making of Japanese Kites: Tradition, Beauty and Creation* by Masaaki Modegi
- *Miniature Kite Plans* by Glenn Davison
- *More Kites for Everyone* by Margaret Greger
- *One-Hour Kites* by Jim Rowlands
- *The Penguin Book of Kites* by David Pelham
- *Rokkaku Kites* by Glenn Davison
- *Stuck* by Oliver Jeffers
- *World on a String: The Story of Kites* by Jane Yolen

DVDs:

- *Black Kite* (2017)
- *Fukrey* (2013)
- *Godsend* (2004)
- *The Kite Runner* (2007)
- *Mary Poppins* (1964)
- *The Peanuts Movie* (2015)

Helpful Advice

- Be especially mindful of ways to make this program as accessible as possible. Go Fly a Kite! is an excellent program to offer to seniors or those in adult residential facilities. Kiting is one of the easiest sports to modify for people with limited mobility or decreased cognitive function. It can be done seated, with perhaps a little help from someone more able-bodied to get it launched, as you should hold it as high in the air as you can to catch the wind (but this isn't necessary; on a windy day, it will even catch from the ground at the right angle!). The mechanics are simple enough to understand that someone with limited cognitive function can enjoy the bliss of flying with the support of a care worker nearby. Those with sensory issues may find the kites noisy, but you can minimize this with the types of materials you choose (cotton is much quieter than paper, plastic, or nylon).

- Advise guests to wear weather-appropriate clothing and to steer away from anything with loose straps, billowy sleeves, or buckles that the lines can get tangled in. They may want to leave their purses or bags locked up somewhere safe in the library or their vehicle, unless they need them on hand. If you are going somewhere with uneven ground (like a park), closed-toe shoes or sneakers are best. Someone may show up in platforms or flip-flops, but thankfully, you should never run with a kite anyway, so hopefully they won't trip and fall. Gloves are highly recommended to avoid string burn. Sunglasses are helpful, too, if you are staring upward on a bright day. Sunscreen is also a good choice, depending on the conditions and how long you are out for. If it is windy enough to fly and you are wearing a hat, make sure it cinches on the head, or it may blow away!
- DON'T RUN WITH A KITE! If you must run to get the kite in the air, it isn't windy enough, and your kite will definitely crash. It isn't satisfying to try to launch a kite over and over for it to only stay in the air for a few seconds. Better to postpone for another day.
- Test the wind. If you are new to kiting, you may not be aware that the wind can change quickly (especially if you live on the coast) and can dramatically affect your ability to launch. An hour or two before the program, go out and test the wind, if possible, to see if it is strong enough to sustain a kite.
- Further kite plans can be found at www.kite.org/about-kites/kite-plans/.
- For a nerdier version of piloting in the great outdoors, why not try this event with drones instead of kites? No fighting, just flying! Patrons would have to supply their own (unless you've got a really huge grant or something!). It would likely be easy to find a local enthusiast to volunteer to run the program. You could take them to a local park or open space and fly them together. Check your local bylaws, though; some municipalities ban or restrict them. For drones with video recording and stills capability, make sure to check privacy bylaws as well, and make sure everyone in the group is okay with being recorded before you begin.

Further Health and Wellness Program Ideas

As mentioned earlier, I've written two full books about health and wellness programming (*Get Your Community Moving: Physical Literacy Programs for All Ages* and *Yoga and Meditation at the Library: A Practical Guide for Librarians*), and I highly recommend you check out Noah Lenstra's *Healthy Living at the Library: Programs for All Ages* or our Let's Move in Libraries initiative (https://letsmovelibraries.org/) for a plethora of programming ideas.[17] But here are a few more to get your brain juices flowing:

- Mental Health Workshops—There's nothing I love more than providing free mental health programs in our community. They are *desperately* needed and always well attended. Support groups, workshops, information sessions, and even one-on-one counseling services are just a few of the amazing options available if you partner with your regional or national mental health organizations, such as the Canadian Mental Health Association (CHMA). The best part is they will often offer these services for free or at a sliding scale or reduced cost to the institution. Sometimes they will even cover the cost of childcare and travel for people to attend. This isn't just for patrons; we've hosted many trainings for staff over the years, my favorite being ASIST (Applied Suicide Intervention Skills Training), which helps recognize invitations to help, signs of suicidality, how to review risks, how to intervene and provide mental health first aid to someone in crisis, and an overview of community resources. These types of trainings are invaluable tools for people working with the public, especially at-risk populations, but they are just as valuable for the patrons themselves. I recommended Sara K. Zettervall and Dr. Mary C. Nienow's *Whole Person Librarianship: A Social Work Approach to Patron Services* for a thorough approach to involving the field of social work in your library program offerings.[18]
- Body Image Bootcamp—A few years ago, a non-binary staff member from the Canadian Mental Health Association (Lee Thomas) and I created a program called Body Image Bootcamp, and we tag-teamed to lead community members through monthly sessions where we used mindfulness techniques to explore topics such as media literacy, mindful eating, sports, and peer pressure. It was open to any gender over the age of twelve. Every session involved some mindful movement (yoga stretches led by me), a presentation and discussion (led by our CMHA staffer), a sharing of online and print resources (led by both of us), and healthy snacks. The program was free, and we also provided workbooks to all participants. Consider teaming up with a mental health professional to offer something similar.
- Learn-to-Play Series—There are endless opportunities to recruit enthusiastic staff, volunteers, or community partners to share their love of sport with your patrons. It could be a one-time offering that leads to a regular event (such as offering a Learn-to-Run clinic and then starting to host a weekly Run Club), or it could be an entire series of Learn to [INSERT FUN THING]. Don't assume adults only want to do things that are "serious." We really, *really* need more opportunities to laugh and play. Here are some (slightly zany) ideas: Learn to Kayak on Dry Land, Learn to Use Hiking Poles, Learn to Belly Dance, Learn to Play Hopscotch, Learn to Fly a Kite (see what I did there?), Learn to Sing the National Anthem (surprisingly helpful at sporting events), Learn to Catch a Baseball, Learn to Hit a Home Run, Learn to Hold a Hockey Stick, Learn to Skateboard, Learn to Hula-Hoop, Learn to Rollerblade, Learn to Play Musical Chairs, Learn to Play Disc Golf, Learn to Wash Your Bike, Learn to Pop a Wheelie, Learn to Ride a Scooter, Learn to Play Four Square, Learn to Tie Knots, Learn to Throw a Punch, Learn to Block a Punch, Learn to Ride a Unicycle, Learn to Build a Snow Fort, Learn to Play Cricket, Learn to Dribble a Basketball, Learn to Lawn Bowl, Learn to Play Darts, Learn to Throw a Horseshoe, Learn to do a Handstand, Learn to Hold a Tennis Racket,

Learn to Skip Rope, Learn to Lift Hand Weights, Learn to Long Jump, Learn to Wear Snowshoes, Learn to Swing a Golf Club, Learn to Set Up a Tent, Learn to Read a Compass, and so on.

- No-Cook Healthy Cooking Classes—Don't have a big community kitchen at your library? Or a chef's training? No problem. Teach patrons how to make healthy snacks without turning on a stove, such as juice, smoothies, yogurt bowls, no-bake granola bars or energy balls, hummus, veggie dips, fruit-and-cheese kabobs, trail mix, and so on.
- Build Your Own Rickshaw (or Frankenbike)—Did you know it is possible to build a rickshaw (two-wheeled people-mover popular in many countries) with spare bicycle parts? I didn't, until I recruited a local bike enthusiast to teach myself, a bunch of parents, teachers, and super-excited kids to do it over the course of one morning at a local school. We then painted the rickshaws, and the kids played with them for days (see figures 8.12 and 8.13). You could use the same process (and more power tools) to build "frankenbikes" (crazy

Figure 8.9 The author learning to kayak on dry land. *Source*: Ebony Scott.

Figure 8.10　Learn to pop a wheelie in the park next to the library. *Source*: Becci Taylor.

bikes made out of spare parts). Find makers in your community with unique skills, and ask them to teach classes at your library. You'll be amazed at how creative people can get with what looks like junk! Time to think outside the (craft) box and get people moving outdoors in funky ways. What about new ways to use old skis? Or toboggans? Or old broken and dusty exercise equipment (who doesn't have some of that lying around their basement or garage)?

- Community Fridge—Look into starting your library's own community fridge or pantry program. Never heard of such a thing? You host a fridge or cupboard in your building that patrons have access to, and you fill it with fruit, vegetables, water bottles, juice, and dry goods donated from local markets, farms, and food security organizations.[19] (See figure 8.11.)
- Create a Quiet Corner—Somewhere in your library (in a low-traffic setting), find a spot to set up a meditation cushion, some noise-canceling headphones (and wipes to clean them with), and a deck of meditation cards. If you have

Figure 8.11 Juice bar promotional poster. *Source*: Brendan Helmuth.

enough space, you can also set up a yoga mat and some yoga cards. I review these card decks on my website: www.yogainthelibrary.com.

- Lending Collections—There are so many great wellness items you can lend as part of an alternative collection: yoga mats and other props, hand weights, snowshoes, hiking poles, board games, toboggans, skateboards, fitness kits, frisbees, kites, play parachutes, lawn games, skipping ropes, Hula-Hoops, bicycles, scooters, exercise ball, resistance bands, ping-pong sets, balance trainers, hiking packs, tents and other camping gear, ice cleats, bicycle pumps, life jackets, canoe paddles, and so on. (See figure 8.14.)

Figure 8.12 Building rickshaws. *Source*: Tegan Wong-Daugherty.

Whether this is your first time offering a movement-based adult program or you've written the book on library wellness, I hope this chapter inspired you to think a little broader about what it means to address the social determinants of health in your community. Sometimes the best thing we can do as a library is offer opportunities in a safe, accessible, friendly manner so that patrons who may feel too intimidated or lack the resources to seek out the services elsewhere feel

Figure 8.13 Building rickshaws with old parts. *Source*: Ryan Garnhum.

Figure 8.14 Guided snowshoe hike to celebrate launch of the library's snowshoe collection.
Source: Holly Melanson.

comfortable coming to us. We can't possibly be all things to all people—we're just (awesome) humans after all—and we also need to make our own health and wellness a priority. I hope this chapter helped you think about ways you could get moving, laughing, and learning in your own life.

Notes

1. Jenn Carson, *Yoga and Meditation at the Library: A Practical Guide for Librarians* (Lanham, MD: Roman & Littlefield, 2019); Jenn Carson, *Get Your Community Moving: Physical Literacy Programs for All Ages* (Chicago: ALA Editions, 2018).

2. Government of Canada, "Social Determinants of Health and Health Inequalities," *Government of Canada* online, last modified October 7, 2020, https://www.canada.ca/en/public-health/services/health-promotion/population-health/what-determines-health.html.

3. "Food Desert," *Wikipedia*, accessed January 20, 2022, https://en.wikipedia.org/wiki/Food_desert.

4. You can find many recordings of webinars I've given over the years on the subject of staff health and wellness and nonnegotiable self-care tactics on my website: www.jenncarson.com.

5. You can find links to examples of these waivers on my website at www.jenncarson.com.

6. Jenn Carson, "Trauma Informed BJJ—Thumbs Up Approach with Jenn Carson," *YouTube*, June 14, 2021. https://youtu.be/00-nS8Ro7uo.

7. Check out this cool video of kite fighting in Rio from *The New York Times*, "Kite Fight | Op-Docs," *YouTube*, July 17, 2014, https://www.youtube.com/watch?v=sl3qWHkqfI8.

8. Jenn Carson, "Go Fly a Kite!," *Children & Libraries Magazine* 19, no. 1 (2021), https://journals.ala.org/index.php/cal/article/view/7542/10424?fbclid=IwAR3ZWZB7rQbxKxsJDdWmv_WXXQ0Y-qgy9hwSiyUJaV4Az2bb4IgHY2nPmks.

9. "Start a Joyful Practice," *Little Cloud Kites*, accessed January 12, 2022, https://littlecloudkites.com/.

10. From *Little Cloud Kites* online (ibid.): "Your kite has a lifetime guarantee. That means that we will repair and replace your kite for its lifetime. Please try not to get it stuck in a tree. If this actually happens (which it can) please send a picture of the offending tree and the poor kite in it! If, for any reason, you are not completely satisfied, just return your purchase. You can choose to either exchange the product or receive a complete refund (including our regular shipping charges); we will also refund your return parcel post costs at the ground mail rate."

11. "Kite Plans," *American Kitefliers Association* online, accessed March 4, 2022, https://www.kite.org/about-kites/kite-plans/.

12. "The 8 Types of Kites and How to Fly Them," *Recreation Insider*, March 21, 2020, https://recreationinsider.com/kites/types-of-kites/.

13. "Brazilian Capucheta Paper Kites," *Little Cloud Kites*, accessed January 12, 2022, https://littlecloudkites.com/pages/paper-kite-downloads.

14. "Toronto Bans Kite Flying in City Park," *CBC News* online, last modified August 17, 2010, https://www.cbc.ca/news/canada/toronto/toronto-bans-kite-flying-in-city-park-1.933181#:~:text=The%20City%20of%20Toronto%20has,of%20a%20danger%20to%20animal.

15. "Radar," *National Weather Service*, accessed March 18, 2022, https://radar.weather.gov/?settings=v1_eyJhZ2VuZGEiOnsiaWQiOm51bGwsImNlbnRlciI6Wy05NC45OCwzNy4wMl0sImxvY2F0aW9uIjpudWxsLCJib29tIjo0fSwiYW5pbWF0aW9uIjpmYWxzZSwiYmFzZSI6Im0xYW5kYXJkIiwiYXJ0Y2MiOmZhbHNlLCJjb3VudHkiOmZhbHNlLCJjd2EiOmZhbHNlLCJyZmMiOmZhbHNlLCJzdGF0ZSI6ZmFsc2UsIm1lbnUiOnRydWUsInNob3J0RnVzZWRPbmx5IjpmYWxzZSwib3BhY2l0eSI6eyJhbGVydHMiOjAuOCwib2pYWwiOjAuNiwibG9jYWxTdGF0aW9ucyI6MC44LCJuYXRpb25hbCI6MC42fX0%3D#/.

16. "*Kiting Magazine*: The World's Leading Kite Magazine Is Free to Members," *The American Kitefliers Association*, accessed April 3, 2022, https://www.kite.org/community/kiting-magazine/.

17. Noah Lenstra, *Healthy Living at the Library: Programs for All Ages* (Santa Barbara, CA: Libraries Unlimited, 2020).

18. Sara K. Zettervall and Dr. Mary C. Nienow, *Whole Person Librarianship: A Social Work Approach to Patron Services* (Santa Barbara, CA: Libraries Unlimited, 2019).

19. Al Donato, "How Canadians Started Community Fridges in Their Cities," *Huffington Post*, January 5, 2021, https://www.huffingtonpost.ca/entry/community-fridges-canada_ca_5fe13c8bc5b66809cb2cbed6.

9

✛

Business and Finance Programs

I can hear the collective sigh now. Ugh, math stuff. Accounting. Capitalism. Taxes. Budgeting. It's enough to send a deep shudder through our (book) spines. The last fourteen years of working in public and school libraries have taught me that these are some of the least represented (and enthused about) subjects for programming librarians everywhere. Give us glitter, give us Hula-Hoops, give us bags of garbage to turn into upcycled crafts, give us anything but a calculator and an Excel spreadsheet. We hate them. Or most of us do. And that's okay. Admitting your weakness is the first step in getting better at something. For many people (librarians or otherwise), dealing with finances is at best a high-executive-function task that delivers a low dopamine reward; at worst, it is a downright sweat-inducing nightmare to be avoided at all costs. This is exactly why libraries are in the perfect position to offer these services. We are free, accessible, and much less intimidating than an accountant's office, the Internal Revenue Service, or the Canadian Revenue Agency. Plus, we are a great place for businesses, nonprofits, and entrepreneurs to get information, network, and reserve free (or very affordable) rooms for meetings.

Financial illiteracy isn't something that only affects certain stereotyped demographics, such as people that are economically disadvantaged. I once hired a university student from a well-to-do family. He came to me with his first paycheck and a puzzled look on his face asking, "What's this piece of paper mean?" I replied, "That's your paycheck. From working the last two weeks." He didn't understand why the money didn't go right into his bank account. I explained that he hadn't set up direct deposit by completing the necessary paperwork at the payroll office, so when I submitted his timesheet (which he'd signed), they issued him a check instead. He said, "But, I don't know what to do with this. How do I spend it?" He was visibly anxious. I explained he'd need to take it to his bank and cash it or else deposit it in his account at the bank machine. He just stood there, staring at me and fidgeting. He finally said, "I don't know how to do that." So, I took him across the street to the bank machine at his branch and showed him how to deposit his paycheck and how to withdraw funds from his account. The student wasn't only clueless, he was genuinely horrified at the idea of standing in front of the machine (or worse, a teller) and not knowing what to do (or say). His parents and teachers had clearly never taught him anything about checks or how to use a bank machine. He'd only been given a bank card and used it to make purchases, never really knowing where the money came from or how to manage it. This was a highly intelligent man in his early twenties. Anyone who works with young adults today can tell you that many of them are not ready to face the real, everyday financial workings of adulthood, such as cashing a check, applying for a car loan, negotiating a mortgage, making (and following) a budget, submitting their taxes, understanding their student loan, buying health or car insurance, signing a lease, or even how to split a bill when buying food with friends during a night out. Not only do they find these fundamental tasks challenging, but they are also sometimes so stressed out at the prospect that they avoid doing them at all. Libraries—especially public, high school, and post-secondary libraries—are in the perfect position to offer accessible (non-condescending) lessons on how to navigate these tasks. Programs could be as complex as having a consultant come in and meet one-on-one to discuss investment portfolio options with individual patrons, to as simple as having a group class on how to use an online shopping platform (something surprisingly difficult to navigate for those with low computer literacy rates).

Statistics Canada also reports that there is a significant gap between males and females when it comes to financial literacy, with women on average scoring 57.7 percent on the Canadian Financial Capability Survey, which measures objective financial knowledge (compared to 62.8 percent for men).[1] The gap seems to be higher among the older generation, which likely comes from years of women being socialized to think that money was a "man's domain" and not being given or allowed control over the household finances, even if they worked outside the home. Hopefully, as we work toward gender parity in the workforce, these numbers will even out, but as it stands, we have a responsibility as a community to make sure women have equal access to financial advice and business opportunities.

Other underserved library populations are small business owners and operators. Here in Canada, small businesses employ about 70 percent of private-sector workers or 7.7 million people across the country.[2] In the United States, there are 30.7 million small businesses, which account for 99.9 percent of all businesses in the country.[3] Unfortunately, about 50 percent of them won't make it past five years. The COVID-19 pandemic has been especially rough to endure, with many small businesses closing their doors for good or suffering huge losses. Libraries can help business owners apply for grants and other funding to help keep them afloat or assist budding entrepreneurs with market research before jumping into a project that may not be sustainable in the long term.

There is also a skilled labor shortage in many industries, which gives libraries an opportunity to present skill-building opportunities to the community, such as classes on how to use Microsoft Office Suite, how to craft a professional-looking resume and cover letter, and how to navigate job-search websites. It has been my experience that there are many adults in our communities with a plethora of highly applicable skills in the trades but that don't have the digital literacy to be able to present themselves as competent potential employees because of their lack of aptitude with online webforms, uploading materials, or tailoring their resumes to what the employer is looking for. This information literacy skill set is something library staff are uniquely equipped to provide. Sometimes it even comes down to a lack of wardrobe opportunities when an interview presents itself. Many patrons trying to reenter the workforce after a lengthy break due to layoff, jail time, caregiving requirements, sick leave, or other issues may find they don't have the right clothing to wear to an interview, and it isn't in their budget to purchase an outfit they are only going to wear a few times because the onsite job requires a uniform or non-dressy attire. Unfortunately, social custom dictates that even if you are applying for a job as a janitor or machinist or electrician, you are usually expected to show up for the interview wearing a suit and tie (or skirt suit), or at least dress pants and a nice shirt and shoes. If a person only has a limited clothing budget, that money needs to be spent on the attire they will actually need for the job (such as steel-toed boots or a welding helmet). Some libraries have seen this discrepancy and offered not only workshops to help people prepare for the interview process (including fashion tips) but also offered donated clothing as well for patrons to take home freely. These days, because of the increase in remote work (and because of the pandemic), many employers are now requiring video interviews online. This adds a whole other layer of stress to the interview process for patrons who may not have a device or access to the internet or the skills to navigate a Zoom or Skype call. Luckily, libraries can also help with this by offering study rooms with free Wi-Fi or workshops and assistance on how to use videoconferencing software.

I encourage you to survey your existing volunteer and staff members to see who has financial and business-related skills that you may be able to tap into. For example, my board treasurer also happens to be a mortgage broker, and she is willing to offer appointments at the library for credit counseling and to help people understand how to apply for or refinance their mortgage and understand their credit score. What a valuable service she is able to provide for free to our community! Many of our small business owners regularly volunteer at events or donate goods (such as local farmers donating watermelons for a Summer Reading Club program or pumpkins for decorating in the fall) or cash to sponsor a program. We'll add their logo to any promotional material, or they'll give us a banner or sandwich board to display during the event to promote their services. Don't be afraid to visit the Chamber of Commerce or other local business organizations to network with entrepreneurs in your community; you never know where these partnerships can lead! This chapter's program model is going to discuss a fabulous business conference idea that came together when I partnered with Amy Anderson, our deputy mayor (who also happens to be a small business owner), to hold a visionary conference in our downtown core (where the library happens to be located). This is something that could easily be replicated in your own branch and will draw a lot of first-timers through your doors that would otherwise never think of using the library.

Program Model: Host a Local Business Conference

When business groups gather to plan a conference or big event, the library might not be on their list of places to call for hosting, but why not? We have generous meeting room policies, bathrooms, some of us have cafes and restaurants, projectors and whiteboards, free Wi-Fi, photocopier and computer facilities, and we are usually centrally located with decent access to (sometimes free) parking. In this program model, I'll discuss a partnership created with our town's deputy mayor to host the first-ever Imagine Woodstock Conference at the library on October 12, 2019. This was done pre-pandemic, and there was a distinct lack of videoconferencing that we are all-too-familiar with now. This program could easily be replicated with more digital options for those who would like to attend offsite, and we'll discuss that in the "Helpful Advice" section. If you haven't been lucky enough to be approached by a local business leader in your community to host a conference, there is no reason you can't organize one yourself, with the help of library staff, volunteers, and members of the Chamber of Commerce or other business organizations in your area. Let's get started!

Advance Planning

Step 1. Decide the subject and scope of your conference. Amy Anderson, our conference's main organizer, described Imagine Woodstock to me as "a free conference intended to gather twenty to thirty really keen people together to discuss, share ideas, network, build skills, and, most importantly, build a sense of togetherness around where we want Woodstock to go in the future. [I]t is built around the idea that small business[es] and engaged citizens have a key role to play in the future of the place we love and call home."[4] We live in a town of fewer than six thousand people, so holding a one-day conference with a broad agenda was a realistic undertaking for us. If you live in a large urban center where you have a (potentially) larger audience, you may need to narrow your focus considerably. You could want to concentrate on just one business sector, such as a conference for local restauranteurs and food truck owners, or a conference for local artists and gallery owners. There are so many possibilities. Why not try out a couple of different events over the course of a year or two?

Or perhaps you want to go really big and plan a jam-packed multi-day schedule offering loads of sessions, keynote addresses, breakout rooms, offsite mingling events, and a giant vendor fair? That is beyond the scope of this chapter, but there are plenty of good resources available on the subject of conference planning and event organizing (perhaps even some on the shelves of your library, such as *Meeting and Event Planning for Dummies*).[5] Feel free to survey your local businesses or Chamber of Commerce members to see what they most want/need in networking and educational opportunities.

Step 2. Once you've settled on the scope of your conference (I recommend starting small for your first attempt!), then you've got to find a way to pay for it. With conferences come vendors. Usually, the way to finance a conference is with corporate sponsorship and an exhibition space for vendors to rent a stall or table to hawk their wares, plus registration fees from participants. Our conference was small and low-key enough we didn't need (much) sponsorship and didn't bother with a vendor fair. Admission was limited but free. The space for the conference sessions was provided at no cost, and the library also provided most of the AV equipment or people brought their own. Delegates were served lunch, which was donated through the Greater Woodstock Chamber of Commerce and was catered by a local business. The small printing costs and an honorarium for the keynote speaker were paid out of pocket by Anderson.[6] I certainly don't expect anyone to pay for anything themselves, and there are small-business promotional incentives and grants available through local, state/provincial, and federal-funding offices to support projects like this. See "Budget Details" section for a more fleshed-out examination of your possible expenses.

Step 3. What's your schedule for the day(s) look like? How many speaker sessions do you plan on hosting? Will you have keynote talks? Workshops? Movement or meditation breaks? Will the entire program be in person, or will you offer online components? How will you recruit speakers and decide on the topics? For our conference, Anderson reached out to members of the community she thought would have something valuable to contribute and wouldn't mind volunteering their time to do so. You can find our schedule in the textbox 9.1, which you can use as an example of a simple one-day conference.

TEXTBOX 9.1

Imagine Woodstock: Supporting DIY Culture & Downtown Revitalization

L. P. Fisher Public Library // Saturday, October 12th, 2019
10:00 a.m. Library Opens
10:15 a.m. Registration—Admission is free
10:30 a.m. Welcome and Opening Remarks—Amy Anderson
10:50 a.m. Imagine Woodstock Presentations:

1. Brittney Toner—"Building Our Community, One Step at a Time"
2. Emily Silva—"Access and Inclusion"
3. Lance Minard—"Buy Local, Support Local"
4. Katie Bursey—"From Employee to Entrepreneur"
5. Jenn Carson—"Community Partnerships"
6. Oumesh Arjoon—"Together We Flourished: Supporting Woodstock's Tourism Growth while Preserving the Existing Value"

12:00 p.m. Discussion Break and Refreshments—Sponsored by the Greater Woodstock Chamber of Commerce
12:30 p.m. Keynote Address—Gilliane Nadeau "5 Steps to Building a Successful Tourism Business"
1:30 p.m. Panel Discussion—"Woodstock 2030: Strengthening Our Town and the Tourism Economy" Featuring Gilliane Nadeau, *Uncorked Tours and Tastings*; Jeremiah Clark, *Moonshine Creek Distillery*; and Oumesh Arjoon, multilingual hospitality professional
2:30 p.m. "Let's Get Practical: Tips from Experienced People"
Attendees will have a choice of sessions to attend from the following:

1. Julie Calhoun Williams—"Getting Involved and Staying Involved"
2. Paul Twyford—"How to Promote Your Small Business on Almost No Money"
3. Brittney Toner—"Mastering Canva: How to Take Your DIY to the Next Level"
4. Jeff Kimball—"Heads, Hearts, and Hands: A Simple Model for Change Management"

Step 4. Settle on dates and times and book the space. Make sure to not conflict with any holidays or special events. Most conferences are generally held in the fall or spring, as winter is too difficult for travel or runs the risk of storm days (depending on your climate), and in summer, many people are away on vacation.

Step 5. Determine how many staff and volunteers you will need to pull this off. Make sure they realize they might be signing up for more than just a one-day commitment, as the prep can take a lot of time to get a conference off the ground, especially a large one. Remember, you'll need moderators for each session, as well as someone to manage the technology.

Step 6. Make a list of supplies you'll need in advance and begin to gather them (you'll find a detailed list of ideas in the "Materials Required" section). Add to it as needed. It's probably going to be a long list.

Step 7. Acquire the necessary technology you'll need and book it in advance if outsourcing or test the equipment if you are providing it. If you'll be hosting an online event, determine which platform you'll be using and consider hiring a support firm to handle the backend during the conference so you can focus on hosting and moderating sessions.

Step 8. Recruit and book speakers. This can be done through a general call for proposals or through recommendations in the community. For our event, Anderson reached out to business owners and professionals she thought might be interested in speaking on a variety of topics related to the theme. Make sure you have a clear vision in advance of what sort of sessions you want to offer and their length. If you need inspiration, look at the schedules from many business conferences available online by searching "business conference programs." You can either decide the session topics in advance and ask people you think would be able to speak on those topics, or else put out a general call and see what interested parties propose; you might get some fun topics you'd never have thought of!

Step 9. What is your conference's branding? Find a tagline that works with your theme and name, such as "Imagine Woodstock: Supporting DIY Culture and Downtown Revitalization."

Step 10. Consider creating an email inbox just for the conference to receive registration requests, correspond with presenters, vendors and attendees, and field questions. Does the conference need a simple website or just a Facebook event?

Step 11. Once the speaker, dates/times, and venue are confirmed, go ahead and put out a call for attendees, but *only* do this once the proper registration process is in place. If you've decided to charge a fee to cover costs, make sure you have a payment method in place that is accessible (with options to pay via check, credit card, e-transfer, etc.). Make sure the registration process is as smooth as possible. Do you have an online form that requires submission or a fillable PDF that must be sent via email? Make sure you have all the bugs for this worked out ahead of time. If your conference is online and you've hired a support company to host, they may also handle the registration, depending on your contract. If not, who on your team is in charge of this? What's the deadline for registration? The limit? Who will process the registrations from start to finish?

Remember, you don't have to put out a finalized schedule before you put out the call for attendees. Let people know about the conference so they can save the date and tease them with information about the keynote speaker(s), several sessions, and/or the general theme with "more to follow!" Registrations will begin to trickle in. You can release the finalized schedule a week or two before the actual event. Don't forget that speakers need to register too!

Step 12. Once you have an idea of the numbers attending, book the catering (if using). Make sure to provide ample choice for varied digestive needs. It's always better to have a bit too much food left, which staff will happily take home, than a paltry offering that looks picked over after the first few hungry delegates reach the table. If you aren't providing meals, at least make sure you are well-stocked with tea, coffee, sugar, honey, creamers and milk, and pitchers of water. Don't forget cups and stir-sticks and napkins! If you are providing snacks, peanut-free granola bars, fresh fruit such as apples and bananas, and individually wrapped cheese strings and yogurt cups make healthy and sanitary choices.

Step 13. Figure out how attendees will register or decide which session to attend. Make sure that you have the space to accommodate them. If you are only offering one session at a time, everyone will be in the same room: easy peasy. If you have overlapping sessions, determine your occupancy limit, and you may need to ask people to register for sessions in advance so you don't overflow. Or, it can be first-come, first-seated. Whatever you decide, make a plan, and don't leave it up to chance. Likewise, I'll remind you to put a cap on your registrations and register-by date, as you may get a lot of last-minute requests.

Step 14. If you plan to record the sessions, make sure presenters are okay with this. Photo and video waivers should be prepared in advance for all delegates to sign, preferably when they register, permitting your library to share their image and conference participation on social media or in library promotional materials. If you are offering movement-based breaks, consider liability waivers (hold harmless forms).

Step 15. Have presenters send you any handouts well in advance for printing. Confirm the equipment needed for each of their sessions, and make sure you are on the same page about who is responsible for what (i.e., are they providing a slideshow on a USB stick for you to upload; will they be bringing their own device; do they need speakers; etc.). Make sure to let them know what resolution you prefer for presentation files (4:3 or 16:9). If you are holding your conference online, make sure to have all the presentations backed up and do a test run using the platform software with each presenter ahead of time to make sure everyone is comfortable.

Step 16. Consider organizing a vendor fair or isolated pop-up tables if you are short on space for vendors to share information about their products. Charge a set-rate per table or else create a tier-level of sponsorship (see textbox 9.2) that can include such a space. Sponsors can also donate goods in kind, which can be useful, such as swag for delegates or catering or IT services.

Step 17. Prepare blurbs for moderators to introduce speakers and thank sponsors and give any land/territory acknowledgments, if using.

TEXTBOX 9.2

An example of what a tiered system could look like for a large, two-day conference:

Diamond Sponsorship: $1,500 or more

- Acknowledgment at Opening Session
- Prominent logo and description on program and website
- Six free registrations for organization
- Free table at vendor fair for both days in prominent location

Platinum Sponsorship: $1,000–$1,499

- Medium logo and description on program and website
- Four free registrations for organization
- Free table at vendor fair for both days

Gold Sponsorship: $500–$999

- Logo on program and website
- Two free registrations for organization
- Free table at vendor fair for both days

Silver Sponsorship: $250–$499

- Logo on program and website
- One free registration for organization

Bronze Sponsorship: In-kind donation of goods (swag or catering goods, etc.)

- Logo on program and website

Materials Required

- Photo/video and liability waivers, if using
- Laptop (if presenters aren't using their own), projector, all the necessary cables, speakers (if required), a mic, a screen
- Whiteboard and markers/eraser or large pad of paper and markers for facilitators to use
- Tables and chairs
- Writing instruments and note pads for delegates to take notes

- Refreshments and cutlery, if needed
- Any printouts needed and copies of the schedule
- Swag from vendors packaged for distribution, if using
- Name tags (we like those easy peel 'n' stick ones, but you can get fancy and preprint and put them in plastic sleeves on a lanyard)

Budget Details

$200–$500+. As mentioned in previous sections, this program can be as complicated (and expensive) or as simple (and cheap) as you are willing to make it. The major expenses will come from speaker fees (unless people are volunteering), refreshments (unless you aren't providing them), and printing costs for programs and handouts (which are nonexistent if you go digital). You can mitigate costs and perhaps break even if you are willing to accept sponsorship from vendors in exchange for putting their logo on your conference materials and possibly giving them a spot to show off their wares. Sometimes, this can happily translate to swag (free promotional materials) to be given to delegates or donations of services, such as free printing from a local office supply company. You can also recoup costs by charging a small entry fee for the conference. I recommend you review your library's policies on charging for programs and soliciting sponsorship or donations before committing to any conference model. Save on catering costs by recommending everyone go out for lunch together at local restaurants within walking distance from the library, perhaps securing table reservations for the group ahead of time. Delegates can pay for their own meals (some will be reimbursed by their employers anyway). By going offsite, you can promote local businesses (who may even offer a discount to attendees), and you can encourage further networking opportunities. Likewise, bring in a local yoga teacher to teach a fifteen-minute stretch break between sessions and allow them to promote their services and studio in exchange.

There are many thoughtful ways to save costs during this program with a little creativity. I encourage you to reach out to other libraries, individual librarians, or people you may know who have served on conference-organizing committees and ask for their budgeting advice. Come find us on social media in library groups; we're usually the ones promoting library conferences!

Day-of-Event

Step 1. The big day is finally here! Gather your volunteers and staff and go over the day's game plan.
Step 2. Test your audio-visual equipment nice and early! Set up the tables and chairs. Make sure washrooms and exits are clearly identified. Call the caterer to confirm times. Set out any refreshment supplies needed. Post copies of the schedule in high-visibility areas. Send out a tweet or Facebook post to remind delegates of the event.
Step 3. Grab your attendee list and set up a check-in table. Hand out name tags, either paper ones you've prepared ahead of time or (my preferred method) peel 'n' stick ones (let them write their own names, as they may prefer a nickname

or want to identify pronouns on it). Have them sign liability or photo/video waivers (if using). Hand out swag bags to delegates (if using) when they sign in.

Step 4. Make sure moderators have their speaking notes, and introduce them to their session presenters.

Step 5. Welcome everyone in the opening plenary, go over the schedule for the day, thank any sponsors, and introduce the opening keynote.

Step 6. Follow the schedule, stepping in to manage any IT gaffs, refill water pitchers, greet caterers, and attend to speaker and guest needs. Don't forget to eat, take bathroom breaks, and hydrate!

Step 7. If this is a multi-day event, repeat Steps 1 through 6 all over again for each day! If not, move to Step 8.

Step 8. After thanking all delegates, sponsors, and presenters at the closing ceremony, clean up and celebrate a successful event with staff and volunteers. Take home leftover swag or save for future program prizes. I recommend sending a short email follow-up survey to participants to gather constructive feedback and thank them again for coming.

Step 9. Don't forget to record your stats for the event and file those waivers! Make notes of what went well and what you could do better for next time.

Step 10. Reach out to members of the business community (who attended) a few weeks after the event to see if they are putting to use any ideas gathered or connections made during the conference. This would also be a good time to reach out to organizations who didn't attend to see what would entice them in the future if you decided to repeat it annually.

Literacy Tie-In

Having lots of people intentionally focusing on a concentrated topic is a great opportunity to promote the library's resources (while you are *already in* the library!). Why not make registration for a library card part of the conference registration process? Create displays that correspond with the topics of each session to have in the conference room(s). Create booklists of pertinent topics to share with delegates (this can also be easily done for an online conference with links to the digital catalog). Lists of helpful websites, databases, and business-related grant-funding organizations would also surely be appreciated by attendees. We put out a bunch of carts full of resources available for check-out in one of the main meeting rooms (see figure 9.1). These are projects that can easily be worked on by volunteers, students, and staff from the time the conference is announced until the opening day. The topic of this program (a business-related conference) is too broad for me to recommend specific titles, but that's what your staff and volunteers do best: set them to it!

Helpful Advice

- I find having a large posterboard of the daily schedule (with assigned room numbers) situated in a highly visible location serves as a helpful touchstone for all volunteers and delegates. It also serves as a place to congregate and network.

Figure 9.1   **Book cart full of resources for Imagine Woodstock Conference.** *Source*: Amy Anderson.

- Don't have a lot of space at your library or are worried a conference will conflict too much with your other programs? Consider holding the conference on days the library is traditionally closed to the public if that is an option with your administration or municipality (or whomever owns the building). You could also hold the conference outdoors, in a nearby park or green space. Consider how that may appeal to different businesses, especially outdoor-based ones such as landscaping companies, adventure travel and tourism organizations, sporting goods stores and rental shops, local forest schools or outdoor education venues, and a whole host of others.
- If all else fails and you just can't make a conference happen in person, why not try online? You could start by offering one or two free sessions from local businesspeople online (as discussed in the "Further Business and Finance Program Ideas" section), see how they are received, and then plan for something more complex.

- Look up resources for hosting comic, gaming, or other conventions at libraries and steal some of their ideas, just skewed for a business-themed model. Instead of prizes for best costume, you could have fun gifts for "biggest briefcase" or "most colorful pantsuit" or "best socks." Let participants know the categories ahead of time so they can play along. Inject a little fun into the party to make it light and memorable.
- If your local business community gives out annual awards or prizes, consider asking them to do it at the conference, which will boost attendance and lend a potentially different audience to the awards.
- With permission from participants, share contact information after the event. We had everyone who was interested in sharing sign a form listing their name, email, phone number, website, title, and company. Then we shared the compiled data with everyone via email and Dropbox. Sometimes business cards get lost or names get forgotten during the busyness of a conference, so having a list after the fact can jog your memory about who you wanted to touch base with. Or you might not have had a chance to connect with someone during the conference and now you have a way to reach out to them without seeming intrusive. In lieu of filling out a form, people could also leave stacks of their business cards on a specially designated table and delegates could pick up the ones they were interested in during the conference.

Further Business and Finance Program Ideas

I understand that organizing an entire business conference may be way more than you are willing or able to take on. But I also know you really want to meet the needs of your adult patrons that might be budding entrepreneurs, small business owners, managers, bankers, accountants, finance geeks, business students, or just laypeople seeking financial information at the library. Here are some scaled-back ideas that are still equally effective at reaching new patrons and helping to get your library known as a place to go to enhance financial literacy skills and that supports business owners.

- Mortgage Basics—Invite a local mortgage broker or other specialists to volunteer to give a talk explaining all the different jargon and terms related to home financing in a way the average person can understand. Have them include recommendations based on your specific region and tips such as, for example, how much people should save for a down payment in advance, how much of a household's net income should go toward monthly payments, and the benefits and drawbacks of renting versus owning. If you'd like to really bump this program up, also bring a home inspector in to discuss what to look for in a used-home purchase and what is worth renovating and what to avoid.
- Car Smarts—Bring in a mechanic or former car salesperson or auto expert to share their tips on how to buy a used car successfully without getting duped into driving off with a lemon. Bonus points if they can also talk the patrons through a new car purchase situation and demystify some of the jargon and give them a real understanding of the manufacturer's suggested

retail price (MSRP) versus the "sticker" price versus the invoice price, which is usually radically different.

- Local Love: Small Business Speed Dating—Ever heard of "speed dating"? It's a bit like musical chairs, but people are playing for love and attraction. You set a timer for three to five minutes, which gives attendees just a few moments to get to know each other, and then a bell or buzzer rings, and they progress to the next person. This continues until everyone has had a chance to meet each other and then there is some free time for mingling at the end, where people who hit it off can have a chance to exchange contact information or keep chatting. If it seems you have nothing in common with the person across from you, you only need to wait a few minutes to move to the next "date." Why not host something similar but instead pair local small businesses with interested patrons? Form two lines of chairs facing each other and have a business member in one and a patron in the other. The business rep has three to five minutes to share samples, talk about their product, give out swag or coupons, or answer questions. For example, a yoga studio could ask "dates" about their experience with yoga and hand out passes for free classes. A local dairy could give out free cheese samples and talk about their cheese-making process and show pictures of the cows/goats/sheep. If patrons aren't interested in what the particular business in front of them is selling, at least they are now aware the product or service exists and may be able to make recommendations to friends and family. Think of it like a really condensed, free trade show in miniature that takes very little time to prepare; just put a call out to your Chamber of Commerce or other local business organizations (don't forget the farmer's market or artist co-op!).
- Disaster Renos: Finding the Right Contractor—Almost every homeowner has a horror story to tell about a renovation gone wrong. Bring in a panel of local builders or building inspectors to tell your patrons what to look for in a reliable, experienced contractor and handy(wo)man.
- Free Credit Counselling—We're lucky enough to have a Library Board Treasurer that is also a mortgage associate by day, and she kindly volunteers at the library to offer one-on-one confidential credit counseling sessions for free on Saturday afternoons. Patrons can learn how credit is reported, the impact their credit score has on their financial situation, and how to correct errors that may be on their credit report. Patrons can also receive post-bankruptcy and consumer proposal credit updates. Our sessions are one hour long and are booked on a first come, first served basis. All we need to do is provide the study room with two chairs (sometimes three, if a couple comes) and keep track of the bookings. Mine your existing volunteer pool to see who may have been a banker or accountant in a past (or current) life or reach out to your local financial institutions to see if they'd be willing to donate some time to provide this valuable service. This program is a great way to increase your patron's financial literacy and reach underserved and vulnerable populations.
- Free Tax Clinics—Another great way to reach underserved populations is by having volunteer certified tax consultants prepare simple tax returns for patrons who have income below a certain amount. In Canada, we have a

program in partnership with the federal government called the Community Volunteer Income Tax Program that matches volunteers with clinic locations.[7] We provide the space, advertise the service, and the volunteers do the rest. During the COVID-19 pandemic, instead of offering in-person sessions, we created a locked drop box in the lobby where patrons who qualified for the program could put their tax information into a provided sealed envelope and a volunteer would stop by once a week to empty the box and complete their returns with them during a phone consultation. Reach out to any retired accountants or other financially literate volunteers to see if this is a program you could consider setting up.

- Understanding Your Student Loan—Whether you're on an academic campus or public library, bring in someone from the student loan office to explain to people what a student loan is, why they should (or shouldn't be) applying for one, how much it is going to cost them in the long run, and what all the rates, terms, and jargon mean. Please!!! It's terrifying how many of our young people take on debt without understanding the (possible) life sentence they are signing up for. There may also be grants and other programs that low-income, disabled, minority, or otherwise disadvantaged students can register for through the student loan program that may allow them to go to school when they thought it might otherwise be financially impossible. Provide this simple service to your community and potentially help so many! Don't assume that because some students on your campus already have a student loan that they know what to do with it. This is also an excellent outreach program to provide to local high schools (if it doesn't already exist at their school library).

I hope this chapter helped you overcome any boredom, anxiety, or inertia you may have felt about offering financial literacy programs and maybe even have increased your own financial literacy slightly. Because the truth of the matter is that most of us don't like dealing with "money stuff" and find it overwhelming or just plain tedious, but it has the potential to actually be fun! The library, whether public or academic, is a safe, accessible place for patrons to seek more information about their entrepreneurial and financial needs, and is much less intimidating than a banker, broker, accountant, or loan officer's office. Familiarize yourself deeply with your collection of resources and then you'll be able to have the right book or website to share when you aren't busy offering one of the valuable (pun intended!) programs listed in this chapter.

Notes

1. Loprespub (screen name), "The State of Financial Literacy in Canada: How Much Do We Know?," *Library of Parliament: HillNotes*, May 9, 2019, https://hillnotes.ca/2019/05/09/the-state-of-financial-literacy-in-canada-how-much-do-we-know/.

2. "10 Things You (Probably) Didn't Know about Canadian SMEs," *BDC (Business Development Bank of Canada)* online, accessed March 20, 2022, https://www.bdc.ca/en/articles-tools/business-strategy-planning/manage-business/10-things-didnt-know-canadian-sme.

3. Maryam Mohsin, "10 Small Business Statistics Every Future Entrepreneur Should Know in 2022," *Oberlo*, January 1, 2022, https://www.oberlo.ca/blog/small-business-statistics.

4. Taken from various personal electronic correspondence with Amy Anderson, circa 2019.

5. Susan Friedmann, *Meeting and Event Planning for Dummies* (Hoboken, NJ: John Wiley & Sons, 2013).

6. When I asked Amy Anderson why she didn't seek funding for this, she said she was happy to pay for it herself as it was a special project of hers and a "labor of love."

7. "Free Tax Clinics," *Government of Canada* online, last modified December 13, 2021, https://www.canada.ca/en/revenue-agency/services/tax/individuals/community-volunteer-income-tax-program.html.

10

✣

Nature and Gardening Programs

The first time I visited our region's largest branch and resource center, I was delighted to find a beautiful garden in its courtyard, complete with wrought iron fencing, a gazebo, and benches amid the perennials. My staff and I were there attending a professional development day, and the library was closed to the public. During our lunch hour, I sat outside in the sunshine with my colleagues and enjoyed my meal at one of the tables. I pulled out my knitting and relaxed, imagining patrons curling up on the benches with books or sitting at tables to play chess together. I let my imagination drift to creating a space like this at our own branch. I casually mentioned this to my boss, our regional manager, and he stopped me mid-sentence to explain that the garden had been nothing but a headache and was more trouble than it was worth. What!? I did a second take, looking around at the beautiful grounds. How was this possible? He rattled off a list of complications: fundraising through the Friends group, the design plan and execution, upkeep, scheduling volunteers to tend the garden, issues with vandalism, and disagreements between the Board, Friends, municipality, volunteers, and staff. He actively discouraged me from pursuing something similar at my own branch and made me see the green space in an entirely different light. No library director in the world welcomes extra logistical and budgeting nightmares—we have enough to deal with already! I walked away that day resigned that I'd just have to be happy offering our outdoor programming on our library's tiny lawn, sidewalks, and, sometimes, the cordoned-off parking lot. Luckily, the mood didn't last.

Fast-forward a year later, and the empty lot of weeds and rubble next to our library (a former demolished doctor's office) was still sitting vacant, begging to be made into a useable space in our downtown and not just a repository for litter and dog poop. At various meetings and opportunities since my appointment as director, I'd discussed the space with town councilors, the mayor, the deputy mayor, the police chief, the head of Parks and Rec, the head of Public Works, the town CAO, the town CFO, my Board, my staff, local business owners, reporters for the local paper and radio . . . pretty much anyone who had an interest in the community and who would listen. Several people reassured me the council was working on the issue and plans were in the making and that someday I'd have a beautiful space to use. I offered to help in any way I could: writing grant proposals, preparing potential program plans for donors to see its potential, offering advice about landscaping and layout to maximize patron enjoyment. I was hoping for a space we could demo vegetable growing to go with our seed library and some interactive play equipment. I was cautiously optimistic it would really happen but still somewhat skeptical. After the conversation I'd had with my boss, I was pretty resigned about not pursuing the funding or planning myself. I mean, the lot was a municipally owned piece of property, and technically, I didn't even work for the municipality, just with them. So even though I was probably one of the people who would use the space the most for community programming (and had good ideas!), my opinions felt mostly ignored.

It was finally a high-ranking official (who shall remain unnamed) who snuck my architectural drawings of the proposed layout options, which initially included a bandstand. I could see right away what they had planned wasn't ideal for all the different kinds of programming we do and wasn't the most accessible for people with disabilities. It was basically a large, raised patio with some shrubs and trees. It looked like something that would appeal to an able-bodied, middle-aged citizen with grown children and a penchant for perennials. I enthusiastically shared my more (ahem!) "creative" suggestions, and while they were acknowledged and appreciated by my covert comrade, she assured me the wheels were already greased on the project, and the mayor and council were going to steamroll ahead with their own ideas. I hated admitting my boss was right. This *was* complicated. No one seemed to be asking the potential users—the citizens themselves and the library staff—what a pocket park next to a busy downtown library (overrun with kids and teens) should look like and what services and features it should provide.

Fast-forward another year, and the park was finally installed, with proper lighting to make it safe at night, no raised bandstand/stage (one of my concerns for accessibility), electrical plug-ins for charging and program use, benches, and landscaping. Young trees were added a bit later. While the bricks chosen for the pathways and common area aren't ideal, they are decent, but the on-ramp area to the parking lot contains sand that fetches up strollers, walkers, and other wheels. There is zero shade (until the trees grow in a decade) or overhead covering that makes it a requirement to erect a pop-up tent in rain or the harsh sunshine. There are a few panels commemorating past provincial premiers and a dedication plaque with a big stone that kids like to climb on (not its purpose but a happy coincidence). There is a garbage/recycling bin. There are no tables to encourage eating or board games or other play.

It isn't perfect, but we are happy to have it. Those first years it was used as a meeting and stretching location for our Run Club and annual Kids Kilometre Fun Run, a place to hold outdoor yoga classes, Summer Reading Club programs, chalk-drawing contests, water balloon tosses, bike clinic demos, and other events, such as concerts (see figure 10.1). During the deepest, darkest days of the pandemic, people escaped lockdown to go for an allowable stroll to the post office and stopped by the park for a breath of fresh air and to let their kids run for a moment. As things

Figure 10.1   **Run registration in the pocket park.** *Source*: Ebony Scott.

opened up a bit, we were allowed to offer in-person outdoor programming, and the park became a haven for the community to be able to meet again, with masks and proper distancing (see figure 10.2). Now, two years into the pandemic at the time of writing, the park is still being used regularly, and I'm so happy to no longer need to cordon off our busy parking lot and divert cranky drivers elsewhere or worry about kids getting hit while they play or walk with their nose in a book. The landscaping and other maintenance are supplied by the municipality, and if I ever notice something amiss, I can call them to deal with it. Honestly, the biggest issues we have are people using or selling drugs in the park and people littering or leaving behind articles of clothing. Our library is across the street from a chain coffee shop, and its parking lot is the go-to hangout for many of our most marginalized citizens. They often wander over to the library or park. Sometimes, there is a lot of yelling and swearing. We try to avoid calling the police, if possible, but sometimes it becomes necessary when people's behavior turns violent, threatening, or especially disruptive. This makes it hard when programming, especially for kids.

A quick scan of my librarian-related social media accounts lets me know I'm not the only one struggling with "outside space" issues. Lots of people in the profession claim to not have any access to a green space at all, which makes me feel very lucky indeed. Others complain their administration isn't supportive of outdoor programming. I can relate. I've been told more than once I should stay inside the library where I "belong" (insert giant eye roll). And then there are concerns about graffiti and vandalism or worse (we've been lucky so far, especially considering we don't even have security cameras in the park, despite my asking for them).

Figure 10.2 Masked runners in April 2021 at the height of the COVID-19 pandemic. *Source*: Kate Waller.

Today, I even saw a post on Facebook that read: "Looking for recommendations to remove & prevent the cat urine smell in our outdoor meeting space. Thanks!" Other people complain about stray dogs (or feral children).

As COVID cases rose again in the autumn of 2021, we were placed back under an emergency order and forced to cancel all in-person programming indoors. When I approached my administration about taking a week-long Forest School practitioner training and partnering with our local nature preserve (which maintains trails and waterfront access within walking distance from the library) in order to offer educational opportunities outdoors, I was met with further resistance. I was basically told I didn't need a degree in outdoor education to offer a storytime next to the river. Despite the fact our province-wide strategic plan calls for more outdoor programming and outreach, more partnerships, and more physical literacy programs, there remains a real disconnect in how some library professionals understand how this also relates to our work to further literacy in our communities. I've written entire books on the subject, and so have other people, so I won't beleaguer the point here.[1]

When we're limited by what indoor programming we can offer due to space or pandemic restrictions, or else we wish to reach a different type of audience or offer more enriching experiences, I think it makes sense to turn to the outdoors. As Kirsteen MacLeod outlines in her book, *In Praise of Retreat: Finding Sanctuary in the Modern World*, humans have been turning to nature for emotional, spiritual, and intellectual fulfillment for millennia, and why should we, in the modern era, be any different?[2] In this time of a global pandemic, seemingly unending wars and oppressive regimes, cases of police brutality, climate disaster, systemic racism, and highly divided political tensions, why shouldn't the public or academic library try to offer a little respite in the form of some nature therapy? Or teach patrons how to be more self-sufficient through gardening and seed-saving programs? Or help our community members be more aware of the lands we inhabit, learn about First Nations who were their original stewards, and how we may maintain that sacred bond with a planet we need?

If this seems like a radical effort beyond the scope of your library degree, feel free to skip this chapter, but I believe reconnecting our patrons with the actual soil our buildings rest upon, and the plants and creatures that surround them, is some of the most rewarding work we can do. Even (perhaps especially) those of us who live and work in concrete jungles, far removed from an immersive countryside retreat. As I have outlined, it might not always be easy, and your plans or concerns might not always be taken seriously, but as we'll explore together in the rest of the chapter, there are many creative ways you can sneak nature and gardening programming into your library's offerings. Join us in the movement toward a more inclusive, nature-centered way of connecting!

Program Model: Seedy Saturday

Since 2016, we have launched the annual opening of our seed library each spring with a "Seedy Saturday" to celebrate all things gardening and home-grown food! If you'd like to start your own seed-lending program, I highly recommend the book *Seed Libraries: And Other Means of Keeping Seeds in the Hands of the People* by Cindy Connor.[3] Even if you don't have an existing catalog of seeds to share, you can still build an awesome display of gardening books and materials and invite

Figure 10.3 **A local farmer shares their knowledge.** *Source*: Brendan Helmuth.

local gardening legends to share their expertise (see figure 10.3). Bonus points for bringing in home cooks to share their fresh produce recipes and having environmental groups share their knowledge of how to keep home gardens free of GMOs and pesticides! Don't think just because you are at an urban or academic library you can't offer a Seedy Saturday (or any other day of the week) program. People can grow plants indoors, on windowsills and balconies, and in community garden spaces. I'll explore the different program offerings we've held every year in this chapter (including online workshops during the pandemic!), and hopefully, this will inspire you to try something new. Be willing to start small. And remember, nature gives us new seasons all the time, so you can always try again next year if something flopped! Wise gardeners know that not every seed will sprout and that sometimes the weeds win the war. That's okay!

Figure 10.4   Seedy Saturday poster 2022. *Source*: Brendan Helmuth.

Figure 10.5 Seedy Saturday poster 2018. *Source*: Brendan Helmuth.

Check out the posters from our 2018 and 2022 events to give you an idea of what a Seedy Saturday program schedule could look like (see figures 10.4 and 10.5). Our general format is to start mid-morning with our library launch, do some yoga for gardeners, and then go through to an afternoon of workshops, with a potluck at lunchtime. This all changed with pandemic restrictions, as we had to move most of the program online or off-site, only offering socially distanced seed-swapping in person at the library. Each year of the pandemic, I gathered with one of our partners at the library, and we sat down and stuffed the seed envelopes prior to the events so patrons could still collect seeds in person after attending the launch. In early spring 2020, in those uncertain and alarming days at the beginning of the pandemic, we moved the program off-site, to our partner's location (The Knowlesville Art and Nature School), where much of the program could be held outdoors, in greenhouses, gardens, and fields (something that wasn't possible in our downtown environment). In 2021, with more practice hosting digital events, we held the entire thing online, with speakers joining us from the library and at our partner's location via Zoom. This online event was still well attended, though not as popular as our in-person Seedy Saturdays. Above all else, be adaptable, just like a good gardener!

Advance Planning

Step 1. Figure out the length of time and what format this program is going to entail. Will it be an all-day event? A few hours? Indoors or out? Or a mixture? How much effort do you want to put in? Will there be multiple speakers and different workshops, or will you be leading this solo? Check out the textbox 10.1 to get some ideas and scratch down some of your own. Many of these suggestions can be done either in person or online. I've added some display suggestions in the "Literary Tie-In" section.

TEXTBOX 10.1

Possible Seedy Saturday Workshop Topics

- Attracting Pollinators to Your Garden: Sharing Stories and Successes
    Attracting pollinators (such as bees, butterflies, wasps, moths, and hummingbirds) benefits every plant in your garden, and they are beautiful too! Have expert gardeners, birders, or beekeepers share some of their experiences building pollinator gardens and patches in rural and urban areas, including at businesses and at home. What can we plant? What other considerations can help, like windbreaks, habitat, and water sources? Have patrons share their tips on attracting pollinators to their spaces.
- Winter Apple Pruning: Get Those Trees Ready for Fruit!
    Many people plant apple trees and other fruiting trees such as pears, plums, or cherries but don't know how to tend to them in the off-season. Have an expert orchard-owner share their knowledge of pruning and fruit tree–care basics for those who may even just want one backyard specimen. More advanced topics could include pollinating, grafting, and pest removal and prevention.
- Gardening 101: Planting Your First Vegetable Garden
    Learn tips and tricks on what to plant, how to plant and tend them, and what to avoid on your first growing adventure. Hint: Don't try to do too much!
- Speak Seed: Decoding the Language on Seed Packages
    Varieties, germination rate, planting depth and spacing, perennial/annual/biannual, and zones—oh my! Learn what all the jargon on your

seed packages means and how to make that information work for you. Help patrons look through the seed catalogue and discover which varieties best suit their landscape and ability.

- Patio Gardening: Containers for Small Spaces

   Don't have a lot of room to grow flowers and vegetables but still have a lot of enthusiasm? Learn what varieties grow best in pots, what soil to use and what amendments it needs, how to ensure good drainage, and what to use for trellises and supports when your plants start climbing out of their homes!

- Yoga for Gardeners: Beginner Stretches for Every *Body*

   Ask a yoga teacher to deliver a short series of poses that all levels can use to keep them limber during this year's growing season. Common points of complaint are overstretched lumbar muscles from bending over, knee issues from kneeling, tight hips during squatting and crouching, and sore upper back and shoulders while raking and shoveling. Necks and arms can get tight from looking up and down and reaching. Hand stretches to ward off arthritis are always welcome! Anything that can be done in a chair is great for those that have a hard time getting down to the floor (or back up!).

- Sprouting Magic: Fresh Veggies All Year Long

   Did you know you can grow sprouts in your kitchen using nothing but seeds, water, a jar, and some cheesecloth (or with a commercial tray)? Learn how to force seeds using various methods (paper towel, rock wool, glass jar, etc.). Seeds can be spouted to get a head start in the garden or for nutritious snacking! This real-life magic can increase food security and access to micro-greens all year long. Why not provide participants with their own sprouting kits to take home to try and have some already-sprouted varieties on hand to taste-test? Learn which seeds you should sprout early to grow in the garden, and which seeds you should sprout to eat. A nice display of cookbooks with recipes involving sprouts takes this session to the next level.

- Singing in the Garden: Digging with Kids

   Would you like to involve little ones in the garden but aren't sure how to keep them from trampling your flowers or pulling up "weeds" thinking they are helpful? Share the same tips and tricks we use during storytimes to keep kids focused and engaged: give them tools their size, involve kids by giving them real jobs to do, have fun with nature-themed songs and games, slow down and follow their wonder, enjoy tactile sensations (mud! leaves! flower petals! water!), rhymes and word play matter, and keep reasonable expectations. For more tips for dealing with littles, visit my blog post on the Programming Librarian blog.[4]

- Basic Seed Saving for the Nervous Hoarder

   When we first realize we can save seeds from the produce right in our very own garden, we sometimes go a little crazy and try to save everything! Learn how to properly wash (or not), dry, sort, label, and store your seeds from one year to the next. Learn from experts how to proof for germination, how long they stay viable, and what's the difference between an heirloom you want to keep and a hybrid (that you might not). Encourage participants to share their excess seed with the Seed Library, or friends!

- Seed Swap

  Set up tables for participants to bring their saved seeds from last year and swap envelopes (or bags, depending on the size of the seeds) with each other. Make sure all varieties are labeled and provide reused plastic bags for everyone to take their treasures home with them. Leftover seed can be donated to the Seed Library or local community garden.

- Plant Swap

  Same as a seed swap but gardeners bring in their seedlings they've started at home, houseplant cuttings, or divided perennials to share. These are placed out on tables, and people take what they want. You can make it more formal by offering tickets so everyone who brings a plant is eligible to take a plant, but often, gardeners are more than happy to share and sometimes don't want (or have room for) anything in return. We usually provide some cast-off plastic pots for re-use and a bag of soil to help people divide and share more easily.

- Raising Heritage Hens (or Ducks or Quails or Turkeys) at Home

  Ever wanted to raise birds for meat, eggs, or just pets but don't know where to start? Have a poultry farmer come to the library to share the basics of coops, feed, water, keeping them warm in the winter and cool in the summer, protection from predators, and how to raise them from peeps to layers. What a great opportunity to display all those backyard chicken books you've got in the nonfiction section!

- Listen for the Pop! Canning and Freezing Your Produce for Year-Round Enjoyment

  Once you've grown all these amazing things in the garden, what do you do with them? Recruit a seasoned canner or enthusiastic prepper (is there any other kind?) to give your patrons the low-down on how to safely store their fruits, vegetables, and grains for the short and long term. Demonstrations are great if you have an available kitchen and are licensed for food preparation; if not, you can share videos and books that patrons can use to follow along at home. Don't forget to talk about dehydration—everyone loves fruit leather!

- Healthy Pest Management

  Learn how to control insect and animal pests in the garden without the use of toxic pesticides and other chemicals. Have someone share their knowledge of companion planting and how it can minimize invasive weeds and pest attacks.

Step 2. What time of year will you host this program? Depending on your geographic location, this could vary widely. Here in New Brunswick, Canada, we're under snow and ice from early December until early-to-mid April, so it usually makes sense to host this program sometime between late February and the middle of April, which is when people start their seeds indoors and plan out their garden for the warmer months. If you live in a more tropical or desert-like climate, you are going to have a drastically different growing season (and perhaps different topics than the ones I've suggested), so plan accordingly.

Choose your day and time and make sure to book the room. If you don't have room at the library for a large gathering, look to partner organizations where you could host off-site. A local nursery or greenhouse that has free space might be ideal! Another option is to host online through Zoom, Skype, or another online platform.

Step 3. Figure out your budget for the event. Do you plan to offer a stipend to the speakers? Will you be providing refreshments? Do you need to purchase seeds or envelopes or zip-top baggies? Funding may be available, so see "Budget Details" section for more thoughts on this.

Step 4. This part becomes a bit "chicken or egg." What comes first: recruiting expert session speakers and seeing what topics they'd like to offer, or picking the topics ahead of time and trying to find people with knowledge in those subject areas? We tend to go for a more collaborative approach. I may jot down a few ideas of what I think might be popular based on past years' events or something new I'd like to see, but first, I'll approach people in each field to see if first they are available on the chosen day, and second, what they are willing to talk about. Sometimes they surprise me with great ideas I've never even imagined! I always reach out to our nonprofit partners first; in our case, that would be instructors at the Knowlesville Art and Nature School, the Meduxneakeag River Association staff, members of the Woodstock Community Garden, vendors and staff and the Woodstock Farm and Craft Market, and members and staff at the Multicultural Association. I always make sure to ask my own staff (who are avid gardeners and practice animal husbandry) and volunteers if they'd like to contribute to the program and if they are available that day (staff is paid to participate if it is during their regularly scheduled working day, of course). Then I'd reach out to local businesses, such as other local farmers, local nurseries and greenhouses, and local food producers (such as the nearby organic grain mill and sprout vendors). Local gardening and environmental groups and tours are great places to recruit knowledgeable speakers; you can probably find them on Facebook gardening groups easily, or through posters on bulletin boards at churches or community halls. If your town has a botanical garden, they likely have a Friends group you can mine for talent.

Don't forget to keep in mind the proposed length of the entire program and suggested length for each session when discussing the day with your potential speakers. Also advise them on the preferred format, and some may not be comfortable with presenting online. Is there a way you could host them locally (i.e., at the library) so they don't need to worry about navigating the technology alone?

Step 5. Gather any materials needed in advance of the event (see "Materials Required" section for suggestions). If you think you'll be taking pictures or video, make sure to write up some photo/video release waivers, and if you are offering yoga or some other physical activity, it might be prudent to have hold harmless forms (liability waivers) prepared to distribute. If the program is digital, make sure you have all the necessary technology required to run it. For in-person, will you need extra chairs, a projector and screen, a mic and amp, access to a sink, extra garbage cans? Walk through each program in your head, and imagine how it will play out and what supplies you might need. You can also ask the presenters if they'll be requiring any special equipment.

Step 6. How will you get the word out about the event? Our usual methods are a digital newsletter, posting a Facebook event, a print calendar, a print poster, a Facebook tile, and, most importantly, word of mouth. Sometimes I'll do a free public service announcement on local radio, especially if it is something geared toward older adults, as many of them still listen to the radio in their vehicles and at home. I would make sure to contact local groups that may be interested (perhaps the same ones you mined for presenters) and let them know about the program so they can tell their members. The timing of this release is crucial, as experienced gardeners will already be planning their next season's potential harvest well in advance and so you want them to know ahead of time that there will be workshops available (perhaps in their area of special interest) and that there may be access to free seeds, seedlings, and cuttings, so they can budget that into their planning process. Likewise, it is also helpful to alert new gardeners to the impending growing season and that they should be thinking ahead if they want to get seeds in the ground on time. Waiting until the last minute can mean lack of access to the best (or any) supplies, feelings of panic/overwhelm or apathy/procrastination, which can lead to a stressful and disappointing experience. Decide your top three to five methods for getting the word out and get started on designing posters, websites, promo videos, and so on.

Step 7. Line up any extra volunteers needed to run the event. If you are hosting a digital event, for example, you may wish to have program moderators, as well as someone to handle tech support. For an in-person program, if there are sessions running concurrently, you will definitely want program moderators to present guest speakers or handle the interactions with (and between) a panel. Even if you are keeping things simple and streamlined, have extra hands on deck so you don't have to deal with everything yourself when surprises happen (and they always do when working with humans and technology!). Create an Excel chart of who is doing what to keep things nice and organized.

Step 8. If your program is complicated, with multiple speakers in multiple rooms at different times, I'd highly suggest creating a color-coded schedule that you can share in advance, so attendees and presenters know what to expect. You can also print schedules on the day of the event to post in the venue (or post on your website or as a landing page during your online event).

Step 9. Is the event catered? Will there be a potluck? What is your library's policy on preparing and sharing food? Will you serve tea and coffee, or at least provide water? Consider what (if any) refreshments will be provided, and make sure to order or acquire the supplies in advance. Don't forget about things needed to serve the items! Are your cutlery and plates/cups environmentally friendly? You don't want to be offering a nature-based program and then serving coffee in non-recyclable Styrofoam cups, right?

Step 10. Put some form of registration plan in place, and be sure to address this in your marketing material. If Seedy Saturday is going to be a digital offering, make sure people know how they can join. Do they register by email for a Zoom link? Do they tune in to FB Live at a certain time? Do they watch the recorded sessions on YouTube via an unlisted link sent to them through email or will the videos be public? Likewise, if Seedy Saturday (or Wednesday or whatever) is going to be in person, do people just show up? Do they need to call or email to register? Do your front desk staff have the details of this event and a sign-up sheet? Who is manning the registration email? Do you have a template created they can reply with to make sure no information is missed? How many people can you accommodate in each session comfortably (keeping in mind physical distancing measures if these are in place or numbers assigned by the fire marshal)? If your event is happening outside, what if people off the street wander over to see what is going on? Who is going to keep track of attendance stats during the event?

Step 11. Set up book displays well in advance if you can, or at least order the books in from other branches you know you'll need.

Step 12. A week prior to the event, confirm the attendance of all presenters and double-check what they'll need for their sessions (cables for laptops, USB sticks for their slides, certain gardening equipment, etc.) and establish expectations of who is responsible for what. If you are paying to have them present, a signed contract or memorandum of agreement should be drafted and received (signed by both parties) by now. For an online event, do a test run with all presenters to check their slides and equipment and make sure everyone is comfortable with the medium.

Materials Required

- Audiovisual equipment needed for in-person presentations (projector, laptop, screen, speakers, mic and amp, etc.) or online presentation (online conferencing software, webcam, speakers/mic, etc.)
- Photo/video release forms and liability waivers (if using)
- Camera for recording sessions
- Printouts of the day's schedule (if using)
- Refreshments
- Plates, cups, napkins, and so on required for food and drink
- Contact tracing form (useful for pandemic protocols if they are in place but also for follow-up with participants if the presenters wish to share slide decks, recipes, etc.)
- Potting soil, small pots, trowels, seeds, and so on or any other supplies needed for your individual programs (if not provided by the presenters)
- Tables and chairs, garbage cans, recycling bin
- If offering a yoga or mobility class, you may want to provide yoga mats, straps, blocks, and so on.
- If offering events outdoors, you may want a sunshade, umbrellas, sunscreen, or anything else needed to deal with uncomfortable weather conditions
- Books and other materials needed for related displays (see "Literacy Tie-In" section for ideas)
- Evaluation forms (if using)

Budget Details

$0–$100+. This program can be delivered for very cheap (or pretty much for zero cost) if done digitally with volunteer presenters. Likewise, it can also easily blow the budget out of the water in printing costs, honorariums for speakers, gardening tools and seed supplies, refreshments, and so on. Really spend some time thinking about how to modify the program to your budget. Every year, we spend about $100 restocking our seed catalog (including the printing cost for envelopes and labels), and that catalog plays a big draw in people attending our Seedy Saturday event (see figure 10.6). Other than that, our costs are minimal and usually center around refreshments and a few bags of soil for people who want to repot plant divisions to share during the plant swap. If you want to offer honorarium for presenters, I generally aim for $60 to $100 per hour, depending on their level of expertise. Funding may be available through wellness, gardening, or nature organizations. Check out a fundraising database like Grant Connect to see what is available. You may need to tailor your program offering to fit the grant's criteria, so do this search and application process well in advance of booking the event line-up.

Figure 10.6   Seed Library collection. *Source*: Jenn Carson.

Day-of-Event

Step 1. It's the big day! Make sure you gather all staff and volunteers and go over the day's itinerary. Make adjustments and contingency plans for any potential fires (a presenter calls in sick, the Wi-Fi goes down, the weather is foul when you planned to hold some sessions outside, etc.). Appoint someone to keep track of program attendance for stats and someone to check people in at the door (if this isn't a drop-in event). Who is the MC or moderator for the day? Do they have a little welcome speech ready? Do you use land acknowledgments?

Step 2. Put out any schedules needed or put up necessary directional signage.

Step 3. Test out any audiovisual equipment or software (for online programs). Make sure your mics and cameras work, your software is running properly, your internet is smooth, your devices are charged or have fresh batteries, your projector and laptop have all the needed cables, and so on.

Step 4. Pick up any last-minute supplies, catering, or accept delivery of said items. Put out supplies and arrange furniture accordingly.

Step 5. Set up book displays if you haven't done this already.

Step 6. Welcome patrons (either online or in person) and enjoy the day!

Step 7. Collect evaluation forms and debrief the event with staff and volunteers. What worked well? What didn't? Will you do this again next year? Clean up and celebrate your accomplishment!

Literacy Tie-In

If your public library is anything like my public library, we have an overabundance of gardening, cooking, and nature-related books and periodicals. There is truly something for everyone! Here are some suggestions to build great displays that will appeal to your patrons at Seedy Saturday. If you are offering a digital event, why not curate an online list in your catalog or email a recommended reading list? Don't forget to ask presenters for their top choices and then you can make a display of their picks! A little sticky note on each book saying "Sally's pick!" (or whomever) helps personalize it.

Periodicals:

- *Amateur Gardening*
- *American Bee Journal*
- *Bee Culture: The Magazine of American Beekeeping*
- *Better Homes and Gardens*
- *Birds & Blooms*
- *Canadian Gardening*
- *Country Living*
- *Countryside & Small Stock Journal*
- *Country Woman Magazine*
- *Easy Gardens*
- *Farm & Ranch Living*
- *Fine Gardening*
- *Gardener's World*

- *Gardens Illustrated*
- *Germination*
- *Grit*
- *Hobby Farms*
- *Home & Gardens*
- *House & Garden*
- *Kitchen Garden*
- *Mother Earth News*
- *Nature*
- *Organic Farming*
- *Orion Magazine*
- *The Prairie Garden Magazine*
- *The Progressive Farmer*
- *Resurgence & Ecologist*
- *Saltscapes*
- *Saving Earth Magazine*
- *Small Farm Canada*
- *Sustainable Farming*
- *Taproot Magazine*
- *Urban Farm*
- *Wildlife*

Print or audiobooks:

- *100 Plants to Feed the Bees: Provide a Healthy Habitat to Help Pollinators Thrive* by The Xerces Society
- *The Backyard Homestead: Produce All the Food You Need on Just a Quarter Acre!* by Carleen Madigan
- *The Beginner's Guide to Raising Chickens: How to Raise a Happy Backyard Flock* by Anne Kuo
- *The Best-Ever Step-by-Step Kid's First Gardening: Fantastic Gardening Ideas for 5–12 Year Olds, from Growing Fruit and Vegetables and Fun with Flowers to Wildlife Gardening and Outdoor Crafts* by Jenny Hendy
- *The Book of Gardening Projects for Kids: 101 Ways to Get Kids Outside, Dirty, and Having Fun* by Whitney Cohen and John Fisher
- *Bringing It to the Table: On Farming and Food* by Wendell Berry
- *Bringing Nature Home: How You Can Sustain Wildlife with Native Plants* by Douglas W. Tallamy
- *Carrots Love Tomatoes: Secrets of Companion Planting for Successful Gardening* by Louise Riotte
- *The Complete Book of Small-Batch Preserving: Over 300 Recipes to Use Year-Round* by Ellie Topp and Margaret Howard
- *The Complete Guide to Saving Seeds: 322 Vegetables, Herbs, Fruits, Flowers, Trees, and Shrubs* by Robert E. Gough and Cheryl Moore-Gough
- *Container Gardening: A Complete Beginner's Guide to Growing Vegetables, Fruits, Herbs, and Edible Flowers in Tubes, Pots, and Other Containers* by Eric Jason

- *Floret Farm's Cut Flower Garden: Grow, Harvest, and Arrange Stunning Seasonal Blooms* by Erin Benzakein, Julie Chai, et al.
- *Four-Season Harvest: Organic Vegetables from Your Home Garden All Year Long* by Eliot Coleman
- *The Garden Primer: The Completely Revised Gardener's Bible* by Barbara Damrosch
- *Gardener's Yoga: 40 Yoga Poses to Help Your Garden Flow* by Veronica D'Orazio and Frida Clements
- *Gardening for Birds, Butterflies, and Bees: Everything You Need to Know to Create a Wildlife Habitat in Your Backyard* by the Editors at *Birds and Blooms*
- *Gardening with Emma: Grow and Have Fun (A Kid-to-Kid Guide)* by Emma Biggs and Steven Biggs
- *Gardening Without Work: For the Aging, the Busy, and the Indolent* by Ruth Stout
- *Greenhouse Gardening: A Beginners Guide to Growing Fruit and Vegetables All Year Round: Everything You Need to Know about Owning a Greenhouse* by Jason Johns
- *Grow Fruit: Gardens, Yards, Balconies, Roof Terraces* by Alan Buckingham
- *Grow Fruit Naturally: A Hands-On Guide to Luscious, Homegrown Fruit* by Lee Reich
- *Grow Vegetables* by Alan Buckingham
- *Growing Tomorrow: A Farm-to-Table Journey in Photos and Recipes: Behind the Scenes with 18 Extraordinary Sustainable Farmers Who Are Changing the Way We Eat* by Forrest Prichard
- *Guide to Canadian Vegetable Gardening* by Douglas Green
- *The Homesteader's Natural Chicken Keeping Handbook: Raising a Healthy Flock from Start to Finish* by Amy K. Fewell
- *Homesteading: A Backyard Guide to Growing Your Own Food, Canning, Keeping Chickens, Generating Your Own Energy, Crafting, Herbal Medicine, and More* by Abigail Gehring
- *The Illustrated Encyclopedia of Country Living: Beekeeping, Canning and Preserving, Cheese Making, Disaster Preparedness, Fermenting, Growing Vegetables, Keeping Chickens, Raising Livestock, Soap Making, and more!* by Abigail Gehring
- *Microgreens: How to Grow Nature's Own Superfood* by Fionna Hill
- *Nature's Best Hope: A New Approach to Conservation That Starts in Your Yard* by Douglas W. Tallamy
- *Pollinator Friendly Gardening: Gardening for Bees, Butterflies, and Other Pollinators* by Rhonda Fleming Hayes
- *The Pollinator Victory Garden: Win the War on Pollinator Decline with Ecological Gardening; Attract and Support Bees, Beetles, Butterflies, Bats, and Other Pollinators* by Kim Eierman
- *Seed to Seed: Seed Saving and Growing Techniques for Vegetable Gardeners* by Suzanne Ashworth, Kent Whealy, et al.
- *The Sprout Book: Tap into the Power of the Planet's Most Nutritious Food* by Doug Evans
- *The Vegetable Gardener's Bible: Discover Ed's High-Yield W-O-R-D System for All North American Gardening Regions* by Edward C. Smith
- *The Vegetable Gardener's Container Bible: How to Grow a Bounty of Food in Pots, Tubs, and Other Containers* by Edward C. Smith

- *Vertical Gardening: Grow Up, Not Out, for More Vegetables and Flowers in Much Less Space* by Derek Fell
- *Week-by-Week Vegetable Gardener's Handbook: Perfectly Timed Gardening for Your Most Bountiful Harvest Ever* by Jennifer Kujawski and Ron Kujawski
- *The Winter Harvest Handbook: Year Round Vegetable Production Using Deep-Organic Techniques and Unheated Greenhouses* by Eliot Coleman
- *The Woodland Homestead: How to Make Your Land More Productive and Live More Self-Sufficiently in the Woods* by Brett McLeod and Philip Ackerman-Leis
- *The Year-Round Vegetable Gardener: How to Grow Your Own Food 365 Days a Year, No Matter Where You Live* by Niki Jabbour

DVDs:

- *Back to Eden* (2011)
- *The Biggest Little Farm* (2018)
- *Dare to Be Wild* (2015)
- *Dirt! The Movie* (2009)
- *Eating Animals* (2017)
- *Farmland* (2014)
- *Ferngully: The Last Rainforest* (1992)
- *Foodchains* (2014)
- *Food, Inc.* (2008)
- *Forks over Knives* (2011)
- *Game Changers* (2019)
- *The Gardener* (2016)
- *Greenfingers* (2000)
- *Growing Cities* (2013)
- *Kiss the Ground* (2020)
- *Minari* (2020)
- *The Organic Life* (2013)
- *The Pollinators* (2019)
- *SEED: The Untold Story* (2016)
- *The Trader* (2018)
- *Vanishing of the Bees* (2009)

Helpful Advice

- Think of ways to include underserved and underrepresented populations in your program, such as hosting BIPOC presenters and making sure the event is free (and the supplies required to complete the projects are free, cheap, or easily accessible). Consider offering the programs in various languages and having translators available, depending on your community's demographics (for example, in my library, we offer programs in French or English, but what about Spanish or Chinese or American Sign Language?). Is your event location wheelchair accessible? Are there enough seats for people with mobility issues? Does your video feed have closed captions or subtitles? Is there gender parity in your presenters? Have you made an effort to reach out to the LGBTQ+ community to see if there are any inclusive gardening or farming groups that might be interested in attending?

- My experience is that many gardening/farming folks tend to have a subjective view of time. Don't be surprised if sessions run over, people have side conversations, things get off-topic, presenters are late and bring children with them, and the day goes a bit off-kilter. Try to go with the flow as best you can while keeping things running smoothly.

- You might find that the demographic of patrons most interested in Seedy Saturday skews north of mid-life. While that may seem typical, it's actually not. Now more than ever, especially with the recent pandemic, more and more young people are getting interested in farming, gardening, and self-sufficiency. The key is to figure out how to reach out to them. Social media and word-of-mouth are your best bets. Make a Facebook event, a TikTok, story it on Instagram, show up at the local community garden or farmer's market to hand out flyers or chat with the growers, and reach out to your local homesteading or urban farming YouTubers (I guarantee they exist within a fifty-mile radius).

- Is this going to be a family-friendly event? My suggestion is to make sure of it. Many parents/guardians don't have easy access to childcare on the weekends, so making sure families feel welcome to participate is a way to be more inclusive while also upping program numbers. You are also introducing the next generation of potential gardeners to the joy of playing in the dirt and the satisfaction derived from growing your own food. Why not host a special session geared just for them, where they can plant their own seeds to take home and care for? Children *love* pulling seeds out of a giant dried sunflower head (see figure 10.7). And sunflower seeds are easy to plant and grow. Or offer child-minding in the children's section of the library staffed by kid-friendly volunteers (with clean criminal record checks). Why not host a garden-themed storytime on the same day?

Figure 10.7   Dried sunflower head. *Source*: Jenn Carson.

Further Nature and Gardening Program Ideas

If Seedy Saturday feels like too much commitment or too complicated, or there just isn't enough staff or time or budget money available, why not bring in a community partner or involve your Board or Friends group? Here are some further program ideas that will help your patrons get more involved in the great outdoors and nurture their green thumbs.

- Backyard Composting—Ask a local composting enthusiast or representative from your solid waste commission to come give a presentation on how to build or buy a proper compost bin, what is allowed according to your municipality's bylaws, the reasons behind why we compost, what to do with "finished" compost, and how to build and maintain a productive compost pile (hint: it's not just a pile of kitchen scraps rotting in a wastebin).
- Pet Worms that Work: Vermicomposting for All Ages—Invite a local vermiculture or vermicomposting enthusiast to bring in some worms and dirt and show local families how to raise pet worms that will happily eat kitchen scraps and give back lovely compost to add to gardens and houseplant soil. Learn what sort of worms are used for the process, what sort of housing they need to be happy and healthy, what they can and can't eat, and how to nurture a livable environment that reaps the rewards of their digestive prowess. A great program for all ages but especially popular with kids. The type of pet that cleans up after itself is a real selling feature to parents!
- Giant Plant Sale—Every spring, my assistant and our Board Trustees organize a giant plant sale. They recruit volunteers to work the cash box and ask local gardeners, farmers, and greenhouses to donate spare seedlings, cuttings, and divisions, and set up tables in our activity room to display the wares. Each item is priced, and all proceeds go toward library programs and collections.
- Grow and Harvest Your Own Mushrooms—Invite a local mycologist or mushroom enthusiast (local universities/colleges, mushroom-hunting groups, or farmer's markets are good places to find them) to teach your patrons how to grow and harvest their own mushrooms at home. All they will need is a moist log to inoculate and some spores, which can be ordered online. In fact, some types of mushrooms will even grow in straw or haybales, manure, sawdust, or grain. It is not recommended to grow mushrooms indoors, unless you have a specially designed environment, as they can cause excessive humidity and lead to mold growth and other issues in the home. An alternative would be to host a Mushroom Walk where a local mushroom hunter takes patrons around the neighborhood park, field, or woodland to find specimens that are safe and tasty to eat. There is some risk that patrons won't heed the expert's advice and may try to gather mushrooms on their own following the outing, which could lead to someone ingesting contaminated or poisonous specimens. Or that they don't gather sustainably. It's also much easier in the countryside as there is more access to woodlands and fields. If you live in a rural environment with fairly level-headed patrons, it may be worth the risk; I'll leave that up to you (and your administration!).

- Tree/Plant Identification—We have an excellent partnership with our local nature preserve. They will happily send volunteers to our packed flora ID events. Sometimes they focus on local trees, and sometimes they focus on other plants in the watershed. This can also be done to identify mushrooms, lichen, houseplants, weeds, geology (rocks), birds, insects, and so on. The plant person will bring some photos and real-life specimens to share, and then they teach everyone the distinguishing characteristics to help people recognize them in the wild. There are also excellent phone apps available, and you can share library resources, such as printed ID guides for your area. (See figure 10.8.) Sometimes we tie this in with a nature walk (which is an excellent way to promote our snowshoe and hiking pole lending library). Reach out to your local university, botanical garden, nature preserve, state or provincial park, or hiking/plant groups to see who might be interested in volunteering. (See figure 10.9.)
- Farmer's Market Pop-Up Library—Sometimes the programs that benefit adults means keeping their kids busy! I love to do a bilingual storytime at the farmer's market in the summer. (See figure 10.10.) There are many farming families who bring their kids to the stalls and would love nothing more than for you to keep them busy for a while. Same goes for local families shopping or tourists visiting. With permission from the market, I set up a blanket on the porch and surround myself with bilingual picture books and a bunch of toys (like sensory-friendly play sand, blocks, noisemakers, puppets, and other fidget gadgets). I also have a large sandwich board or banner indicating

Figure 10.8   A display of books and tree branch specimens. *Source*: Jenn Carson.

Figure 10.9 A patron looks at a tree branch for identification during a partner-led program.
Source: Jenn Carson.

I'm from the library, so I don't look like a creepy lady sitting alone with toys on a blanket trying to entice kids to play. Rather than having stories read at a certain time, I invite families to come check out the toys and books, and when enough have gathered, I'll ask, "How about a story?" Then, based on their first language, I'll choose either a French or English book, or sometimes I'll read both. Hearing me read usually brings other families closer, and they'll start fiddling with the toys until I'm finished and then I'll read some new stories to the new group. I bring enough stories and toys that usually kids can sit for a good fifteen to twenty minutes without losing interest or hearing the same story twice. When I'm feeling really keen, or have another person with me to help, I'll bring our portable check-out station so I can enroll people in the Summer Reading Club or sign them up for library cards and even let them check out the storybooks on the spot.

- Or why not expand this program for adults? Instead of offering toys and picture books, bring items related to the interests of people at a farmer's market: books about gardening, seeds from your seed library, tools from your tool library, a calendar of events related to nature and gardening programs, directions to local farms that give free tours, a flyer for joining the community

Figure 10.10   Farmer's Market Storytime. *Source*: Jenn Carson.

garden, or maps of local hiking or biking trails. Why not invite the author of a local tour guide or nature book to offer a reading? For more details on the original storytime idea, I wrote a blog post on my first experience with this program at the Programming Librarian website.[5]

- Forest Bathing—In Japan, the Ministry of Agriculture, Forestry, and Fisheries created the term *shinrin-yoku* in 1982, which roughly translates to "forest bathing" or "absorbing the forest atmosphere."[6] This doesn't involve any actual baths but rather encourages people to spend time of quiet contemplation in a natural environment. This is very different from a guided nature walk, where the leader points out different types of flora and fauna and is considered more of an educational opportunity. Likewise, Forest Bathing is not intended to be done for exercise; the focus is not on how far you walk or how many calories you burn. Instead, Forest Bathing is something closer to meditation and more of a spiritual—or if that word bothers you: *restorative—* experience. I belong to a very active Forest Bathing group, mostly made up of retired women, who organize weekly walks in different locations.

- Alternative Outdoor Collections—Opportunities abound to add alternative material formats related to nature and gardening to your collection. At our branch, we have a seed library, a kite lending program, as well as snowshoes and hiking poles with maps of our local nature trails. We're in the process of adding ten adult- and kid-sized skateboards and longboards, helmets, and elbow and knee pads. Bird-watching kits, including binoculars and ID guides, could be popular. Some libraries even lend bikes to encourage people to get moving and get outside! Consider also creating a library of gardening tools that may be expensive or inaccessible to beginners, like trowels, shovels, shears, pruners, edgers, wheelbarrows, tillers, and so on (though you must factor in the maintenance cost of retaining this equipment and also storage and tagging considerations).

- Gardening for Families Program—If you'd like to expand the program offerings for teaching kids and their parents about gardening beyond what I've suggested for Seedy Saturday, check out what the Free Library of Philadelphia's Falls of Schuylkill Library did by reading their story on the Programming Librarian blog.[7]
- Library Greenspace—If I didn't scare you at the beginning of the chapter with my story of getting a park installed next to our branch, consider building a green space of your own. This doesn't have to be as complicated as what I went through. Maybe it's cultivating some window boxes or raised beds with vegetables and flowers planted by patrons? Maybe it's a Zen garden filled with sand and rocks used for meditation by students on your campus? Maybe it's some cheery houseplants placed around the library to create more of a natural atmosphere (which has been shown to reduce stress levels)?[8] What about a rooftop garden? What about a vertical garden climbing up a bare wall in the lobby? Even the most urban library environment can likely come up with a way to increase patron and staff exposure to the good green stuff.

As you've hopefully seen in this chapter, there are myriad possibilities for enticing your adult patrons to learn more about nature and gardening at your library. Whether it is through appealing to young parents with family-friendly programs, tapping into the homesteading and self-sufficiency trends among twenty-to-thirty-somethings, letting outdoor and environmental enthusiasts know what sort of materials are available through their local branch, getting university students thinking about where their food comes from, or involving seniors in community-building programs to enhance their well-being and share their skills, there is something for everyone at your library!

Notes

1. Jenn Carson, *Yoga and Meditation at the Library: A Practical Guide for Librarians* (Lanham, MD: Roman & Littlefield, 2019); Jenn Carson, *Get Your Community Moving: Physical Literacy Programs for All Ages* (Chicago: ALA Editions, 2018).

2. Kirsteen MacLeod, *In Praise of Retreat: Finding Sanctuary in the Modern World* (Toronto: ECW Press, 2021).

3. Cindy Conner, *Seed Libraries and Other Means of Keeping Seeds in the Hands of the People* (Gabriola, BC: New Society Publishers, 2015).

4. Jenn Carson, "Blog: Storytime Stretching," *Programming Librarian*, July 27, 2015, https://programminglibrarian.org/blog/storytime-stretching.

5. Jenn Carson, "Blog: Bilingual Market Storytime," *Programming Librarian*, March 7, 2019, https://programminglibrarian.org/blog/bilingual-market-storytime.

6. Qing Li, *Forest Bathing: How Trees Can Help You Find Health and Happiness* (London: Penguin Life, 2018).

7. Meredith McGovern, "Blog: Gardening for Kids Programs Grow Community Connections," *Programming Librarian*, August 14, 2019, https://programminglibrarian.org/blog/gardening-kids-programs-grow-community-connections.

8. E. Largo-Wight, W. W. Chen, V. Dodd, and R. Weiler, "Healthy Workplaces: The Effects of Nature Contact at Work on Employee Stress and Health," *Public Health Reports* 126, Suppl 1 (2011): 124–30, accessed March 24, 2022, https://www.ncbi.nlm.nih.gov/pmc/articles/PMC3072911/.

Conclusion

A Pandemic-Era Manuscript Requires Outside the Shelf Thinking

When I first started writing this collection of adult program ideas in the summer of 2019, few of us in libraryland had any inkling that we would find ourselves just a few months later scrambling to line our circulation desks with Plexiglas, reminding patrons to wear their masks and stay home if they were coughing, canceling all our programs, or worse, closing our doors or campuses. Some of us even had to deal with the shock of being furloughed or put on indefinite leave (paid or unpaid). Some unlucky library workers got sick with coronavirus or had to care for people at home with it, and sad stories abounded of those who died or were struck with lingering, distressing symptoms.

In the spring of 2020, our town went into lockdown, and my library was closed for seven weeks, with no indication of when we would reopen or what program delivery might look like at that time. I worked from home, desperately trying to record yoga videos in my living room for patrons to follow on YouTube or Facebook Live, while homeschooling my two children and posting book reviews to encourage patrons to access our e-books. My staff were put on paid leave and weren't required to work. I had regular check-ins with them to see how they were doing and keep them informed of any news from the provincial office. I did the same with my Board Trustees. Even when we returned to the building in June of 2020, everything was uncertain and ever-changing. We were required to quarantine all books for seventy-two hours before circulating or shelving. We couldn't lend other objects. And then suddenly, we could do so, as policies changed. We had to wash everything, including ourselves. Over and over. Patrons couldn't use the computers. And then suddenly, they could, with rigorous cleaning and spacing protocols. More lockdowns, strange "circuit breakers," and the understandable confusion followed.[1]

We started offering curbside pickup and take-home craft kits and screening patrons at the door for symptoms and travel history. One week we could only have digital programs, and the next week we could have in-person programs but only outdoors, then restrictions relaxed, and we could go back to having indoor events, but they had to be masked and physically distanced and with low numbers. Then things tightened up again, and we required proof of vaccination for any program, even outdoor ones. We had to have staff stationed at the door, screening everyone that walked through. Meanwhile, we were still required to offer digital programs, and I was juggling online author events, video book reviews, digital storytimes, podcast interviews, online conferences and professional development days, a digital newsletter and print calendar, and trying to offer a hybrid Summer Reading Club program. I was also still homeschooling as schools were closed due to exposures, which meant sometimes I had my kids in my office doing online learning, and other times I rushed home at lunch to check on them, and still other times I tried to work at home while teaching them. Some of my staff were deployed for months at a time to work for the Public Health Department in essential services, and others were home sick or on vacation, leaving us perpetually short-staffed and overwhelmed.

Whenever I'd find a few moments to spare to sit down and try to write this book about adult library programs, which was based on a detailed outline of successful in-person events I'd organized and ran the last five years at my public library, I'd have a bit of an existential crisis. The inside of my head sounded like this: *Do libraries even matter when the world is falling apart? My job is nearly obsolete. I'm not saving lives here. Who cares about a salsa dancing program when we aren't even allowed to touch each other and people are looting and holding protests over George Floyd's death and demanding for police reform? What if we're all dead by the time this book is even finished? How can I write in a tone that sounds chipper and encouraging when I feel the exact opposite? None of these programs are applicable to the world we are now living in. I'm going to have to rethink this entire book. Who is even going to want to buy a book like this? My work is irrelevant.*

In other words, I was exhausted—to the point of burnout—probably depressed and overwhelmed with frustration and, sometimes, apathy. But, as the head of my library and the head of my household, I had to just keep going. And so, I told my editor that I was going to rejig the chapters to include digital delivery options, I was going to drop the chapter on object lending and incorporate those ideas into the previous chapters (by subject), and I was going to be very, very late turning in the manuscript. Like, over a year late. Thankfully, as his New York office had also experienced many stops and starts and witnessed much turmoil over the last two years, he was incredibly understanding.

So, it is my hope that as you read over these pages of adult programming ideas as diverse as old-fashioned recipe swaps, kite-flying events, and stop-motion animation classes, you were comforted to know there were alternatives to in-person delivery accompanying them. I also hope you were heartened that there was another librarian in the trenches with you, slogging my way through one program at a time, amid ever-changing health and safety procedures, staff shortages, deaths in the community, and challenges at home. I want you to know that sometimes it is okay to take a step back, reassess, change gears, and, most importantly, take care of yourself and ask for the help or space and time to do that. Because as people of service, we are inclined to give and give, and often, more and more is expected of us, even under exceedingly difficult circumstances. Sometimes we have to say, "Enough. This is what I can do within the reality of the situation."

I always remind my staff to temper their expectations according to what the day brings. If case numbers rise and we get put under tighter restrictions, it means we can't provide the same level of face-to-face service our patrons have come to expect and that we love to deliver. That has to be okay. If technology breaks down and a Zoom program goes sideways, we figure it out as we go along and we apologize for any inconvenience. If our people get sick or go out on bereavement leave, we remind them to take care of themselves and we reduce our workloads accordingly. This may mean rescheduling a program. This may mean the building is running on reduced hours. This may mean we occasionally disappoint people. I know we don't like to do that, but sometimes, in order to protect the health and safety of our staff and ourselves, we have to. It's okay.

I hope this book also broadened your understanding of what is considered a viable "adult" demographic to market to in the library, and why we need to reach out to community partners and underserved populations in order to build the community (either online or in-person) that we all so desperately need for our emotional well-being. I hope you've seen ways that these community partners can fill in the gaps in your skills, or budget, or even your energy deficits, and how much partners get out of the partnership too. During the pandemic, libraries became one of the few places people could go and feel relatively safe and also not have to spend any money when maybe they were out of work or facing medical bills. When movie theaters were closed and concerts were canceled, they could come to the library (or visit us online) and find ways to be entertained. They could travel through stories when they couldn't get into a car or airplane and go anywhere. They could see your friendly face, behind your mask, even when they couldn't be near their loved ones. I hope you know what a difference you are making.

While it's probably too much to ask that the pandemic is done and over by the time you read this conclusion, I want you to be confident in the knowledge that these adult library programs work. And more than that, they are a really, really good time. I know, because I went to them (and so did a lot of other people) and had a blast. And some people might even consider me a "grown-up" (insert winky face emoji). A sense of humor and nonnegotiable self-care tactics are some major adulting best practices, I promise. Happy Programming!

Note

1. Our province instituted something called a "circuit breaker" where a certain section of a specific region of the province went into lockdown if the COVID-19 cases were high in that particular area. Sometimes this would last over a month. This meant that my library might be open but the branch that is a fifteen-minute drive up the river was closed. Or that certain staff or patrons, because of where they lived, couldn't leave their houses except for emergencies. The rules around this were volatile, so sometimes people could travel for essential services, but that was subject to change. So, patrons could come to town to get groceries but not to the library to pick up their holds, for example, or attend a program. It became complicated when we checked their ID at the door and knew they lived in a "circuit breaker" region but weren't allowed to say anything. The rules around quarantining (books and people) also changed multiple times, creating further confusion. There were a lot of angry, unvaccinated people outraged when they weren't allowed in the building, so then we were allowed to let them in but only for certain tasks and certain time limits.

References

"The 8 Types of Kites and How to Fly Them." *Recreation Insider*. March 21, 2020. https://recreationinsider.com/kites/types-of-kites/.

"10 Things You (Probably) Didn't Know about Canadian SMEs." *BDC (Business Development Bank of Canada)* online. Accessed March 20, 2022. https://www.bdc.ca/en/articles-tools/business-strategy-planning/manage-business/10-things-didnt-know-canadian-sme.

"10 Tips to Master Social Media at Your Library." *EBSCO* online. Accessed February 12, 2022. https://www.ebsco.com/sites/g/files/nabnos191/files/acquiadam-assets/10-Social-Media-Tips-for-Public-Libraries-Infographic.pdf.

"20 Somethings' Trivia: *Game of Thrones*." *Baton Rouge Parish Library Infoblog*. July 17, 2013. https://ebrpl.wordpress.com/2013/07/17/20-somethings-trivia-game-of-thrones/.

"The 25 Best Library Websites for 2019." *Piola* online. May 2, 2019. https://meetpiola.com/the-25-best-library-websites-for-2019/.

"About V-Day." *V-Day* online. Accessed March 3, 2022. https://www.vday.org/about-v-day/.

Aiken, Julian, Femi Cadmus, and Fred Shapiro. "Not Your Parents' Law Library: A Tale of Two Academic Law Libraries." *Cornell Law Faculty Publications* (2012): 655. Accessed January 15, 2022. https://scholarship.law.cornell.edu/facpub/655.

"Age of Majority." *Wikipedia*. Accessed January 20, 2022. https://en.wikipedia.org/wiki/Age_of_majority.

Allan, John, and Keith Brown. "Jungian Play Therapy in Elementary Schools." *Elementary School Guidance & Counseling* 28, no. 1 (1993): 30–41. http://www.jstor.org/stable/42869127.

Alessio, Amy J., Katie LaMantia, and Emily Vinci. *A Year of Programs for Millennials and More*. Chicago: ALA Editions, 2015.

American Library Association. *Programming Librarian* (blog). Accessed February 11, 2022. https://programminglibrarian.org/.

Animotion. "Obsession." *AnimotionVEVO*. Video (1985), June 11, 2010, 4:01. https://youtu.be/hIs5StN8J-0.

"Art Battle Artist Frequently Asked Questions and Competition Rules." *Art Battle*. Accessed March 3, 2022. https://artbattle.com/artist-faq/.

Artrageous with Nate. "How Do You Create Stop Motion Animation?" *YouTube*. November 8, 2017. https://youtu.be/nHyc0GAfjJg.

Barbakoff, Audrey. "Learning through Play in Adult Programs." *RA News*. August 2014. https://www.ebscohost.com/novelist/novelistspecial/learning-through-play-in-adult-programs.

Bernstein, Sara Tatyana, and Elise Chatelain. "The Dress Code: Is the Kimono Trend Cultural Appropriation?" *Dismantle* online. Accessed March 3, 2022. https://www.dismantlemag.com/2019/07/22/dress-code-kimono-cultural-appropriation/.

"Brazilian Capucheta Paper Kites." *Little Cloud Kites*. Accessed January 12, 2022. https://littlecloudkites.com/pages/paper-kite-downloads.

Breen, Rachel. "Program Model: *Downton Abbey* Episode Viewing and Afternoon Tea." *Programming Librarian*. February 1, 2016. https://programminglibrarian.org/programs/downton-abbey-episode-viewing-and-afternoon-tea.

"Bringing the Arts to Life." *Canada Council for the Arts* online. Accessed February 12, 2022. https://canadacouncil.ca/.

Butland, Sarah. "The Lethal Librarian." *Maritime Edit*, no. 11 (Winter 2019–2022): 41–43.

"Carnegie Library." *Wikipedia*. Accessed January 20, 2022. https://en.wikipedia.org/wiki/Carnegie_library.

Carson, Jenn. "Blog: Bilingual Market Storytime." *Programming Librarian*. March 7, 2019. https://programminglibrarian.org/blog/bilingual-market-storytime.

———. "Blog: Cursive Writing Course." *Programming Librarian*. July 19, 2018. https://programminglibrarian.org/blog/cursive-writing-course.

———. "Blog: Digital Storytelling in 6 Steps." *Programming Librarian*. March 31, 2020. https://programminglibrarian.org/blog/digital-storytelling-6-steps.

———. "Blog: Eco-Friendly Fall Garland." *Programming Librarian*. September 18, 2019. https://programminglibrarian.org/blog/eco-friendly-fall-garland.

———. "Blog: Libraries Rock." *Programming Librarian*. August 7, 2019. https://programminglibrarian.org/blog/libraries-rock.

———. "Blog: A Range of Ages: Mixed-Age Play at the Library." *Programming Librarian*. September 17, 2018. http://programminglibrarian.org/blog/range-ages-mixed-age-play-library.

———. "Blog: Storytime Stretching." *Programming Librarian*. July 27, 2015. https://programminglibrarian.org/blog/storytime-stretching.

———. "Blog: Tile Art: A Creative Program for All Ages." *Programming Librarian*. December 8, 2018. https://programminglibrarian.org/blog/tile-art-creative-program-all-ages.

———. *Get Your Community Moving: Physical Literacy Programs for All Ages*. Chicago: ALA Editions, 2018.

———. "Go Fly a Kite!" *Children & Libraries Magazine* 19, no. 1 (2021). https://journals.ala.org/index.php/cal/article/view/7542/10424?fbclid=IwAR3ZWZB7rQbxKxsJDdWmv_WXXQ0Y-qgy9hwSiyUJaV4Az2bb4IgHY2nPmks.

———. "Jenn Carson: Author/Librarian/Yogi." *Jenn Carson*. Accessed March 12, 2022. www.jenncarson.com.

———. "Trauma Informed BJJ—Thumbs Up Approach with Jenn Carson." *YouTube*. June 14, 2021. https://youtu.be/00-nS8Ro7uo.

———. *Yoga and Meditation at the Library: A Practical Guide for Librarians*. Lanham, MD: Roman & Littlefield, 2019.

"Categories of Risk." *Heritage Crafts* online. Accessed March 12, 2022. https://heritagecrafts.org.uk/redlist/categories-of-risk/.

CBBAG. Canadian Bookbinders and Book Artists Guild. Accessed March 12, 2022. https://www.cbbag.ca.

CBC News. "Laurier, Kitchener Public Library Collaborate to Offer Free Virtual Concerts." *CBC* online. Last modified November 5, 2020. https://www.cbc.ca/news/canada /kitchener-waterloo/laurier-kitchener-public-library-virtual-concert-series-1.5790659 ?fbclid=IwAR3uFRSH_ouWSLxaEjTs0A3yLZnnvxg6OxWdFTza5mul6E1BvxJZQT6P87A.

Chen, Jenn. "20 Facebook Stats to Guide Your 2021 Facebook Strategy." *Sprout Social* online. February 17, 2021. https://sproutsocial.com/insights/facebook-stats-for-marketers/.

"Child Marriage." *UNICEF* online. October 2021. https://data.unicef.org/topic/child -protection/child-marriage/.

City of Edmonton. "Intergenerational Programming Toolkit." *Edmonton* online. Accessed February 11, 2022. https://www.edmonton.ca/city_government/documents/PDF/afe -intergenerational-toolkit.pdf.

Clubb, Barbara H. "Public Libraries." *Encyclopedia of Library and Information Sciences,* third edition. Boca Raton, FL: Taylor & Francis, 2010.

Conner, Cindy. *Seed Libraries and Other Means of Keeping Seeds in the Hands of the People.* Gabriola, BC: New Society Publishers, 2015.

Deerchild, Rosanna. *Cultural Appropriation vs. Appreciation.* CBC Radio, video, October 27, 2016, 3:46. https://youtu.be/vfAp_G735r0.

Dixon, Jennifer A., and Steven A. Gillis. "Doing Fine(s)? | Fines & Fees." *Library Journal* online. April 4, 2017. https://www.libraryjournal.com/?detailStory=doing-fines-fines -fees.

Donato, Al. "How Canadians Started Community Fridges in Their Cities." *Huffington Post.* January 5, 2021. https://www.huffingtonpost.ca/entry/community-fridges-canada_ca _5fe13c8bc5b66809cb2cbed6.

"Double C's Celebrate 47 Years of Square Dancing in Cove." *Leader Press.* Copperas Cove, TX. May 1, 2017. https://www.coveleaderpress.com/news/double-c%E2%80%99s -celebrate-47-years-square-dancing-cove.

Dowd, Ryan. *The Librarian's Guide to Homelessness: An Empathy-Driven Approach to Solving Problems, Preventing Conflict, and Serving Everyone.* Chicago: ALA Editions, 2018.

"Drag Queen Storytime Is 'Controversial' and 'Potentially Divisive,' Says Okanagan Library CEO." *CBC News* online. September 21, 2019. https://www.cbc.ca/news /canada/british-columbia/kelowna-drag-queen-story-time-1.5292257.

"Food Desert." *Wikipedia.* Accessed January 20, 2022. https://en.wikipedia.org/wiki/Food _desert.

Ford, Anne. "Adulting 101: When Libraries Teach Basic Life Skills." *American Libraries* online. May 1, 2018. https://americanlibrariesmagazine.org/2018/05/01/adulting-101 -library-programming/.

"Free Tax Clinics." *Government of Canada* online. Last modified December 13, 2021. https:// www.canada.ca/en/revenue-agency/services/tax/individuals/community-volunteer -income-tax-program.html.

Friedmann, Susan. *Meeting and Event Planning for Dummies.* Hoboken, NJ: John Wiley & Sons, 2013.

Geiger, A. W. "Millennials Are the Most Likely Generation of Americans to Use Public Libraries." *Pew Research Centre.* June 21, 2017. http://pewrsr.ch/2tOt8gQ.

"Generation Alpha." *Wikipedia.* Accessed January 20, 2022. https://en.wikipedia.org/wiki /Generation_Alpha.

Glasser, William. *Choice Theory: A New Psychology of Personal Freedom.* New York: Harper Perennial, 1999.

Government of Canada. "Household Food Insecurity, 2017/2018." *Statistics Canada.* June 24, 2020. https://www150.statcan.gc.ca/n1/pub/82-625-x/2020001/article/00001-eng .htm.

Government of Canada. "Social Determinants of Health and Health Inequalities." *Government of Canada* online. Last modified October 7, 2020. https://www.canada.ca/en/public-health/services/health-promotion/population-health/what-determines-health.html.

Government of New Brunswick. "Appendix B: Sample Program Evaluation Form." *The New Brunswick Public Library Service Policy 1085* (July 2017). Accessed February 12, 2022. http://www2.gnb.ca/content/dam/gnb/Departments/nbpl-sbpnb/pdf/politiques-policies/1085_library-programs_appendix-b.pdf.

"Grant Connect." *Imagine Canada*. Accessed February 11, 2022. https://www.imaginecanada.ca/en/grant-connect.

Gray, Peter. *Free to Learn*. New York: Basic Books, 2015.

"Guild of Book Workers: The National Organization for All the Book Arts." *Guild of Book Workers*. Accessed March 12, 2022. https://guildofbookworkers.org/.

Gundersen, Craig, and James P. Ziliak. "Food Insecurity and Health Outcomes." *Health Affairs* 34, no. 11 (2015): 1830–39.

Hanby, Elizabeth. "Program Model: Cook the Book Club." *Programming Librarian*. March 25, 2020. https://programminglibrarian.org/programs/cook-book-club.

Haut-Saint-Jean Library Region. *Annual Report 2018-2019*. Edmundston, NB: New Brunswick Public Library Service, 2019.

Hutchins, Michael. "Library Park Brings Music Outdoors." *Herald Democrat* online. Last modified October 14, 2020. https://www.heralddemocrat.com/story/news/2020/10/14/sherman-showcases-native-texas-plant-life-new-library-music-park/3656001001/.

"Indigenous Storyteller in Residence." *Vancouver Public Library* online. Accessed March 3, 2022. https://www.vpl.ca/storyteller.

Inklebarger, Timothy. "Company to Supply Free Narcan to Libraries." *American Libraries* online. October 24, 2018. https://americanlibrariesmagazine.org/blogs/the-scoop/narcan-company-supply-free-narcan-to-libraries/.

Ivers, Louise C., and Kimberly A. Cullen. "Food Insecurity: Special Considerations for Women." *The American Journal of Clinical Nutrition* 94, no. 6 (2011): 1740S–1744S.

"Jerome Bruner." *Wikipedia*. Accessed January 20, 2022. https://en.wikipedia.org/wiki/Jerome_Bruner.

Karasev, Igor. "Which Generation Are You From?" *Igor Karasev* blog. June 22, 2018. https://medium.com/@igorkarasev/which-generation-are-you-from-4ce5410755f7.

"Kite Fight | Op-Docs." *YouTube*. July 17, 2014. https://www.youtube.com/watch?v=sl3qWHkqfI8.

"Kite Plans." *American Kitefliers Association* online. Accessed March 4, 2022. https://www.kite.org/about-kites/kite-plans/.

"*Kiting Magazine*: The World's Leading Kite Magazine Is Free to Members." *The American Kitefliers Association*. Accessed April 3, 2022. https://www.kite.org/community/kiting-magazine/.

Klinenberg, Eric. *Palaces for the People: How Social Infrastructure Can Help Fight Inequality, Polarization, and the Decline of Civic Life*. New York: Crown, 2018.

Largo-Wight, E., W. W. Chen, V. Dodd, and R. Weiler. "Healthy Workplaces: The Effects of Nature Contact at Work on Employee Stress and Health." *Public Health Reports* 126, Suppl 1 (2011): 124–30. Accessed March 24, 2022. https://www.ncbi.nlm.nih.gov/pmc/articles/PMC3072911/.

Lenstra, Noah. *Healthy Living at the Library: Programs for All Ages*. Santa Barbara, CA: Libraries Unlimited, 2020.

———. *Let's Move in Libraries*. Accessed March 1, 2022. https://letsmovelibraries.org/.

Lenstra, Noah, and Christine D'Arpa. "Food Justice in the Public Library: Information, Resources, and Meals." *The International Journal of Information, Diversity, & Inclusion*

(IJIDI) 3, no. 4 (2019). https://jps.library.utoronto.ca/index.php/ijidi/article/view/33010.

"Let's Move: America's Move to Raise a Healthier Generation of Kids." *Let's Move* online. Accessed March 1, 2022. https://letsmove.obamawhitehouse.archives.gov/.

Li, Qing. *Forest Bathing: How Trees Can Help You Find Health and Happiness.* London: Penguin Life, 2018.

"Liability Waivers." *Jenn Carson* online. Accessed February 12, 2022. http://www.jenncarson.com/resources.html.

"List of Enlistment Age by Country." *Wikipedia.* Accessed January 20, 2022. https://en.wikipedia.org/wiki/List_of_enlistment_age_by_country.

"List of the Oldest Living People." *Wikipedia.* Accessed January 20, 2022. https://en.wikipedia.org/wiki/List_of_the_oldest_living_people.

Loprespub (screen name). "The State of Financial Literacy in Canada: How Much Do We Know?" *Library of Parliament: HillNotes.* May 9, 2019. https://hillnotes.ca/2019/05/09/the-state-of-financial-literacy-in-canada-how-much-do-we-know/.

MacLeod, Kirsteen. *In Praise of Retreat: Finding Sanctuary in the Modern World.* Toronto: ECW Press, 2021.

"Marriageable Age." *Wikipedia.* Accessed January 20, 2022. https://en.wikipedia.org/wiki/Marriageable_age.

"Marriage Age in the United States." *Wikipedia.* Accessed January 20, 2022. https://en.wikipedia.org/wiki/Marriage_age_in_the_United_States.

Matczak, Jamie. "Charging Fees for Library Programs." *Wisconsin Valley Library Service (WVLS)* online. September 20, 2018. https://wvls.org/charging-fees-for-library-programs/.

McCarthy, Justin. "In U.S., Library Visits Outpaced Trips to Movies in 2019." *Gallup* online. January 22, 2020. https://news.gallup.com/poll/284009/library-visits-outpaced-trips-movies-2019.aspx.

McGovern, Meredith. "Blog: Gardening for Kids Programs Grow Community Connections." *Programming Librarian.* August 14, 2019. https://programminglibrarian.org/blog/gardening-kids-programs-grow-community-connections.

McMillian, Tracie. "The New Face of Hunger." *National Geographic Magazine* online. Accessed March 1, 2022. https://www.nationalgeographic.com/foodfeatures/hunger/.

Millette, Dominique. "Tintamarre." *The Canadian Encyclopedia* online. Last modified July 15, 2015. https://www.thecanadianencyclopedia.ca/en/article/tintamarre.

Mohsin, Maryam. "10 Small Business Statistics Every Future Entrepreneur Should Know in 2022." *Oberlo.* January 1, 2022. https://www.oberlo.ca/blog/small-business-statistics.

Morrow, Abby. "Program Model: Cooking Matters® Pop-up Grocery Store Tour: Online!" *Programming Librarian.* June 4, 2020. https://programminglibrarian.org/programs/cooking-matters%C2%AE-pop-grocery-store-tour-online.

Office of Disease Prevention and Heath Promotion. "Food Insecurity." *Healthy People.* https://www.healthypeople.gov/2020/topics-objectives/topic/social-determinants-health/interventions-resources/food-insecurity.

Pagliaro, Jennifer. "They're the 'Beating Hearts' of the City's Neighbourhoods. So Why Are Toronto's Public Libraries Still Chronically Underfunded?" *The Toronto Star.* Last modified January 20, 2020. https://www.thestar.com/news/gta/2020/01/18/the-best-thing-a-library-can-be-is open.html?fbclid=IwAR3wckuaop0aDjv6NYb0gPEeMAu2J9hIawlRDT-PslLM9Nz0UEDQPOQEOAg.

"Performance Rights Organisation." *Wikipedia.* Accessed January 20, 2022. https://en.wikipedia.org/wiki/Performance_rights_organisation.

Perley-Dutcher, Shane. *2021 Wild Child Symposium* (online). March 13, 2021.

Pew Charitable Trusts. "The Library in the City: Changing Demands and a Challenging Future." *Philadelphia Research Initiative.* Philadelphia: PEW, 2012.

Price, Chelsea. "Blog: Trivia Night at a Tiny Library: It Can Be Done!" *Programming Librarian.* June 26, 2019. https://programminglibrarian.org/blog/trivia-night-tiny -library-it-can-be-done.

"Radar." *National Weather Service.* Accessed March 18, 2022. https://radar.weather.gov/ ?settings=v1_eyJhZ2VuZGEiOnsiaWQiOm51bGwsImNlbnRlciI6Wy05NC45OCwzNy4 wMl0sImxvY2F0aW9uIjpudWxsLCJ6b29tIjo0fSwiYW5pbWF0aW9uIjpmYWxzZSw iYmFzZSI6Ik50YW5kYXJkIiwiYXJ0Y2MiOmZhbHNlLCJjb3VudHkiOmZhbHNlLCJ jd2EiOmZhbHNlLCJyZmMiOmZhbHNlLCJzdGF0ZSI6ZmFsc2UsIm1lbnUiOnRydWU sInNob3J0RnVzZWRPbmx5IjpmYWxzZSwib3BhY2l0eSI6eyJhbGVydHMiOjAuOCw ibG9jYWwiOjAuNiwibG9jYWxTdGF0aW9ucyI6MC44LCJuYXRpb25hbCI6MC42fX0 %3D#/.

Reid, Ian. "The 2017 Public Library Data Service Report: Characteristics and Trends." *Public Libraries* online. December 4, 2017. http://publiclibrariesonline.org/2017/12/the-2017 -public-library-data-service-report-characteristics-and-trends/.

RequiemScrc (screen name). "How to Re-ink a Typewriter Ribbon." *Instructables.* Accessed March 18, 2022. https://www.instructables.com/How-to-Re-ink-a-Typewriter-Ribbon/.

Rettig, James. "Technology, Cluelessness, Anthropology, and the Memex: The Future of Academic Reference Services." *References Services Review* 31, no. 1 (2003): 17–21.

Rothstein, Pauline, and Diantha Dow Schull. *Boomers and Beyond: Reconsidering the Role of Libraries.* Chicago: ALA Editions, 2010.

"Selective Service System." *Wikipedia.* Accessed January 20, 2022. https://en.wikipedia.org /wiki/Selective_Service_System.

Silverman, David J. "The Vicious Reality behind the Thanksgiving Myth." *New York Times* online. November 27, 2019. https://www.nytimes.com/2019/11/27/opinion /thanksgiving-history-racism.html.

Small, Gary. "Mind Games: A Mental Workout to Help Keep Your Brain Sharp." *The Guardian* online. October 13, 2018. https://www.theguardian.com/lifeandstyle/2018 /oct/13/mental-exercises-to-keep-your-brain-sharp.

Stamburg, Susan. "How Andrew Carnegie Turned His Fortune into a Library Legacy." *NPR.* Last modified August 1, 2013. https://www.npr.org/2013/08/01/207272849 /how-andrew-carnegie-turned-his-fortune-into-a-library-legacy.

"Start a Joyful Practice." *Little Cloud Kites.* Accessed January 12, 2022. https://littlecloudkites .com/.

Statista Research Department. "Distribution of Facebook Users Worldwide as of October 2021, by Gender." *Statista* online. January 28, 2022. https://www.statista.com/statistics /699241/distribution-of-users-on-facebook-worldwide-gender/.

"Stop Motion Lighting Tips." *Stop Motion Central.* July 6, 2018. https://www .stopmotioncentral.com/stop-motion-lighting-tips/.

"Toronto Bans Kite Flying in City Park." *CBC News* online. Last modified August 17, 2010. https://www.cbc.ca/news/canada/toronto/toronto-bans-kite-flying-in-city -park-1.933181#:~:text=The%20City%20of%20Toronto%20has,of%20a%20danger%20to %20animals.

Tracy, Melissa. "Understanding Accessibility Challenges for Patrons." *American Library Association (ALA)* online. February 5, 2018. http://www.ala.org/news/member-news /2018/02/understanding-accessibility-challenges-patrons.

"Tribe of Noise." *Free Music Archive.* Accessed January 12, 2022. https://freemusicarchive .org/.

UNESCO and International Federation of Library Associations and Institutions (IFLA). *IFLA/UNESCO Public Library Manifesto 1994*. Accessed January 20, 2022. https://repository.ifla.org/handle/123456789/168.

"Voting age." *Wikipedia*. Accessed January 20, 2022. https://en.wikipedia.org/wiki/Voting_age.

Wallace, Martin K., Rebecca Tolley-Stokes, and Erik Sean Estep. *The Generation X Librarian: Essays on Leadership, Technology, Pop Culture, Social Responsibility and Professional Identity*. Jefferson, NC: McFarland & Co, 2011.

Warnick, Melody. *This Is Where You Belong: Finding Home Wherever You Are*. New York: Penguin, 2017.

Whitbourne, Susan Krauss. "What's Your True Age?" *Psychology Today* online. June 23, 2012. https://www.psychologytoday.com/ca/blog/fulfillment-any-age/201206/what-s-your-true-age.

Yenigun, Sami. "Play Doesn't End with Childhood: Why Adults Need Recess Too." *NPR*. August 6, 2014. https://www.npr.org/sections/ed/2014/08/06/336360521/play-doesnt-end-with-childhood-why-adults-need-recess-too.

Zettervall, Sarah K., and Mary C. Nienow. *Whole Person Librarianship: A Social Work Approach to Patron Services*. Santa Barbara, CA: Libraries Unlimited, 2019.

Index

About the Author

Jenn Carson is an internationally recognized expert in physical literacy, a professional yoga teacher, and the director of the L. P. Fisher Public Library in Woodstock, New Brunswick, Canada. She is the author of *Get Your Community Moving: Physical Literacy Programs for All Ages* (2018) and *Yoga and Meditation at the Library: A Practical Guide for Librarians* (Rowman & Littlefield, 2019). You can find out more about her programs and research at www.jenncarson.com.

Made in the USA
Monee, IL
11 October 2023

44435759R00122